From Participants in the

TEXT READING PROGRAM

If it were not for these enlightening Text commentaries, we would still be floundering in an intellectual soup. The soup was mighty tasty, but was difficult to get our teeth into without these brilliant observations, comparisons, and analogies. We know this is a vast body of work that has been given us and we are grateful from the bottom of our hearts.
—SYLVIA AND CAP LYONS

A very powerful tool to keep me on track, reading and absorbing just a few pages each day. This process has been an invaluable source of inner peace during this past year.
—CONNIE PORTER

Robert Perry and Greg Mackie are experts at making the sometimes challenging Text not just understandable, but rich with meaning and poignancy. This is a priceless gift to anyone who wants to fully understand the awesome teachings of *A Course in Miracles*. I can think of no better form of support than this!
—JULIA SIMPSON

The Text commentaries offer insights I could not have had alone, because of the deep understanding Robert and Greg have.
—DIETRUN BUCHMAN

An amazing journey into the genius and magnitude of this material. Don't miss this opportunity.
—SHARON EDWARDS

Robert and Greg's insights illuminate Text principles like never before.
—LORETTA M. SIANI, PH.D

I have studied the Text and read it through at least once a year for the last 19 years. I thought I knew it pretty well. However this year has been a real eye-opener. Many of those little question marks I made in the margins have been erased. I shall be forever grateful for this year of Text study.
—WENDY FINNERTY

After 20 years with the Course, I now understand it on a much different level.
—ULLA WALLIN

Robert and Greg's intelligence, insight, and wit, create a fun climate of spiritual scholarship that helps make the Text more intelligible and alive. They're extraordinarily gifted.
—AMY ELLISON

The clear and down-to-earth commentary has helped me connect with the Text as never before.
—NANCY NEVITT

Robert and Greg have a tremendous comprehension of the Course and provide down-to-earth explanations. I know of no better way to learn the message of the Text than this program.
—JAN WORLEY

Translates the beautiful poetry of the Course's Text into everyday common language, making the valuable meaning of each sentence easily understood.
—KATHERINE LATORRACA

Previously, I had never succeeded in completely reading the Text. Participating was the best thing that I did for myself this year.
—DAVID COLWELL

There is nothing else in my years of studying the Course that has helped me so much!
—GEORGE PORTER

I can honestly say I'll finally complete the reading of the entire Text—and I've been at this for 20 years!
—BARBARA OLSON

Robert and Greg's insights helped me understand and assimilate the Course's otherwise complex and difficult passages. I will do this again next year, and the next, and the next. This program is amazing.
—JO CHANDLER

Your program has been a revelation.
—DON DE LENE

I would like to say that this year has been too amazing to actually put into words.
—KATHY CHOMITZ

Having studied the Course faithfully for 28 years, I never imagined the insights and miracles I would receive from these commentaries on the Text!
—MIRKALICE GORE

I can truly say that this program has made an incredible difference to my life. I wholeheartedly recommend it.
—DAVID FLEMING

Nothing less than totally inspiring.
—REV. JERRY CUSIMANO

THE ILLUMINATED TEXT

Commentaries for Deepening Your Connection with
A Course in Miracles

Robert Perry & Greg Mackie

VOLUME 4

Published by Circle Publishing
A division of the Circle of Atonement
P.O. Box 4238 * West Sedona, AZ 86340
(928) 282-0790 * www.circleofa.org
circleoffice@circleofa.org

Cover design by Thunder Mountain Design and Communications
Design & layout by Phillips Associates UK Ltd
Printed in the USA

ISBN 978-1-886602-35-9

Library of Congress Cataloging-in-Publication Data

Perry, Robert, 1960-
  The illuminated text : commentaries for deepening your connection with A course in
miracles / Robert Perry & Greg Mackie.
      p. cm.
  Includes bibliographical references.
  Summary: "Provides in-depth analysis of the Text of A Course in Miracles"--
Provided by publisher.
  ISBN 978-1-886602-35-9
  1. Course in Miracles. 2. Spiritual life. I. Mackie, Greg, 1963- II. Title.
  BP605.C68P455 2010
  299'.93--dc22

                                        2009039354

CONTENTS

Commentaries on Chapter 16: THE FORGIVENESS OF ILLUSIONS

Commentaries on Chapter 17:
FORGIVENESS AND THE HOLY RELATIONSHIP

FOREWORD

The Text is the foundation of *A Course in Miracles*. Doing the Course is simply a process of learning and internalizing its thought system, and the Text is where that thought system is laid out. It is an unparalleled spiritual tour de force. Careful study of it will change your outlook in ways that perhaps nothing else can.

Many students, however, find the Text to be very hard going. Many do not finish it, and even those who make it through, perhaps repeatedly, wish they had a deeper grasp of what they were reading.

For this reason, in 2006, the Circle of Atonement offered the Text Reading Program. This was a year-long tour through the Text of *A Course in Miracles* with commentary on each paragraph, written by myself and Greg Mackie, both teachers for the Circle. Before each weekday, we would send out to all the participants via e-mail the reading for that day. This would usually consist of a single section from the Text, accompanied by our commentary as well as practical exercises.

We often supplemented these sections with material from the Urtext, the original typescript of the Course. Our experience was that, especially in the early chapters of the Text, material from the Urtext that was eventually edited out was very helpful and clarifying. So when we felt it was useful, we included this Urtext material in brackets, and let it inform our commentary. We also indicated where a word had been emphasized in the Urtext, as this too often added clarity.

Note: In this volume, words that were originally emphasized in the Urtext are <u>underlined</u>. So when you see an underlined word here, know that that word was emphasized in the Urtext, but that emphasis was not included in the eventual published Course, which included fewer emphasized words. Again, we did this because quite often that emphasis from the Urtext would add clarity.

The reason we developed this program has a bit of history to it. In 2000, we offered a local program in Sedona that included a daily Text class, using a schedule that took us through the entire Text in a year of weekday readings. (On the sixth and seventh days, we rested!) Our friend, student, and colleague John Perry attended that program. When it ended, he began guiding people through the Text using the same schedule, only doing so online. He sent out the Text material for a given day and interspersed it with his own clarifying comments. In fall 2005 he felt guided to suggest we do something similar. Our guidance told us to go ahead, and so that's what we did. Without John's suggestion, however, it is safe to say we never would have done this.

2006, the year of the program, was an intense one. I would write commentaries for three weeks. Then I got a breather for a week while Greg wrote the commentaries. And then the schedule started over. Each day we wrote the commentary that needed to go out the next day. In addition, we led a weekly phone class for participants, in which we summarized the previous week's sections. (The recordings are still available to students who sign up for the online version of the Text Reading Program.)

The response to our program far exceeded our expectations. We have included a few edited comments at the front of the book, but if you want to read the unadulterated student reactions, straight from the various horses' mouths, then go to www.circlepublishing.org and click on the link for the Text Reading Program. During the year of the program, and actually ever since, we have had consistent requests that we put this material into published form.

So here it is, presented in book form as a multi-volume set. We hope you find these commentaries illuminating, and that they do indeed deepen your understanding of the spiritual masterpiece, *A Course in Miracles*.

ROBERT PERRY
SEPTEMBER 2009
SEDONA, ARIZONA

Commentaries on Chapter 14

TEACHING FOR TRUTH

Introduction
Commentary by Robert Perry

1.   ¹Yes, you are blessed indeed. ²Yet in this world you do not know it. ³But you have the means for <u>learning</u> it and <u>seeing</u> it quite clearly. ⁴The Holy Spirit uses logic as easily and as well as does the ego, except that <u>His</u> conclusions are <u>not</u> insane. ⁵They take a direction <u>exactly</u> opposite, pointing as clearly to Heaven as the ego points to darkness and to death. ⁶We have followed much of the ego's logic, and have seen its logical conclusions. ⁷And <u>having</u> seen them, we have realized that they can<u>not</u> be seen except in illusions, for there alone their <u>seeming</u> clearness <u>seems to be clearly seen</u>. ⁸Let us now turn <u>away</u> from them, and follow the simple logic by which the Holy Spirit teaches the simple conclusions that speak for truth, and <u>only</u> truth.

What a beautiful introduction to this chapter. In the last chapter, we spent so much time looking at the inevitable conclusions to the logic of the ego. Those conclusions are dark indeed. Yet if we really see them, we'll see that they can't be seen, because there's nothing there.

The ego's logic leads to death. And that is how we often see logic itself—if we're being logical, we'll end up depressed. There will be no magic, no wonder. Yet here we are told that the Holy Spirit's logic leads in the exact opposite direction—to Heaven. His logic, if we'll follow it, will lead us to the realization of the one thing that we don't know in this world: how utterly blessed we are.

I. The Conditions of Learning
Commentary by Robert Perry

1.   ¹If you are blessed and do not know it, you need to learn it must be so. ²The knowledge is not taught, but its conditions must be acquired for it is they that have been thrown away. ³You can learn to bless, and cannot give what you have not. ⁴If, then, you offer blessing, it must have come first to yourself. ⁵And you must also have accepted it as yours, for how else could you give it away? ⁶That is why miracles offer *you* the testimony that you are blessed. ⁷If what you offer is complete forgiveness you must have let guilt go, accepting the Atonement for yourself and learning you are guiltless. ⁸How could you learn what has been done for you, unknown to you [Ur: *but which you do not know*], unless you do what you would have to do if it *had* been done for you?

Application: Here we see the Holy Spirit's logic at work. Begin by thinking of a time when you felt you really blessed someone, when you gave them the implicit message that they are worthy of love and free of their past mistakes. Now dwell on the following lines.

> *I cannot give what I don't have.*
> *Therefore, if I offered blessing, it **must** have come first to myself.*
> *And I must have accepted it as mine, for how else could I give it away?*
> *If I offered forgiveness—the affirmation of guiltlessness—I must have accepted my own guiltlessness.*
> *I didn't know I had done this.*
> *But by doing what I **would** do if I **had** done this,*
> *I learn all that has been done for me and all that I have accepted as mine.*

As we have seen many times now, this is the heart of the Course's process. We give miracles, which are in essence the communication of forgiveness, the affirmation of guiltlessness. This reveals to us the guiltlessness we have already received, unbeknownst to us. We thereby learn that we are innocent. We learn that we are blessed. In doing so, we lay hold of the conditions of knowledge. Then we graduate to the absolute knowledge that we are eternally blessed in Heaven.

2. ¹<u>Indirect</u> proof of truth is needed in a world made of denial and without direction. ²You will perceive the need for this if you realize that to <u>deny</u> is the decision <u>not</u> to know. ³The logic of the world <u>must</u> therefore lead to nothing, for its <u>goal</u> is nothing. ⁴If you decide to have and give and <u>be</u> nothing except a dream, you <u>must</u> direct your thoughts unto oblivion. ⁵And if you have and give and are <u>everything</u>, and <u>all this has been denied</u>, your thought system is closed off and wholly separated from the truth. ⁶This *is* an insane world, and do not underestimate the [Ur: actual] extent of its insanity. ⁷There is no area of your perception that it has not touched, and your dream *is* sacred to you. ⁸That is why God placed the Holy Spirit <u>in</u> you, where <u>you</u> placed the dream.

The logic in the previous paragraph was all about proving to us the truth, the truth that we are blessed. But notice how indirect it was. It didn't try to directly affirm our blessedness. It had us bless someone *else*, almost so that the realization of our own blessedness would sneak up on us. This is how the Holy Spirit has to work with us. He has to bring us to the knowledge of our blessedness *indirectly*.

What a strange situation. Why is this so? Because the whole aim of our thought system is to close ourselves off to knowledge. The whole point of denial is "not to know." When someone has closed the door in your face, that's not the time to just keep banging on the door. That's the time for a less direct approach. The next thing that shows up at the front door shouldn't be you, it should be flowers. That's how the Holy Spirit works with us.

If we are slamming the door in the face of our blessedness, then we are insane, far more insane than we realize. After all, part of insanity is turning away from just how insane you are. We have dedicated ourselves to the achievement of nothingness, of complete oblivion. How kindly, then, are we going to greet totality when it shows up at our door?

3. ¹Seeing is <u>always</u> outward. ²Were your thoughts wholly of <u>you</u>, the thought system <u>you</u> made <u>would</u> be forever dark [because all you

would see outside would be the reinforcement of it]. ³The thoughts the mind of God's Son projects or extends <u>have</u> all the power that he gives to them. ⁴The thoughts he shares with God are <u>beyond</u> his belief, but those <u>he</u> made *are* his beliefs. ⁵And it is <u>these,</u> and <u>not</u> the truth, that he has chosen to defend and love. ⁶They will not be taken from him. ⁷But they <u>can</u> be given up *by* him, for the Source of their undoing is <u>in</u> him. ⁸There is <u>nothing</u> in the world to teach him that the logic of the world is totally insane and leads to nothing. ⁹Yet in him who <u>made</u> this insane logic there is One Who <u>knows</u> it leads to nothing, for He knows <u>everything</u>.

When we look without, we merely see the outer reflection of our beliefs. Thus, what we see will simply *reinforce* those beliefs. That's why there is nothing in the world that will teach us that we have been employing insane logic. No, our only hope is for an inside job, for something to quietly creep into our minds and introduce a different kind of thought, which will then show us a different kind of world. That something, of course, is the Holy Spirit.

To get a sense of His role, imagine a therapist who is actually able to enter the mind of a madman. The therapist doesn't change anything on the outside. He simply reasons with the madman from the inside, asking him to question his logic. The madman thinks, "The CIA is after me, so I have to be afraid." And the therapist says, "Let's look at those beliefs. Are you sure you have to be afraid? Aren't you the one who elects to be afraid? Maybe you can elect otherwise. And besides that, are you really certain that the CIA is after you?"

4. ¹Any direction that would lead you where the Holy Spirit leads you <u>not</u>, goes nowhere. ²Anything you deny [reject] that He knows to be true you have denied <u>yourself</u> [deprived yourself of], and He must therefore teach you <u>not</u> to deny it. ³Undoing *is* indirect, as <u>doing</u> is. ⁴You were created <u>only</u> to create, neither to see <u>nor</u> do. ⁵These [seeing and doing] are but <u>indirect</u> expressions of the will to live, which has been blocked by the capricious and unholy whim of death and murder that your Father does not share with [Ur: shares not *with*] you. ⁶You have set yourself the task of sharing what can<u>not</u> be shared. ⁷And while you think it possible to <u>learn</u> to do this, you will <u>not</u> believe all that *is* possible to learn to do.

When we go in a direction apart from the Holy Spirit's leading, we may think we are going to hell. Or maybe we think we are going to Pleasure Island, that place in *Pinocchio* where you enjoy endless pleasures but end up in slavery as a donkey. Yet we are not going to hell or to Pleasure Island. We are going nowhere. We are expending a lot of energy grabbing after nothing. We are denying ourselves what we could have had. As Lesson 133 puts it, we are simply failing to gain.

The Holy Spirit's job is to undo our denial. As "The Way to Remember God" said, we need to deny the denial of truth (12.II.1:5). This is another example of His indirectness. Real directness would simply say, "Totally affirm truth," which He knows we will not do.

In fact, the only really direct thing would be for us to create in Heaven, to express our innate will to create new life. We talk about "being direct"; this is the only way to be truly direct. In this world, not only is undoing indirect, even our *doing* is indirect, along with our seeing. Our true will to create has been blocked by the ego's "death whim," and so now our will to create can't flow out naturally. It can only come out sideways.

> 5. ¹The Holy Spirit, therefore, must begin His teaching by showing you what you can <u>never</u> learn. ²His <u>message</u> is not indirect, but He must introduce the simple truth into a thought system which has become so twisted and so complex you <u>cannot see</u> that it means nothing. ³<u>He</u> merely looks at its foundation and <u>dismisses</u> it. ⁴But <u>you</u> who <u>cannot</u> undo what you have made, nor escape the heavy burden of its dullness that lies upon your mind, cannot see <u>through</u> it. ⁵It <u>deceives</u> you, because you chose to deceive yourself [Ur: *yourselves*]. ⁶Those who choose to <u>be</u> deceived will merely <u>attack</u> direct approaches, because they seem to <u>encroach</u> upon deception and <u>strike</u> at it.

In order to persuade us to undo our denial, the Holy Spirit has to show us our denial as it really is. He has to show us that we are actually choosing nothingness. He has to show us that the castles in the sky that we are chasing are just empty clouds. He sees this instantly, but we do not see it at all ("you…cannot see through it"). Here again we see how indirect He has to be, simply because we would reject a more direct approach. Rather than asking us to create again in our Father's Kingdom, He needs to start all the way on the other end, by showing us the nothingness of *our* kingdom.

He works with us like you work with an alcoholic. You want to say, "Get a life. Start doing what you're really good at again. Be kind to your wife." But instead you need to say, "When you put that drink to your lips, what payoff are you looking for? Is it possible that there is no payoff? Could it be that your 'reward' is nothingness? And is nothingness what you really want?" Only once He shows us that our thought system is just nothingness dressed up like something will we start thinking about undoing it. And only once we undo it will we be ready to return to truth. He is indirect because He is dealing with crazy people.

II. The Happy Learner
Commentary by Robert Perry

This section continues the themes from the previous section, discussing the Holy Spirit's attempt to teach us the simple truth in spite of our resistance.

1. ¹The Holy Spirit needs a happy learner, in whom His mission can be happily accomplished. ²You who are steadfastly devoted to misery <u>must</u> first recognize that you <u>are</u> miserable and <u>not</u> happy. ³The Holy Spirit cannot teach <u>without</u> this contrast, for you believe that misery *is* happiness. ⁴This has so confused you that you have undertaken to learn to do what you can <u>never</u> do [this refers to the sharing of nothing, which is an expression of the ego's unholy whim of death and murder; see I.4:5-7], believing that <u>unless</u> you learn it you will <u>not</u> be happy. ⁵You do <u>not</u> realize that the foundation on which this most peculiar learning goal depends means <u>absolutely nothing</u> [makes no sense]. ⁶Yet it may still make sense to you [Ur: This *does* make sense to you]. ⁷Have faith in nothing and you will <u>find</u> the "treasure" that you seek. ⁸Yet you will add another burden to your <u>already</u> burdened mind [Ur: or you would *not* have sought another]. ⁹You will believe that <u>nothing is of value,</u> and will <u>value</u> it. ¹⁰A little piece of glass, a speck of dust, a body or a war are one to you. ¹¹For if you value <u>one</u> thing made of nothing, you <u>have</u> believed that nothing <u>can</u> be precious, and that you *can* learn how to make the <u>un</u>true true.

Being a happy learner is the opposite of the learner we met in the last section, the person who has to be reached indirectly because he is so defended against learning. To be happy about learning, we must first realize that there is a need for learning. This means realizing that we are miserable, not happy. Are we willing to admit that?

Having confused misery with happiness, we have dedicated ourselves to a confused learning goal. Rather than learning the Holy Spirit's lessons, we are trying to learn how to "have and give and be nothing" (I.2:4). We are trying to lay hold of the nothingness of this world. Because we value this nothingness so deeply, even when we have it in our hands and can

9

see its nothingness, we will still tell ourselves it is valuable. We are like someone who sees an item that looks fantastic on the home shopping network. When it finally arrives, though, it turns out to be a worthless piece of plastic. But we value it so much that we still find a way to convince ourselves it is the most precious thing there is.

The final results are even more pitiful than that. For having valued this one worthless thing, we now value all of this world's worthless pieces of plastic. This uncomfortable fact is particularly evident when you sort through your old junk. Have you ever felt that little pang of regret over throwing away a totally useless piece of crap?

> 2. ¹The Holy Spirit, <u>seeing</u> where you are but <u>knowing</u> you are elsewhere, begins His lesson in simplicity with the fundamental teaching that *truth* <u>is true</u>. ²This is the hardest lesson you will ever learn, and in the end the <u>only</u> one. ³Simplicity is very difficult for twisted minds. ⁴Consider all the distortions you have made of nothing; all the strange forms and feelings and actions and reactions that you have woven out of it. ⁵Nothing is so alien to you as the simple truth, and nothing are you <u>less</u> inclined to listen to. ⁶The contrast between what is true and what is not is <u>perfectly</u> apparent, yet you do <u>not</u> see it. ⁷The simple and the obvious are <u>not</u> apparent to those who would make palaces and royal robes of nothing, believing they are kings with golden crowns <u>because</u> of them.

This paragraph clarifies further why the Holy Spirit has to be so indirect with us (the theme of the previous section). All He wants to do is teach us one incredibly simple lesson: truth is true. It doesn't get any simpler than that. Yet we will only really learn this lesson at the very end of our journey—meaning that we are quite far from understanding it now. We find this lesson unbelievably hard to learn, harder than anything else. It is the single core of all of the Course's lessons, the thing that makes them all seem so challenging.

Yet why would a lesson as simple as "truth is true" be so hard? Because we have spent so long weaving our thoughts and feelings and lives out of nothing, that we think this nothing (rather than truth) is true. We are thus like a really insane version of the emperor in "The Emperor's New Clothes." We have not only woven our royal robes out of nothing; we are actually just peasants who have also woven our crown and palaces out of nothing. We have spent our lives ascending royal steps that aren't there, putting on crowns that aren't there, and ordering around subjects that aren't there, all the while feeling ever-so-special because, after all, we're the king. Now imagine that someone (the Holy Spirit) comes along and says, "Hey, King, you're naked. Your clothes aren't there. And your palace isn't there, either. Oh and one more thing: You're not even a king. You're just a peasant carrying on the elaborate fantasy of being a king." This person is saying the simplest, most obvious thing. Yet would it be simple and obvious to this "king"? This is why the truth is not simple and obvious to us.

3. ¹All this the Holy Spirit sees, and teaches, simply, that <u>all this is not true</u>. ²To those unhappy learners who would teach themselves nothing, and delude themselves into believing that it is <u>not</u> nothing, the Holy Spirit says, with steadfast quietness:

> ³*The truth is true.* ⁴*Nothing else matters, nothing else is real, and* <u>*everything*</u> *beside it is not there.* ⁵*Let Me make the one distinction* <u>*for*</u> *you that you* <u>*cannot*</u> *make, but* <u>*need*</u> *to learn.* ⁶*Your faith in nothing* <u>*is*</u> *deceiving you.* ⁷*Offer your faith to Me, and* <u>*I*</u> *will place it gently in the holy place where it belongs.* ⁸*You will find* <u>*no*</u> *deception there, but only the simple truth.* ⁹*And you will love it because you will* <u>*understand*</u> *it.*

Application: Imagine yourself in a situation like the previous one of the peasant/king. Instead, however, you are a Son of God (rather than a peasant). Yet you think you are a human being, and you think you are wearing clothes, and living in a house or apartment, and occupying a certain place in society. Yet all of these—house, clothes, place in society, identity as human (which includes the body)—are just images in your mind, the mind of God's Son. They are just fantasies. They are nothingness that you have woven to look like something. But none of it is really there. You are living a fantasy existence, without recognizing it for what it is.

Now, keeping this scenario in mind, read the Holy Spirit's above italicized statement to you, hearing it as the Son of God who thinks he's a human.

4.   ¹Like you, the Holy Spirit did <u>not</u> make truth. ²Like God, He <u>knows</u> it to be true. ³He brings the <u>light</u> of truth into the darkness, and <u>lets</u> it shine on you. ⁴And as it shines <u>your brothers</u> see it, and realizing that this light is <u>not</u> what you have made, they see in you <u>more</u> than <u>you</u> see. ⁵They will be happy learners of the lesson this light brings to them, because it teaches them release from nothing and from all the works of nothing. ⁶The heavy chains that <u>seem</u> to bind them to despair they do <u>not</u> see as nothing, until <u>you</u> bring the light <u>to</u> them. ⁷And <u>then</u> they see the chains have disappeared, and so they *must* have been nothing. ⁸And <u>you</u> will see it <u>with</u> them. ⁹<u>Because</u> you taught them gladness and release, they will become <u>your</u> teachers in release and gladness.

This is yet another one of those important statements of the heart of the Course's process. As we actually listen to the Holy Spirit, His light shines on us, and then it shines through us on our brothers, releasing them. They need release, for out of the nothingness they had woven one more thing: *chains*. Maybe their chains were a sick body, or maybe they were some other kind of problem. Yet as our light shines, those chains disappear, setting our brothers free. Now they think, "Hey, if those chains just vanished like that, maybe they weren't real in the first place. Maybe they were made of nothing all along."

Now our brothers look back at us, their liberators, and—here is the crucial part—they see in us *more than we see*. We don't yet fully appreciate how much this light, though within us, comes from *beyond* us. Yet they do, so that when they look at us, they see "us" plus the "light from beyond us." And in that clear sight, *our* chains are revealed to be nothing. Their sight reveals *us* to be God's all-powerful Son wrapped in fantasy chains. Thus, the brothers we healed have turned around and become *our* "teachers of release and gladness."

Application: Have you ever had this experience? Have you ever given someone such a vision of the divine worth in her that she then saw in you more than you saw? If so, don't reject her vision of you in false modesty. Realize she has come as your savior. She has come to teach you what you cannot teach yourself. Let her fulfill her function. Be humble enough to accept from her the gift of your magnitude.

5. ¹When you teach <u>anyone</u> that truth is true, <u>you learn it with him</u>. ²And so you learn that what seemed hardest was the easiest. ³Learn to be a happy learner. ⁴You will <u>never</u> learn how to make nothing everything. ⁵Yet <u>see</u> that this <u>has been</u> your goal, and <u>recognize</u> how foolish it has been. ⁶Be glad it is undone, for when you look at it in simple honesty, it *is* undone. ⁷I said before, "Be not content with nothing" [12.VIII.6:1—here, too, the "nothing" is the "visible" world], for you <u>have</u> believed that nothing <u>could</u> content you. ⁸*It is not so.*

The previous paragraph was actually a description of how we learn that hardest of all lessons: truth is true. We teach it to someone else. We let someone else know that her reality is God's Son and that everthing else is a pile of empty images, spun out of nothingness. She then turns around and releases us from our illusory chains. Now we associate "truth is true" not with fear, but with release. This seemingly threatening lesson has set us free from the nothing that we were so attached to, yet which only imprisoned us.

This, then, is what it means to be a happy learner (a perennial source of confusion for Course students). We release our brothers with the message, "Your nature as God's Son is what's true. Your chains are just illusion." And then she turns around and releases us with the same message, a message we are now *happy* to *learn*.

6. ¹If you would be a happy learner, you must give <u>everything</u> <u>you</u> have learned to the Holy Spirit, to be <u>un</u>learned <u>for</u> you. ²And <u>then</u> begin to learn the joyous lessons that come quickly on the firm foundation that truth is true. ³For what is builded there *is* true, and <u>built</u> on truth. ⁴The universe of learning will open up before you in all its gracious simplicity. ⁵With truth before you, you will not look back [a reference to Lot's wife, who looked back while leaving Sodom and Gomorrah].

To be a happy learner is a two-stage affair. The first stage is unlearning nothingness—we give the thought system we have taught ourselves to the Holy Spirit to be undone. The second stage is learning truth—we start learning His joyous lessons, all of which are founded on the single idea that truth is true. All of them are just permutations of the first and final, the hardest and easiest, the one and only, lesson. With nothingness behind us, we will go onward to truth. We will go from misery and twisted complexity to joy and gracious simplicity. And we will never look back.

7. ¹The happy learner meets the conditions of learning here, as he meets the conditions of knowledge in the Kingdom. ²All this lies in the Holy Spirit's plan to free you from the past, and open up the way to freedom <u>for</u> you. ³For truth *is* true. ⁴What else could ever be, or ever was? ⁵This simple lesson holds the key to the dark door that you believe is locked forever. ⁶You <u>made</u> this door <u>of</u> nothing, and behind it *is* nothing. ⁷The key is only the light that shines away the shapes and forms and fears of nothing. ⁸Accept this key to freedom from the hands of Christ Who gives it to you, that you may join Him in the holy task of bringing light. ⁹For, like your brothers, <u>you</u> do not realize the light has come and freed you from the sleep of darkness.

Application — a visualization:

You stand before a massive dark door.

It is the door to a dark building, the edifice of your ego's thought system.

Behind the door lie all the thoughts and deeds and sins and grudges of the past.

All of these dusty objects lie piled within, knit together by the cobwebs of the ego's beliefs.

The contents of this building seem inaccessible, locked safely away in the unconscious.

It is the building of your sleep. You might even imagine it shaped like a sleeping face—*your* sleeping face.

How do you get through it to the light on the other side?

At that moment, Christ, your true Self, shows up.

In His hand He holds a large silver key, which He offers you—the key to freedom.

You take it from Him and turn to put it in the door.

But before you reach the door, a light shines out from the key.

This light simply shines away the door, revealing that there was no real door to put a key in.

The door was just a scrap of darkness appearing as something.

When the light came on, it automatically vanished.

The light then proceeds to shine away the entire building.

8.   ¹Behold your brothers in their freedom, and learn of them how to be <u>free</u> of darkness. ²The light in you will waken them, and they will not leave <u>you</u> asleep. ³The vision of Christ is <u>given</u> the very instant that it is perceived. ⁴Where everything is clear, it is <u>all</u> holy. ⁵The quietness of its simplicity is so compelling that you will realize <u>it is impossible to deny the simple truth</u>. ⁶For there <u>is</u> nothing else. ⁷God is everywhere, and His Son is <u>in</u> Him <u>with</u> everything. ⁸Can he sing the dirge of sorrow when <u>this</u> is true?

Application continued:

With this key in your hand, you have now joined Christ in the holy task of bringing light.

So you shine the light of this key on your sleeping brothers.

As it shines on them, you can see that behind their veil of sleep, they are already awake.

For this light is the vision of Christ, which sees them as they really are.

And as you see them as awake, they awaken.

They then look down and find the key in their own hands.

So they shine its light on you, and see *you* as awake.

And only then do you really awaken.

When you do, you realize that the light came long ago and freed you from sleep.

You just didn't know it.

Now you realize that sleep was never the truth about you.

Wakefulness was always the only truth.

Now you understand that only truth is true.

It is the only thing that ever was, or ever will be.

III. The Decision for Guiltlessness
Commentary by Robert Perry

This is a very powerful section that divides neatly in two. The first half is an important discussion of the connection between accepting our guiltlessness and being invulnerable in the face of attack.

> 1.   [Ur: Learning will be commensurate with motivation, and the interference in your motivation for learning, is *exactly* the same as that which interferes with *all* your thinking.] ¹The happy learner <u>cannot feel guilty about learning</u>. ²This is so <u>essential</u> to learning that it should never be forgotten. ³The guiltless learner learns [Ur: so] easily <u>because his thoughts are free</u>. ⁴Yet this entails the recognition that <u>guilt is interference, not salvation,</u> and serves <u>no</u> useful function at all.

This paragraph says that we feel guilty about learning, which drains our motivation to learn. As a result, this guilt blocks learning, for "learning will be commensurate with motivation"—in the end, we learn as much as we *want* to learn. Guilt over learning makes us reluctant learners, not happy learners.

Yet why do we feel guilty about learning? I think this guilt could be described as the dues we pay to the status quo. We feel an allegiance to the status quo, and yet learning means *leaving* the status quo. If one is going to leave home, one can at least be decent enough to feel guilty about it. The Course seems to confirm this interpretation in "The Obstacles to Peace," where it speaks of us feeling awful about deserting our friends by lifting the veil and going into God (T-19.IV(D)6). Have you ever felt that way? Of course, the "friends" here are not our brothers; they are sin, guilt, and death—the real pillars of the status quo. Could it be that we feel guilty about learning, because learning means leaving *them*?

> 2.   ¹Perhaps you are accustomed to using guiltlessness merely to offset the pain of guilt, and do not look upon it as having value <u>in itself</u>. ²You believe that guilt <u>and</u> guiltlessness are <u>both</u> of value, each representing an <u>escape</u> from what the other does <u>not</u> offer you. ³You do <u>not</u> want either alone, for without both you do not see yourself [Ur:

yourselves] as whole and therefore happy. ⁴Yet you are whole only in your guiltlessness, and only in your guiltlessness can you be happy. ⁵There is no conflict here. ⁶To wish for guilt in any way, in any form, will lose appreciation of the value of your guiltlessness, and push it from your sight.

We are attached to feeling guilty because it silently affirms to us that we are a decent, honest, responsible person. Remember how the Urtext said it is a device "for asking for pardon without change"? Guilt seems to pay off our wrongdoings. It seems to prove that we are not a callous monster. Yet guilt is no fun, so to relieve the pain of it, we tell ourselves that we are clean and innocent—guiltless—unlike the other guy. This, however, carries the nagging feeling that we are being irresponsible, skirting the truth. Guilt, then, can be likened to going to work: You don't enjoy it, but it leaves you feeling like an upstanding citizen. Guiltlessness can be likened to going on vacation: It's a great relief from the stress of work, but constant vacationing would leave you feeling like a ne'er-do-well. Thus, in our eyes, we need both. Without both, we won't be whole.

We've got it wrong, says Jesus. Only guiltlessness makes us feel whole.

3.   ¹There is no compromise that you can make with guilt, and escape the pain that only guiltlessness allays. ²Learning is living here, as creating is being in Heaven. ³Whenever the pain of guilt seems to attract you, remember that if you yield to it, you are deciding against your happiness, and will not learn how to be happy. ⁴Say therefore, to yourself, gently, but with the conviction born of the Love of God and of His Son:

> ⁵*What I experience I will make manifest.*
> ⁶*If I am guiltless, I have nothing to fear.*
> ⁷*I choose to testify to my acceptance of the Atonement, not to its rejection [Ur: not for its rejection].*
> ⁸*I would accept my guiltlessness by making it manifest and sharing it.*
> ⁹*Let me bring peace to God's Son from his Father.*

This practice is impossible to understand without the context provided later by paragraph 7. The situation is this: People are—directly or indirectly—accusing you of guilt. You feel tempted to accept the guilt as yours, in order to pay off your debt, to be a good person. Instead, realize that this is a decision to be unhappy. Therefore, refuse this temptation by saying the following words with gentle conviction:

> *What I experience* [inwardly] *I will make manifest* [in my behavior toward you].
> *If I am guiltless, I have nothing to fear.* [If I am guiltless, I deserve no punishment and am therefore invulnerable.]
> *I choose to testify* [to you] *to my acceptance of the Atonement* [of my guiltlessness], *not to its rejection.*
> *I would accept my guiltlessness by making it manifest* [by showing you that I am invulnerable to your condemnation] *and sharing it* [by showing you that, since you haven't hurt me, *you* are guiltless].
> *Let me bring peace* [the peace of guiltlessness] *to God's Son* [you and me] *from his Father.*

This practice is not easy to understand, but its meaning is, in the end, quite simple. When someone attacks me (and thus accuses me of guilt), I can choose to embrace my guiltlessness, a state in which I have nothing to fear. And then I can manifest that state in how I respond to the attack. My response can make the statement, "Because I am guiltless, I can't be hurt. And because you haven't hurt me, you are guiltless, too." By making my guiltless manifest, then, I more fully accept my guiltlessness myself *and* I bring peace to my brother. I bring peace to both of us, peace from our Father.

This explains why it is only in our guiltlessness that we can be happy. When we feel guilty, we feel vulnerable to the condemnation of others. Out of that vulnerability, we lash out, prompting retaliation from the other person, and the whole cycle starts over.

Application: Obviously, this practice is meant to be done. Please think of a situation in which someone is directly or indirectly accusing you of guilt, and then repeat the above lines with gentle conviction, perhaps putting this person's name in wherever appropriate.

4.   ¹Each day, each hour and minute, even each second, you are deciding between the crucifixion and the resurrection; between the ego

and the Holy Spirit. ²The ego is the choice for guilt; the Holy Spirit the choice for guiltlessness [Ur: blamelessness]. ³The power of decision is all that is yours. ⁴What you can decide <u>between</u> is fixed, because there are no alternatives <u>except</u> truth and illusion. ⁵And there is no overlap between them, because they are opposites which <u>cannot</u> be reconciled and <u>cannot</u> both be true. ⁶You are guilty <u>or</u> guiltless, bound <u>or</u> free, unhappy <u>or</u> happy.

The above practice, in which we choose guiltlessness when tempted to feel guilty, highlights the choice that is always before us. We are always tempted to feel guilty, and we are always choosing whether we will yield to that temptation or not. This is not an occasional dilemma. We are faced with it all the time, though mostly in forms that we do not recognize.

5.   ¹The miracle teaches you that you have chosen guiltlessness, freedom and joy. ²It is not a cause, but an <u>effect</u>. ³It is the natural result of <u>choosing right</u>, attesting to your happiness that comes from choosing to be <u>free</u> of guilt. ⁴Everyone you offer healing <u>to</u> returns it. ⁵Everyone you attack <u>keeps</u> it and cherishes it by holding it <u>against</u> you. ⁶Whether he <u>does</u> this or does it not will make no difference; <u>you will think he does</u>. ⁷It is impossible to offer <u>what you do not want</u> without this penalty. ⁸The cost of giving *is* receiving. ⁹Either it is a penalty from which you suffer, or the happy purchase of a treasure to hold dear.

This paragraph lays out two cycles. In the first, we choose guilt, though probably don't realize it. Then we attack a brother. He then cherishes this attack and holds it against us—either in fact or in our imagination. This leads us to consciously feel guilty. Our initial choice for guilt has flowered into something much more conscious.

In the second cycle, we choose guiltlessness, though probably don't realize it. Then we give a miracle to a brother; we heal him. He then returns it in gratitude (a process we have seen in several sections). This leads us to consciously feel guiltless. Our initial choice for guiltlessness has flowered into something much more conscious.

The next paragraph discusses the first cycle, while the one after that discusses the second cycle.

6.   ¹No penalty is ever asked of God's Son except <u>by</u> himself and <u>of</u> himself. ²Every chance given him to heal [a brother] is another

19

opportunity to replace darkness with light and fear with love. ³If he refuses it he binds himself <u>to</u> darkness, because he did not choose to free his brother and enter light <u>with</u> him. ⁴By <u>giving</u> power to nothing, he throws away the joyous opportunity to learn that nothing <u>has</u> no power. ⁵And by <u>not dispelling</u> darkness, <u>he</u> became afraid of darkness <u>and</u> of light. ⁶The joy of learning that darkness has no power over the Son of God is the happy lesson the Holy Spirit teaches, and would have <u>you</u> teach <u>with</u> Him. ⁷It is <u>His</u> joy to teach it, as it will be <u>yours</u>.

Application: Think of a time recently when you passed up an opportunity to heal someone. Perhaps someone asked for your forgiveness, but you couldn't bring yourself to give it. Perhaps someone asked for your help, but you were too busy. Perhaps someone attacked you, and you missed the implicit call for help in that act. Realize that by not freeing your brother from darkness, you bound yourself to darkness. By not freeing your brother from his belief in the power of nothing, you threw away your own joyous opportunity to learn that nothing has no power. Realize no one else asked this penalty of you; you asked it of yourself. Be determined, therefore, not to throw away the next such opportunity.

7. ¹The way to teach this simple lesson is merely this: Guiltlessness <u>is</u> invulnerability. ²Therefore, make your <u>invulnerability</u> manifest to everyone. ³Teach him that, <u>whatever</u> he may try to do to you, your perfect freedom from the belief that you can <u>be</u> harmed shows him that <u>he</u> is guiltless. ⁴He can do <u>nothing</u> that can hurt you, and by refusing to allow him to <u>think he can</u>, you teach him that the Atonement, which you have accepted for yourself, <u>is also his</u>. ⁵<u>There is nothing to forgive</u>. ⁶No one can hurt the Son of God. ⁷His guilt is <u>wholly</u> without cause, and being without cause, <u>cannot</u> exist.

This paragraph, as I said, is a clearer explanation of the gist of the practice in paragraph 3. It is also an elaboration on what I called the second cycle from paragraph 5. Here is the idea: You choose guiltlessness, which means that you don't deserve to be hurt and *can't* be hurt. Now someone comes along and attacks you, conveying with his attack that you are guilty (as all attack does). Yet you know that you aren't guilty and so can't really be attacked—can't be injured. You then make this invulnerability manifest to him. You show him that you are unhurt. Rather than an act of defensiveness, this is a gift to him, for if he didn't hurt you, then he didn't sin, and so he must be guiltless, too.

Application: Think of a recent time when someone attacked you, thus implying that you are guilty. Repeat the following lines to this person:

> *You have not really harmed me at all.*
> *No one can hurt the Son of God.*
> *And I **am** the Son of God.*
> *I am guiltless, and therefore invulnerable.*
> *Therefore, you have done nothing that needs forgiveness.*
> *Your guilt is wholly without cause,*
> *And thus cannot exist.*
> *God is the only Cause, and He knows nothing of guilt.*
> *He knows only that we are His guiltless Son.*

8.   ¹God is the only Cause, and guilt is not of Him. ²Teach no one he has hurt you, for if you do, you teach yourself that what is not of God has power over you. ³*The causeless cannot be.* ⁴Do not attest to it, and do not foster belief in it in any mind. ⁵Remember always that mind is one [which means that that other mind is one with yours], and cause is one. ⁶You will learn communication with this oneness only when you learn to deny the causeless, and accept the Cause of God as yours [accept God's causation as yours]. ⁷The power that God has given to His Son *is* his, and nothing else can His Son see or choose to look upon without imposing on himself the penalty of guilt, in place of all the happy teaching the Holy Spirit would gladly offer him.

I love the logic in this paragraph. If God is the only Cause, then only what He causes exists. If He does not cause guilt, then guilt does not exist. If guilt does not exist, then it can have no power over me. If guilt can have no power over me, then my brother's accusation that I am guilty can have no power over me.

We can accept this, and enter a state of total invulnerability, as well as communication with all minds. Or we can reject it, and make ourselves subject to all sorts of plagues that are not of God. It all hinges on this: What do we teach our brother? Do we teach him that he has hurt us or that we can't be hurt?

Does this mean that when our feelings have been hurt, we just hide this fact from our brother? No, because those feelings will inevitably leak out and teach our brother he hurt us. They can't be entirely hidden. Our job is not to hide our feelings but to *heal* our feelings. We need to get in touch with our guiltlessness, which will put us in touch with our invulnerability, which will take away our hurt feelings. Then we can genuinely teach our brother that he never hurt us.

The second half of this section is on the intimate, yet unexpected, connection of decision-making and guilt.

> 9.   ¹Whenever you choose to make decisions <u>for yourself</u> you are thinking destructively, and the decision <u>will be wrong</u>. ²It will hurt you [with guilt] because of the <u>concept</u> of decision that led to it. ³It is not true that you can make decisions <u>by</u> yourself or <u>for</u> yourself alone. ⁴No thought of God's Son <u>can</u> be separate or isolated in its effects. ⁵Every decision is made for the <u>whole Sonship</u>, directed in and out, and influencing a constellation larger than anything you ever dreamed of.

Let's say you make an ordinary decision; say, to pay your rent. If you made this decision on the basis of its effects on you, then your decision was wrong. Even if the form of the decision was right, the content was wrong. For your decision actually affects everyone, every living mind throughout the universe and beyond. This means you were affecting *everyone* while taking into account only *yourself.*

How does this "hurt you"? To answer that, ask yourself how you would feel if you devoured a delicious meal, only to look up and see yourself surrounded by starving children. The hurt that comes from our self-focused decision-making is the pain of guilt.

> 10.   ¹Those who accept the Atonement [and thus accept their guiltlessness] *are* invulnerable [cannot be hurt].²But those who believe they are guilty <u>will</u> respond to guilt, because <u>they think it is salvation</u>, and will <u>not</u> refuse to see it and side <u>with</u> it. ³They <u>believe</u> that <u>increasing</u> guilt is self-<u>protection</u>. ⁴And they will fail to understand

the simple fact that what they do not want [guilt] must hurt them. ⁵All this arises because they do not believe that what they want is good. ⁶Yet will was given them because it is holy, and will bring to them all that they need, coming as naturally as peace that knows no limits. ⁷There is nothing their will fails to provide that offers them anything of value. ⁸Yet because they do not understand their will, the Holy Spirit quietly understands it for them, and gives them what they want [Ur: what *they* will,] without effort, strain, or the impossible burden of deciding what they want and need alone.

Once you believe you are guilty, you enter a deeply self-destructive cycle. Now, you must do your best to *feel* guilty, for this inner self-beating pays off your past sins *and* protects you against sinning in the future. No matter that you don't want to feel guilty because it hurts. You can't go by what you want. You are, in fact, at war with your desires, for they are wicked. Therefore, what you want (your sinful desires) is bad, while what you don't want (guilt) is good. This is the same twisted logic that drove many of us away from organized religion.

The solution is to accept the Atonement—accept the fact that your nature is pure and holy. Now you will feel invulnerable, for you don't deserve to be hurt. And now you will realize that your true will, rather than seething with wayward desires, is itself holy. If you can only bring yourself to trust it, it will bring to you all that you need. Indeed, this will is so holy that the Holy Spirit's role is to stand in for it, bringing to you the blessings of this holy will while you remain out of touch with it. He just gives these blessings to you, "without the impossible burden of deciding what [you] want and need alone."

11. ¹It will never happen that you must make decisions for yourself. ²You are not bereft of help, and Help that knows the answer. ³Would you be content with little, which is all that you alone can offer yourself, when He Who gives you everything will simply offer it to you? ⁴He will never ask what you have done to make you worthy of the gift of God. ⁵Ask it not therefore of yourself. ⁶Instead, accept His answer, for He knows that you are worthy of everything God wills for you. ⁷Do not try to escape the gift of God He so freely and so gladly offers you. ⁸He offers you but what God gave Him for you. ⁹You need not decide whether or not you are deserving of it. ¹⁰God knows you are.

When we hear, "Let the Holy Spirit decide, for He takes everyone into account," we probably imagine that His decisions will make sure we only get one small slice of the pie, whereas our decision was going to give us the whole thing. This paragraph makes clear that we have got it backwards. Instead, His decisions contain the gift of everything—not on a form level, but on a content level. On the inner level, they are like winning the lottery. They drop so much in our laps that we are likely to feel unworthy, to say, "No, this is too much. I don't deserve this." But that is not humility. It is simply refusal of a gift on which God Himself put our name.

Application: Try to think of some bit of guidance you received from the Holy Spirit. This guidance may have felt challenging, but somewhere inside of it was a diamond, a gift so precious that it contained everything. See yourself responding to this gift of everything not with greedy excitement, but with a sense of being deeply undeserving. Now repeat these words:

> *The Holy Spirit will never ask me what I have done to make me worthy of the gift of God.*
> *I will therefore not ask it of myself.*
> *I will instead accept the gift, for He knows I am worthy of everything God wills for me.*
> *I need not decide whether or not I am deserving of it.*
> *God knows I am.*

12. ¹Would you deny the truth of God's decision, and place your pitiful appraisal of yourself in place of His calm and unswerving value of His Son? ²Nothing can shake God's conviction of the perfect purity of everything that He created, for it *is* wholly pure. ³Do not decide against it, for being of Him it must be true. ⁴Peace abides in every mind that quietly accepts the plan [Ur: that *God*] God set for its Atonement, relinquishing its own [Ur: *relinquishing his own*]. ⁵You know not of salvation, for you do not understand it. ⁶Make no decisions about what it is or where it lies, but ask the Holy Spirit everything, and leave all decisions to His gentle counsel.

What a beautiful paragraph! Yet to really appreciate it, we must see it in its specific context. It is talking about not rejecting the Holy Spirit's guidance for our decisions. When we reject that guidance, we are thinking, "Oh, this sounds so great. It is so idealistic. It affirms everyone. But it *screws* me." Isn't this what we are thinking when He tells us to reach Atonement by forgiving that hardest person to forgive? We think, "Actually, I'd feel a lot more guiltless if I just more effectively *blamed* this person."

Yet this is all a bit of a ruse, for underneath this reason for rejecting His guidance is a deeper reason: We sense that this guidance offers us everything, and we don't feel worthy. God may think we are pure and deserving, but we know better. We "know" that we are deserving of only the tiny crumbs that our own decision-making offers us.

> 13. ¹The One Who knows the plan of God that God would have you follow can teach you what it <u>is</u>. ²Only His wisdom is capable of guiding you to follow it. ³Every decision you undertake alone but signifies that you would define what salvation *is*, and what you would be saved *from*. ⁴The Holy Spirit <u>knows</u> that <u>all</u> salvation is escape from guilt. ⁵You have no other "enemy," and against this strange distortion of the purity of the Son of God the Holy Spirit is your <u>only</u> Friend. ⁶He is the strong protector of the innocence that sets you free. ⁷And it is <u>His</u> decision to undo <u>everything</u> that would obscure your innocence from your unclouded mind.

Here we have further clarification on how our decisions differ from the Holy Spirit's guidance for us. Our decisions grab stuff for us, while taking on the collateral damage of guilt, guilt that we think we can handle. How many decisions have we made that are just like this? We don't realize that the stuff we grab is worthless, while the guilt costs us everything.

The Holy Spirit's decisions, in contrast, give us "escape from guilt." We have no idea how precious, how all-important this is. We don't realize that guilt is our only enemy. We don't realize that guilt blocks out our holiness, which contains the gift of everything. Because we don't understand these things, we need to follow the Holy Spirit like an uncoordinated hiker would follow a Sherpa up a treacherous mountain trail, full of sheer cliffs and ice fissures. Right now, He is our only Friend.

25

We are not just uncoordinated; we are a bit possessed, and we keep trying to throw ourselves over the cliff into the chasm of guilt. That is what our self-made decisions do.

14. ¹Let Him, therefore, be the only Guide that you would follow to salvation. ²He knows the way, and leads you gladly on it. ³<u>With</u> Him you will not fail to learn that what God wills <u>for</u> you *is* your will. ⁴<u>Without</u> His guidance you will think you know alone, and will decide <u>against</u> your peace as surely as you decided [Ur: as surely as you made the wrong decision in ever thinking] that salvation lay in you alone. ⁵Salvation is of Him to Whom God <u>gave</u> it <u>for</u> you. ⁶He has not forgotten it. ⁷Forget <u>Him</u> not and He will make <u>every</u> decision for you, for <u>your</u> salvation and the peace of God in you.

This paragraph reiterates the message of the preceding ones: Our own decision-making is not our friend, for its self-absorbed nature just stacks on more guilt. The Holy Spirit's decision-making *is* our friend, for it delivers us from guilt and thus allows us to claim God's gift of everything.

In other words, we need to see ourselves in the arena of decision-making like a wise alcoholic sees himself while inside a bar. Just as the alcoholic knows that he can't trust his impulses to have a drink, so we should know that we can't trust our impulses in decision-making, for we are likely to grab a tumbler full of guilt.

Application: Think of a decision currently facing you. Then say to yourself:

Without His guidance I will think I know alone.
And I will decide against my peace.
I will decide to take on more guilt.
Yet guilt is my only "enemy."
And against this "enemy," the Holy Spirit's guidance is my only
friend.

15. ¹Seek not to appraise the worth of God's Son whom He created holy, for to do so is <u>to evaluate his Father</u> and judge <u>against</u> Him. ²And

you *will* feel guilty for this imagined crime, which no one in this world or Heaven could possibly [Ur: *can possibly*] commit. ³The Holy Spirit [Ur: God's Spirit] teaches only that the "sin" of <u>self</u>-replacement on the throne of God is <u>not</u> a source of guilt. ⁴What <u>cannot</u> happen can have no effects to fear. ⁵Be quiet in your faith in Him Who loves you, and would lead you out of insanity. ⁶Madness may be your <u>choice</u>, but <u>not</u> your reality. ⁷Never forget the Love of God, Who <u>has</u> remembered you. ⁸For it is quite impossible that He could ever let His Son drop from the loving Mind wherein he was created, and where his abode was fixed in perfect peace forever.

Application: To take in the meaning of the above paragraph, slowly repeat these lines to yourself:

To decide that I am guilty when God created me holy, is to evaluate God and judge against Him.
It is to place myself on God's throne in His stead.
I do feel guilty for this imagined crime.
But it cannot be committed, and so can have no effects.
I am therefore still innocent.
It is quite impossible that God could ever let me, His beloved Son, drop from the loving Mind wherein my abode was fixed in peace forever.
Therefore, I will trust the only One Who knows this, the Holy Spirit.
He Who leads me out of the madness of guilt into my reality as God's perfect Son.

16. ¹Say to the Holy Spirit only, "Decide for me," and it is done. ²For His decisions are reflections of <u>what God knows about you,</u> and in this light, error of <u>any</u> kind becomes impossible. ³Why would you struggle so frantically to anticipate all you <u>cannot</u> know, when <u>all</u> knowledge lies behind <u>every</u> decision the Holy Spirit makes <u>for you</u>? ⁴Learn of His wisdom and His Love, and teach His answer to everyone who struggles in the dark. ⁵For you decide for <u>them and</u> for yourself.

You might say that there is a surface level to this paragraph and a deeper level. The surface level message is that it's ridiculous for us to try, in our decision-making, to anticipate all we cannot know. Why? Because there is Someone there Who knows everything. He simply makes better decisions, because He has access to more information, infinitely more.

The deeper message is that what He knows is not simply information (though He definitely knows that—see M-10.3-4). What He knows is "what God knows about you." In other words, His decisions may seem to be about form, about what to do. But contained in each one is God's perfect knowledge of who we are, and of our infinite holiness and worth. Thus, if we *act out* that decision, we *take in* that knowledge.

> 17. ¹How gracious it is to decide all things through Him Whose equal Love is given equally to all alike! ²He leaves you no one <u>outside</u> you [Ur: *outside* yourself, alone *without* you]. ³And so He gives you what is yours, because your Father would have you share it <u>with</u> Him. ⁴In everything be led by Him, and do not reconsider. ⁵Trust Him to answer quickly, surely, and with Love for everyone who will be touched in any way by the decision. ⁶And <u>everyone</u> will be. ⁷Would you take unto yourself the sole responsibility for deciding what can bring <u>only</u> good to everyone? ⁸Would you <u>know</u> this?
> 18. ¹You taught yourself [Ur: *yourselves*] the most unnatural habit of <u>not</u> communicating with your Creator. ²Yet you remain in close communication with Him, and with everything that is within Him, as it is within <u>yourself</u>. ³<u>Un</u>learn isolation through His loving guidance, and learn of all the happy communication that you have thrown away but could <u>not</u> lose.

Imagine you had a person with you who was the ultimate guide for decision-making. This person had access to detailed information on every single person alive and knew how your decisions would affect each one. Based on that information, he made sure that your decisions factored in everyone. After he told you exactly how a particular decision of yours would positively affect a whole list of people you had never met, delivering needed blessings into their lives, wouldn't you feel more connected to those people? As this happened with decision after decision, wouldn't you start feeling connected to everyone? Wouldn't it seem as if you were in communication with everyone? Wouldn't you, in fact, feel that you were unlearning isolation? And would you ever want to go back to making decisions by yourself again?

19. ¹Whenever you are in doubt what you should do, think of His Presence in you, and tell yourself this, and <u>only</u> this:

> ²*He leadeth me and knows the way, which I know not.*
> ³*Yet He will never keep from me what He would have me learn.*
> ⁴*And so I trust Him to communicate to me all that He knows for me.*

⁵Then let Him teach you quietly how to perceive your guiltlessness, which is <u>already</u> there.

Application: Think of some situation in which you are in doubt about what to do. Then think of the Holy Spirit's Presence in you. Then tell yourself,

> *He leadeth me and knows the way, which I know not.*
> *Yet He will never keep from me what He would have me learn.*
> *And so I trust Him to communicate to me all that He knows for me.*

Then say to Him, *"Decide for me,"* trusting that His decision will help you perceive your guiltlessness.

Then still your mind and listen for His guidance. Listen in patience and confidence. Repeat your question as often as you like.

IV. Your Function in the Atonement
Commentary by Robert Perry

1. ¹When you accept a brother's guiltlessness you will <u>see</u> the Atonement in him. ²For by proclaiming it in <u>him</u> you make it <u>yours</u>, and you <u>will</u> see what you sought. ³You will not see the symbol of your brother's guiltlessness [the Atonement] shining within him while you still believe <u>it is not there</u>. ⁴<u>His</u> guiltlessness is *your* Atonement. ⁵Grant it to him, and you will see the truth of what you have acknowledged. ⁶Yet truth is offered <u>first</u> to be received, even as God gave it first to His Son. ⁷The first in time means nothing, but the First in eternity is God the Father, Who is both First and One. ⁸Beyond the First there is no other, for there is no order, no second or third, and nothing <u>but</u> the First.

Application: Choose a couple of people at random and silently say these lines to them:

I accept your guiltlessness, [name].
I therefore see the Atonement shining within you.
For by seeing it in you, I will see it in myself.
*Your guiltlessness is **my** Atonement.*

The principle in this paragraph is, as we probably know by now, central to the Course. We have to first offer truth to our brother—the truth of guiltlessness—before we can receive that truth for ourselves. Jesus keeps telling us this in a hundred different ways.

I have always found the last two sentences to be very beautiful. They echo the Hindu saying about God being "one without a second." God's Son, therefore, is not a true second, not a true other, but is part of, included in, the One.

2. ¹You who belong to the First Cause, created by Him like unto Himself and part of Him, are more than merely guiltless. ²The state of guiltlessness is only the condition in which what is <u>not</u> there [guilt] has

been <u>removed</u> from the disordered mind that <u>thought</u> it <u>was</u>. ³This state, and only this, must <u>you</u> attain, with God beside you. ⁴For until you do, you will still think that you are separate <u>from</u> Him. ⁵You can perhaps feel His Presence <u>next</u> to you, but <u>cannot</u> know that you are one with Him. ⁶This cannot be taught. ⁷Learning applies <u>only</u> to the condition <u>in which it</u> [knowing you are one with Him] <u>happens</u> of itself.

We are not a second to God; we are part of the One Who is without a second. Yet as long as we feel guilty, we cannot know this. Guilt says to us, "You are alone in your sins, cut off from the Holy One." As long as we carry guilt, then, we may feel Him walking alongside us, but we will not know that we are part of His very Being. Our whole journey, then, is one of realizing that guilt is an illusion in our disordered mind. It is no more a real part of our mind than a mirage is a real part of the desert. And when we finally do learn this, we will awaken to knowledge that cannot be described nor learned, in which we know with infinite certainty that we are part of God.

3.   ¹When you have let all that obscured the truth in your most holy mind be undone for you, and therefore stand in grace [freedom from sin] before your Father, He will give Himself to you as He has <u>always</u> done. ²Giving Himself is all He knows, and so it is <u>all</u> knowledge. ³For what He knows <u>not</u> cannot be, and therefore <u>cannot be given</u>. ⁴Ask not to <u>be</u> forgiven, for this has already been accomplished. ⁵Ask, rather, to <u>learn</u> how to forgive, and to restore <u>what always was</u> [the knowledge of God giving Himself to us] to your unforgiving mind. ⁶Atonement becomes real and visible to those who <u>use</u> it [who give it to others]. ⁷On earth this is your <u>only</u> function, and you must learn that it is <u>all you want to learn</u>. ⁸You <u>will</u> feel guilty till you learn this. ⁹For in the end, whatever form it takes, your guilt arises from your failure to fulfill your function in God's Mind with <u>all of yours</u>. ¹⁰Can you <u>escape</u> this guilt by failing to fulfill your function <u>here</u>?

I love everything in this paragraph. First it says that when you have finally let the truth shine away the vaporous clouds of guilt in your mind, you will stand in sinlessness before your Father, and "He will give Himself to you as He has *always* done." This giving goes on eternally. This is the sun that shines forever. Your job is merely to clear away the clouds, so it can once again shine on your upturned face.

Then it says a line that, in light of Western tradition, can scarcely be believed: "Giving Himself is all He knows." What a beautiful vision of God! And it continues. Since giving Himself is all God knows, then it is all knowledge; it is all *we* can know. This is the knowledge we are returning to, as we allow our guilt to be wiped away, the knowledge of God giving Himself to us continually—the only thing we can know.

If we truly understood that God has always given Himself to us, would we ask Him to forgive us? Asking Him to forgive us does entail a recognition that guilt is what keeps us from Him, but it also makes guilt real. Would you say to someone who is absolutely in love with you, "Stop hating me"?

No. Rather than asking God to forgive our real guilt, we need to ask Him to help us do what clears the *illusion* of guilt from our mind. "Ask, rather, to learn how to forgive." This is our great need, *to learn how to forgive*. Guiltlessness will only become real to us as we give it to others. Atonement will only become visible in us as we use it to free our brothers. *This* is how we clear the clouds of guilt from our mind.

Finally, the paragraph says that we *will* feel guilty until we fulfill our only function of giving Atonement to others. This is because not fulfilling our function on earth is a reflection, a repetition, of not fulfilling our function in Heaven (our function of creation), which is the ultimate source of all our guilt.

> 4. ¹You need not understand creation to do what must be done <u>before</u> that knowledge would be meaningful to you. ²God breaks no barriers; neither did He <u>make</u> them. ³When <u>you</u> release them they are gone. ⁴God will not fail, nor ever has in anything. ⁵Decide that God is right and <u>you</u> are wrong about yourself. ⁶He created you out of Himself, but still <u>within</u> Him. ⁷He knows what you are. ⁸Remember that there is no second to Him. ⁹There cannot, therefore, be anyone <u>without</u> His Holiness, nor anyone unworthy of His perfect Love. ¹⁰Fail not in your function of loving in a loveless place made out of darkness and deceit, for thus are darkness and deceit <u>undone</u>. ¹¹<u>Fail not yourself</u>, but instead offer to God <u>and you</u> His blameless Son. ¹²For this small gift of appreciation <u>for</u> His Love, God will Himself exchange your gift for <u>His</u> [the gift of Himself].

We don't need to have knowledge in order to make way for it. That would be a cruel system, wouldn't it? We simply need to clear away the barriers—which are made of our belief in our sinfulness. This is the whole path. Extending forgiveness and love to others is an act of repeatedly, and in the end, constantly, teaching ourselves that we are guiltless.

Application: Reflect on the list from "The 'Dynamics' of the Ego" (11.V.9:1). You have called yourself contemptuously condescending, unbelieving, insufficiently serious, distant, emotionally shallow, callous, uninvolved, and desperate. You think you *are* these qualities. Yet God knows otherwise. He knows that, since "there is no second to Him," you are part of Him, and thus share in His Holiness, and are worthy of His perfect Love. Say, then, the following line as an acknowledgment that He knows who you are:

I decide that God is right and I am wrong about myself.

Holding this new view of yourself in mind, repeat these lines:

I will fail not in my function of loving in a loveless place.
For thus do I shine away the cloud of guilt in my own mind.

5.   ¹Before you make <u>any</u> decisions for yourself, remember that <u>you have decided against your function in Heaven</u>, and then consider carefully whether you <u>want</u> to make decisions here. ²Your function here is only to decide <u>against</u> deciding what you want, in recognition that <u>you do not know</u>. ³How, then, <u>can</u> you decide what you should do? ⁴Leave <u>all</u> decisions to the One Who speaks for God, and for your function as He <u>knows</u> it. ⁵So will He teach you to remove the awful burden you have laid upon yourself by loving not the Son of God, and trying to teach him guilt <u>instead</u> of love. ⁶Give up this frantic and insane attempt that cheats you of the joy of living with your God and Father, and of waking gladly to His Love and Holiness that join together as the truth in <u>you</u>, making you one with Him.

This paragraph repeats a key idea from the previous section. We need to be incredibly suspicious of our own decision-making, for it chronically dumps guilt into our mind. We need to remember that we decided against our function in Heaven, and are therefore liable to inject that content into even the most "obvious" decisions now. Those decisions, then, will become subtle perpetuations of deciding not to do our function here. And that will lead to guilt—"the awful burden you have laid upon yourself by loving not the Son of God."

Application: Think of a decision facing you and remember this:

My own decision will make me feel guilty.
It will contain the decision to love not my brother,
and will thus be a refusal of my function here on earth.
And this will repeat my refusal of my function in Heaven.
I give up the lovelessness that cheats me of the joy of living with
*   God.*
Holy Spirit, decide for me.

6.   ¹When you have learned how to decide <u>with</u> God, <u>all</u> decisions become as easy and as right as breathing. ²There is no effort, and you will be led as gently as if you were being carried down a quiet path in summer. ³Only your own volition seems to make deciding hard. ⁴The Holy Spirit will not delay in answering your <u>every</u> question what to do. ⁵He <u>knows</u>. ⁶And He will <u>tell</u> you, and then do it <u>for</u> you. ⁷You who are tired will find this is [Ur: You who are tired might consider whether this is not] more restful than sleep. ⁸For you can bring your guilt into sleeping, but <u>not</u> into this.

This is a beautiful paragraph. Decision-making can be so difficult, as we struggle to choose between competing alternatives, and as we strive to predict a future we cannot know. What a wonderful thought to think that God can carry us through our decisions as if we are "being carried down a quiet path in summer." How amazing to think that we can find decision-making more restful than sleep!

The subtle message here is that what makes decision-making so hard is only our own unloving volition, and what makes us so tired is our own guilt. How can this be? Our decisions, I think, are usually wrestling matches between our desire to express our lovelessness and our desire to redeem ourselves for past lovelessness. "Which one should I do?"

becomes so much of the whole struggle. Then, after the decision is made, we are left with guilt, either guilt over expressing our lovelessness or guilt over the lovelessness we concealed with our "redemptive" act. This guilt is an "awful burden," and carrying this burden is what makes us tired. That is why we can wake after a full night's sleep and still not feel rested.

> 7. ¹Unless you are guiltless you cannot know God, Whose Will is that you know Him. ²Therefore, you *must* be guiltless [for His Will cannot be thwarted]. ³Yet if you do not accept the necessary conditions for knowing Him, you have denied Him and do not recognize Him, though He is all around you. ⁴He cannot be known without His Son, whose guiltlessness is the condition for knowing Him. ⁵Accepting His Son [in yourself and others] as guilty is denial of the Father so complete, that knowledge is swept away from recognition in the very mind where God Himself has placed it. ⁶If you would but listen, and learn how impossible this is! ⁷Do not endow Him with attributes you understand. ⁸You made Him not, and anything you understand is not of Him.

The first lines deserve real reflection. I will lay their logic out in my own words:

> I cannot know God if I have even the slightest shred of guilt.
> Yet God wills that I know Him and His Will cannot be thwarted.
> Therefore, I *must* be guiltless. Every last shred of my guilt must be unreal.
> Thinking that I have any guilt, then, blinds me to the truth.
> It causes me to not recognize God, even though He is all around me.

This last line is not how we see things. We think that we have actually blotted the knowledge of God from our mind. Yet this is utterly impossible. That would mean that we either managed to overpower God, or that He decided to punish us by withdrawing from us. Either one implies a God that is simply a product of our very human thinking.

> 8. ¹Your task is not to make reality. ²It is here without your making, but not without you. ³You who have tried to throw yourself away [Ur: who have thrown your selves away] and valued God so little, hear me

35

speak for Him and for yourself. ⁴You cannot understand how much your Father loves you, for there is no parallel in your experience of the world to help you understand it. ⁵There is nothing on earth with which it can compare, and nothing you have ever felt <u>apart</u> from Him resembles it ever so faintly. ⁶You cannot even give a blessing in perfect gentleness. ⁷Would you know of One Who gives forever, and Who knows of nothing <u>except</u> giving?

We think we have banished the knowledge of God from our mind. We think we have thrown away something we can do without. We assume that the knowledge of God can't stack up to the pleasures this world has to offer. We just don't get it. Quite simply, we have no comprehension of the magnitude of God's Love. How could we? There is literally no earthly parallel. The love of a lover does not compare. The love of a mother does not compare. The most intense love in this world doesn't even come close. Nothing here even faintly compares. Surely our own love doesn't compare. The love we give is such a mixed bag, so full of hidden fangs. How, then, can we understand a Love that is not remotely a mixed bag, a Love that only gives, that gives forever, that knows of nothing except giving? How can we understand a Love that is *pure* love?

This is why, even though Jesus yearns to tell us what this Love is like, words fail him:

> I cannot tell you what this will be like, for your heart is not ready. (T-11.III.3:6)

> O my brothers, if you only knew the peace that will envelop you and hold you safe and pure and lovely in the Mind of God... (C-4.8:1)

> [The body] cannot enter Heaven. But I can take you there any time you choose. Together we can watch the world disappear and its symbol [the body] vanish as it does so. And then, and then—I cannot speak of that. (Guidance on the resurrection from *Absence from Felicity*, by Kenneth Wapnick, p. 399)

9. ¹The children of Heaven live in the light of the blessing of their Father, because <u>they know that they are sinless</u>. ²The Atonement was established as the means of restoring guiltlessness to minds that have denied it, and thus denied Heaven to themselves. ³Atonement teaches

you the true condition of the Son of God. ⁴It does <u>not</u> teach you what you are, or what your Father is. ⁵The Holy Spirit, Who remembers this <u>for</u> you, merely teaches you how to <u>remove</u> the blocks that stand between you and what <u>you</u> know. ⁶His memory is <u>yours</u>. ⁷If you remember what <u>you</u> have made, you are remembering nothing. ⁸Remembrance of reality is in <u>Him</u>, and <u>therefore</u> in you.

This is what the whole journey is about—restoring the awareness of our guiltlessness. All of the work we do along the way is for this. We are not here to remember the knowledge of who we are or Who God is. We are here to learn that we never did the things we thought we did. We are here to learn that we never made a devil of God's Son. Then we will remember the knowledge we threw away.

This is why it is so crucial to be in touch with our guilt and realize its debilitating effects. To the extent that we do not, we will lack the motivation to do what Jesus asks of us here; for instance, the motivation to forgive our brothers, and the motivation to ask for the Holy Spirit's guidance.

10. ¹The guiltless and the guilty are totally incapable of understanding one another. ²Each perceives the other <u>as like himself</u>, making both unable to communicate, because each sees the other <u>unlike</u> the way he [the other] sees <u>himself</u>. ³God can communicate <u>only</u> to the Holy Spirit in your mind, because only He shares the knowledge of what you are <u>with</u> God. ⁴And only the Holy Spirit can answer God for <u>you</u>, for only He knows what God <u>is</u>. ⁵Everything <u>else</u> that <u>you</u> have placed within your mind <u>cannot</u> exist, for what is not in communication with the Mind of God has never been. ⁶Communication with God is life. ⁷Nothing without it <u>is</u> at all.

I've always found this passage fascinating. It explains why we can't communicate with God directly. The reason is that communication requires that you, the communicator, see the other party the way he sees himself. If, for instance, you spoke to your boss while seeing your boss as your dog, would any real communication take place?

This is analogous to what happens when we communicate with God. Feeling guilty, we imagine a guilty God and speak to that God. We, in essence, say, "Hey Jehovah, could you stop sending all those plagues and instead forgive me down here?" God's natural response is, "Are you talking to Me?" Further, God, being innocent, knows us as innocent. So He says to us, "You are My holy Son. You've always been in Heaven." We quite naturally look around and say, "Who the hell is He talking to?"

This is why God must communicate with us through the Holy Spirit. The Holy Spirit can receive God's communications to us because the Holy Spirit sees us the way God's communications portray us. And the Holy Spirit can pass on our communications to God, for He knows God the way God knows Himself.

Everything else in our mind—everything besides this Holy Spirit-mediated communication with God—is not really there. This is because nothing that is not in communication with God exists. As this paragraph says, "Communication with God is life."

V. The Circle of Atonement
Commentary by Robert Perry

1.   ¹The only part of your mind that has reality is the part that links you still with God. ²Would you have all of it transformed into a radiant message of God's Love, to share with all the lonely ones who have denied Him [Ur: with you]? ³*God makes this possible.* ⁴Would you deny His yearning to be known? ⁵You yearn for Him, as He for you. ⁶This is forever changeless. ⁷Accept, then, the immutable. ⁸Leave the world of death behind, and return quietly to Heaven. ⁹There is nothing of value here, and everything of value there. ¹⁰Listen to the Holy Spirit, and to God through Him. ¹¹He speaks of you to *you.* ¹²There is no guilt in you, for God is blessed in His Son as the Son is blessed in Him.

The first sentence picks up from the closing lines of the previous section. It says that only the part of our mind that is in communication with God is actually real. For similar passages, see W-pI.49.1-2 and C-1.3-4.

Application: Ask yourself,

>*Do I want all of my mind transformed into a radiant message of God's Love, to share with all the lonely ones of this world?*

Then say to yourself,

>***God makes this possible.***

Now reflect for a moment on the fact that you yearn for God. Perhaps you aren't aware of this, but this is the yearning behind *every* yearning. Then reflect on the fact that God yearns for you. This may be hard to believe, but the Course says it repeatedly (see W-pI.76.10:6 and W-pII.7.3:1). Then say,

>*I cannot change my yearning for Him, nor His yearning for me.*
>*I will accept, then, the changeless.*

2. ¹Everyone [Ur: Each one of you] has a special part to play in the Atonement, but the message given to each one [Ur: to share] is always the same; *God's Son is guiltless.* ²Each one teaches the message differently, and learns it differently. ³Yet <u>until</u> he teaches it and learns it, he will suffer the pain of dim awareness [the pain of guilt] that his true function remains unfulfilled in him. ⁴The burden of guilt is heavy, but God would not have you bound by it. ⁵<u>His</u> plan for your awaking is as perfect as yours is fallible. ⁶You know not what you do [you don't realize that your plan for being happy just makes you feel guilty], but He Who knows is with you. ⁷His gentleness is yours, and all the love you share with God He holds in trust for you. ⁸He would teach you nothing except how to be happy.

Each one of us has been assigned a special part in the overall plan of salvation. The essence, however, of each part is exactly the same: We give the message to others that "God's Son is guiltless." We tell everyone, with our attitudes and actions, and occasionally our words, that they are God's Son and that their mistakes have left them untainted. Until we devote every day to imparting this message, we will be haunted by a dim pain we can't put our finger on, a lingering sense that we are leaving our true job here undone. And what is this "sense" but another way of talking about guilt? We think we know the path to happiness. We have no idea that our decisions are just more choices to stay home from work. They thus simply add rocks onto our already heavy burden of guilt. Only the Holy Spirit knows the way to happiness for us, and that way is fulfilling our special part in His plan.

I have always found it odd that the message given to each one is essentially that of Course-based forgiveness. This implies that forgiveness is the active ingredient in the ministry of every teacher, healer, yogi, mystic, saint, pastor, and rabbi—whether that person is fully aware of it or not.

3. ¹Blessed Son of a wholly blessing Father, joy was created <u>for</u> you. ²Who can condemn whom God has blessed [you]? ³There is nothing in the Mind of God that does not share His shining innocence. ⁴Creation is the natural extension of perfect purity. ⁵Your only calling here is to devote yourself, with active willingness, to the denial of guilt in <u>all</u> its forms. ⁶To accuse is *not to understand.* ⁷The happy learners of the Atonement become the teachers of the innocence that is the <u>right</u> of all

that God created. ⁸Deny them [all that God created] not what is their due, for you will not withhold it from them alone.

God created us by extending His perfect purity. That extension became our being, making innocence the very fabric of our eternal nature. We cannot change our nature, but we can deny it. We do this by denying the innocence of others.

Application: Reflect on what you see as your calling or callings here on earth. Maybe it is being a mother, or a teacher, or a provider, or a healer. Maybe it is a collection of various roles that you carry out. Now dwell on this line:

> *My only calling here is to devote myself to the denial of guilt in all its forms.*

Realize that this is the real, intended content of whatever role you have been given.

4.   ¹The inheritance of the Kingdom is the right of God's Son, given him in his creation. ²Do not try to steal it from him [a reference to Jacob stealing Esau's inheritance from him], or you will <u>ask for</u> guilt and <u>will</u> experience it. ³<u>Protect</u> his purity from every thought that would steal it away and keep it from his sight. ⁴<u>Bring innocence to light</u>, in answer to the call of the Atonement. ⁵Never allow purity to remain hidden, but shine away the heavy veils of guilt within which the Son of God has hidden himself from his own sight.

How do we try to steal our brother's inheritance from him? By accusing him of guilt, for guilt makes him undeserving of the Kingdom that God willed to him. Doing this is actually a covert request to experience guilt ourselves, a request which we will grant. Instead of taking away our brother's purity, we need to swing all the way to the other side and become the *protector* of it.

Application: Think of someone whose purity you have tried to take away, realizing that in doing so, you've tried to steal this person's inheritance. Be determined to reverse this. Say the following lines to this person, as formal vows for the future:

> *[Name], I will protect your purity from every thought that would steal it away and keep it from your sight.*
> *I will bring your innocence to light, in answer to the call of the Atonement.*
> *I will never allow your purity to remain hidden.*
> *Instead, my love will shine away the heavy veils of guilt with which you have hidden your divinity from your own sight.*

5. ¹We are all joined in the Atonement here, and nothing else can unite us in this world. ²So will the world of separation slip away, and full communication be restored between the Father and the Son. ³The miracle acknowledges the guiltlessness that <u>must</u> have been denied to produce the <u>need</u> of healing. ⁴Do not withhold [from your brother] this glad acknowledgment [of guiltlessness], for hope of happiness and release from suffering of <u>every</u> kind lie in it. ⁵Who is there but wishes to be free of pain? ⁶He may not yet have learned how to exchange guilt for innocence, nor realize that <u>only</u> in this exchange can freedom from pain be his. ⁷Yet those who have failed to learn need <u>teaching,</u> <u>not</u> attack. ⁸To attack those who have need of teaching is to fail to learn <u>from</u> them.

We seem to join in all sorts of things, but the only thing that can really unite us here is joining in the Atonement, joining in the purpose of releasing everyone from guilt. If that is not the underlying purpose behind a relationship, then that relationship is just separateness masquerading as relationship.

Notice that the miracle is really extending to another the "glad acknowledgment" of guiltlessness. That's how the miracle heals, for guilt is what makes us sick.

Application: Think of someone who seems bent on attacking you, someone whose innocence you find very hard to see. Then say to yourself,

> *Don't I think he wishes to be free of pain?*

Clearly, he has not learned that only by relinquishing guilt can he be free of pain.
He has also not learned that only by relinquishing attack can he be free of guilt.
Yet those who have failed to learn need teaching, not attack.
It is my job to teach him that he is guiltless.

6.   ¹Teachers of innocence, each in his own way, have joined together, taking their part in the unified curriculum of the Atonement. ²There is no unity of learning goals apart from this. ³There is no conflict in this curriculum, which has one aim however it is taught. ⁴Each effort made on its behalf is offered for the single purpose of <u>release</u> from guilt, to the eternal glory of God and His creation. ⁵And every teaching that points to this points straight to Heaven, and the peace of God. ⁶There is no pain, no trial, no fear that teaching this can fail to overcome. ⁷The power of God Himself supports this teaching, and <u>guarantees</u> its limitless results.

This is Jesus' view of the global community of teachers of God. What defines them is not that they teach about oneness, or even about God. What defines them is that they teach *guiltlessness*. Each teaches this in his or her own way. Most may not even think of it in these terms. Yet this is the underlying content that unites them all. On the surface, they may compete and may disparage each other, but beneath that, they are united in "the single purpose of release from guilt." This teaching has all of God's power behind it. Nothing can stand in its way. This is where the miracles come from.

Therefore, the real litmus test of a spiritual teacher is not whether he talks about God or about oneness. It is whether he is really promoting— in his teachings and in his attitudes—the idea that we are not defined by the bad things we have done. Given this, an atheist can be a more powerful teacher of God than many believers.

7.   ¹Join your own efforts to the power [the power of God that supports this teaching] that cannot fail and <u>must</u> result in peace. ²No one can be untouched by teaching such as this. ³You will not see yourself <u>beyond</u> the power of God if you teach only this. ⁴You will <u>not</u> be exempt from the effects of this most holy lesson, which seeks but to restore what is

the right of God's creation. ⁵From everyone whom you accord release from guilt you will <u>inevitably</u> learn <u>your</u> innocence. ⁶The circle of Atonement <u>has</u> no end. ⁷And you will find ever-increasing confidence in your safe inclusion in the circle [Ur: inclusion in what is for all,] with everyone you bring within its safety and its perfect peace.

8.   ¹Peace, then, be unto everyone who becomes a teacher of peace. ²For peace is the acknowledgment of perfect purity, from which no one is excluded. ³Within its holy circle is everyone whom God created as His Son. ⁴Joy is its unifying attribute, with no one left outside to suffer guilt alone. ⁵The power of God draws everyone to its safe embrace of love and union. ⁶Stand quietly within this circle, and attract all tortured minds to join with you in the safety of its peace and holiness. ⁷Abide with me within it, as a teacher of Atonement, <u>not</u> of guilt.

The circle of Atonement is such a beautiful image. It is a "circle" both in the sense of a sphere or area within which something acts (e.g., a circle of influence) and in the sense of a number of persons bound by a common tie (e.g., a circle of friends). Inside the circle are all those who are reconciled with God through guiltlessness (reconciliation with God being what Atonement is about). It is therefore a place of joy, in which everyone feels bound together by the common experience of being with God. It is not a physical place but a mental space, a space occupied by advanced individuals scattered all over the globe.

In truth, everyone is within the circle: "Within its holy circle is everyone whom God created as His Son." This tight-knit club, then, is the entire Sonship. This well-defined sphere is the entire Kingdom.

Even though everyone is inside, most don't *realize* they are inside, because they think they are guilty. They look in on this holy party from the outside, shivering out in the darkness, alone in their guilt.

Our task, then, is to realize that we are already inside; our experience of standing outside is a perceptual illusion. How do we do this? By standing within the circle and drawing *others* inside. We do this by giving them the message that they are guiltless. We thereby become teachers of Atonement, of guiltlessness. With each person we bring into the circle, we find ever-increasing confidence in our own safe inclusion in the circle. As Edgar Cayce said, "You'll not be in heaven if you're not leaning on the arm of someone you have helped."

9.   ¹Blessed are you * who teach with me. ²Our power * comes not of us, but of our Father. ³In guiltlessness we know Him, as He knows us guiltless. ⁴I stand within the circle *, calling you to peace. ⁵Teach peace with me *, and stand with me on holy ground. ⁶Remember for everyone your Father's power [of guiltlessness] that He has given him. ⁷Believe not * that you cannot teach His perfect peace [the peace that comes from guiltlessness]. ⁸Stand not outside *, but join with me within. ⁹Fail not the only purpose to which my teaching calls you *. ¹⁰Restore to God His Son as He created him, by teaching him his innocence.

Application: Please read this again very slowly, inserting your name at the asterisks, and imagining that Jesus is speaking this paragraph personally to you.

Then go within for guidance. Jesus is calling you using poetic imagery, in which you stand inside the circle with him, stand on holy ground with him, and call to those who think they are outside, inviting them in with the proclamation of their guiltlessness. The question you need to ask the Holy Spirit within is, "What would standing with Jesus on holy ground and teaching guiltlessness with him mean for me *in literal terms*?"

10.   ¹The crucifixion had no part in the Atonement. ²Only the resurrection became my part in it. ³That is the symbol of the release from guilt by guiltlessness. ⁴Whom you perceive as guilty you would crucify. ⁵Yet you restore guiltlessness to whomever you see as guiltless. ⁶Crucifixion is always the ego's aim. ⁷It sees everyone as guilty [Ur: It *sees as guilty*], and by its condemnation it would kill. ⁸The Holy Spirit sees only guiltlessness, and in His gentleness He would release from fear and re-establish the reign of love. ⁹The power of love is in His gentleness, which is of God and therefore cannot crucify nor suffer crucifixion. ¹⁰The temple you restore [in your brother] becomes your altar, for it was rebuilt through you. ¹¹And everything you give to God is yours. ¹²Thus He creates, and thus must you restore.

This paragraph repeats points made in "Salvation Without Compromise," where we were told, "The crucifixion did not establish the Atonement; the resurrection did" (T-3.I.1:2). The resurrection was the symbol of being freed from the crucifixion of guilt and lifted into eternal life. In contrast, the crucifixion was the symbol of guilt, for that is exactly what guilt does: it crucifies. More specifically, *seeing as guilty* crucifies. This is the ego's full-time job. (Crucifixion is always the ego's aim.) While seeing others as guilty crucifies them, seeing them as guiltless resurrects them. It releases them from crucifixion and raises them to new life.

This is our job while on earth. We are here to be temple restorers. We restore our brother's temple by affirming that our brother really does have the presence and purity of God inside of him. And once we have done that, his temple becomes the altar at which we ourselves kneel, at which we ourselves approach our God.

> 11. ¹Each one you see you place within the holy circle of Atonement or leave outside, judging him fit for crucifixion or for redemption. ²If you bring him <u>into</u> the circle of purity, you will rest there <u>with</u> him. ³If you leave him without, you <u>join</u> him there. ⁴Judge not except in quietness which is <u>not</u> of you. ⁵Refuse to accept anyone as <u>without</u> the blessing of Atonement, and bring him <u>into</u> it by blessing him. ⁶Holiness <u>must</u> be shared, for therein lies everything that makes it holy. ⁷Come gladly to the holy circle, and look out in peace on all who think they are outside. ⁸Cast no one out, for here [in the circle] is what <u>he</u> seeks along with you. ⁹Come, let us join him in the holy place of peace which is for all of us, united as one within the Cause of peace.

Application: A visualization:

See yourself in an area illuminated by a vast circle of light from
　　above....
Within this circle you see the great teachers of God:
Buddha, St. Francis, Gandhi, Lao Tzu, Mother Teresa, and hundreds
　　of others.
At the very center of the circle stands Jesus.
You might see everyone, yourself included, as wearing robes of
　　holiness....
There is no sense of difference among these many teachers.
In the light from above each one is literally shining with purity.
And everyone sees each other as totally pure—guiltless.
Everyone loves each other with a pure, unrestrained brotherly love.

The light from above is the power and love of God.

It is as if God is smiling on everyone as one, and this light is the warmth of His smile.

In short, it is the experience of perfect community, perfect brotherhood, in which all are united in the Love of God.

Being there is the most wonderful feeling you could imagine.

Yet you have this hidden doubt: Do I really belong in this place? Am I pure enough?

You are standing towards the edge of the circle.

And now you peer just beyond it, into the darkness outside its boundaries.

There you see the dim figure of someone you have been resenting lately....

As you look closer you realize that he is nailed to a cross.

He has been crucified by his own guilt and by your condemnation.

You see how miserable he is, left outside the circle to suffer guilt alone.

You also realize that *you* are now outside the circle.

Your resentment toward him has made you feel unworthy to be in it.

Your robes of holiness are gone now and you are in your old attire.

So remind yourself, "My only calling here is to devote myself, with active willingness, to the denial of guilt in all its forms."

"My only purpose is release from guilt, to the eternal glory of God and His creation."

Say to this person, "You are God's Son,

And God's Son is guiltless.

Come into the circle, where you belong."

Walk up and pull the nails out of his hands and feet.

Help him down off the cross.

Lift the crown of thorns from his head.

Take him by the hand and lead him into the holy circle.

And as you and he stand together in the circle, on holy ground,

Both of you clad in the robes of holiness.

All who are there silently bow their heads and join hands
In honor of this new member,
And in honor of you who fulfilled your holy function and brought him
in.
As you stand there, hands joined with your friend and with the entire
community of the teachers of God, you realize at last that you do
belong here,
That this is your home
Where you will be for all eternity.

VI. The Light of Communication
Commentary by Robert Perry

1. ¹The journey that we undertake together is the exchange [Ur: change] of dark for light, of ignorance for understanding. ²<u>Nothing you understand is fearful</u>. ³It is only in darkness and in ignorance that you perceive the frightening, and shrink away from it to further darkness. ⁴And yet it is only the hidden that <u>can</u> terrify, <u>not</u> for what it is, but <u>for</u> its hiddenness. ⁵The obscure is frightening <u>because</u> you do not understand its meaning. ⁶If you did, <u>it</u> would be clear and <u>you</u> would be no longer in the dark. ⁷Nothing has <u>hidden</u> value, for what is hidden <u>cannot</u> be shared, and so its value is unknown. ⁸The hidden is <u>kept apart,</u> but value <u>always</u> lies in joint appreciation. ⁹What is concealed <u>cannot</u> be loved, and so it <u>must</u> be feared.

In this world, there seem to be things that are legitimately frightening. However, this paragraph begs to differ. It says that everything we fear is, in the end, an irrational fear, where we are afraid of something we only imagine is there. All our fears, then, are like the classic fear of the monster under the bed. You can only fear the monster as long as you don't look under the bed. When you look, the fear is gone.

The final sentences provide an argument as to why this is so.

- Value can only be known through sharing.
- What is hidden cannot be shared.
- The value of what is hidden is therefore unknown.
- You therefore cannot value what is hidden.
- To love is to value.
- Since you cannot value what is hidden, you cannot love what is hidden.
- What is not loved is feared.
- What is hidden must be feared.

This sounds roundabout and obscure, but I think the essence of it is very simple. The hidden is the unknown. It's hard to love the unknown, isn't it? And this vacuum of love is easily filled by fear.

49

> 2.   ¹The quiet light in which the Holy Spirit dwells within you is merely perfect openness, in which nothing is hidden and therefore nothing is fearful. ²Attack will <u>always</u> yield to love if it is brought <u>to</u> love, not hidden <u>from</u> it. ³There is no darkness that the light of love will not dispel, unless it is concealed from love's beneficence. ⁴What is <u>kept apart</u> from love <u>cannot</u> share its healing power, because it has been separated off and <u>kept in darkness</u>. ⁵The sentinels of darkness watch over it carefully, and you who made these guardians of illusion out of nothing are now <u>afraid</u> of them.

The Holy Spirit is the complete opposite of hiddenness and mystery. He dwells within us in the light of perfect openness. So what is the "hidden" that Jesus is talking about? It's our ego's darkness. Jesus specifically mentions "attack" in the second sentence. What we are doing is hiding our ego's hate-filled darkness from the light of love, for that light would automatically shine it away.

What we have done is shut our darkness up in the basement, and to make sure that the light never shines in there, we have stationed guards at the door. These are "the sentinels of darkness." What are they? They are very much like the censor which the Urtext speaks of (and which is borrowed from Freud), which is stationed at the border of the consciousness and is there to ensure that our unconscious fear doesn't flood into consciousness.

> 3.   ¹Would you continue to give imagined power to these strange ideas of safety [the sentinels]? ²They are neither safe nor unsafe. ³They do not protect; <u>neither do they attack</u>. ⁴They <u>do</u> nothing at all, <u>being</u> nothing at all. ⁵As guardians of darkness and of ignorance look to them <u>only</u> for fear, for what they keep obscure <u>is</u> fearful. ⁶But let them go, and what <u>was</u> fearful will be so no longer. ⁷Without protection of obscurity <u>only</u> the light of love remains, for only this <u>has</u> meaning and <u>can</u> live in light. ⁸Everything else <u>must</u> disappear.

The sentinels are mental functions that we have stationed in our mind to keep our ego's darkness hidden behind closed doors, where it can never be exposed to the light. We think the sentinels keep us safe. Yet actually, they keep us afraid. Imagine that you are walking around in your mind and there, down a set of dark stairs, is a dark door, and at this door are stationed two guards, dressed in black military uniforms. As you approach, they say, "I'm sorry, sir, but you can never, ever, *ever* go in there." What would you feel but fear?

Without the sentinels, you could just walk up and open the door. The light would then shine in and reveal that there is nothing there, nothing at all. Therefore, oddly enough, it's not what's behind the doors, but the sentinels themselves, that make you afraid.

> 4.   ¹Death yields to life simply because destruction is not true. ²The light of guiltlessness shines guilt away because, when they are brought together, the truth of one must make the falsity of its opposite perfectly clear. ³Keep not guilt and guiltlessness apart, for your belief that you can have them both [see III.2] is meaningless. ⁴All you have done by keeping them apart is lose their meaning by confusing them with each other. ⁵And so you do not realize that only one means anything. ⁶The other is wholly without sense of any kind.

Based on the section so far, what lies behind the door is attack (second paragraph), death, destruction, and guilt (first two sentences of this paragraph). Those certainly don't sound like nothing. However, they only seem dark and weighty and foreboding when the light is not allowed to shine on them. The light would reveal them to be absolutely vacuous and empty.

That is why we have to bring the light and darkness together. This paragraph talks specifically of exposing our guilt to the light of guiltlessness. Our guilt seems to always carry this unspoken attitude: "You'd like to let yourself off the hook here, but you know better than that. Honesty requires you to feel guilty." This convincing lie, however, can only survive when our guilt is partitioned off, when it is protected from the light of guiltlessness. If we would just let them come together, our tune would change to "Honesty requires me to feel *guiltless*."

> 5.   ¹You have regarded the separation as a means for breaking your communication with your Father. ²The Holy Spirit reinterprets it as a means of re-establishing what was not broken, but *has* been made obscure. ³All things you made have use to Him, for His most holy purpose. ⁴He knows you are not separate from God, but He perceives much in your mind that lets you think you are. ⁵All this and nothing else would He separate from you. ⁶The power of decision, which you made in place of the power of creation, He would teach you how to use

on your behalf. ⁷You who made it to crucify yourself must learn of Him how to apply it to the holy cause of restoration.

In the separation, we broke communication with God. We refused to "talk" to Him anymore. The Holy Spirit, however, takes everything we made as a block to communication and reinterprets it as a means for re-establishing communication. For instance, He knows we made the power of decision to crucify ourselves. He teaches us, however, to use it to restore ourselves, to raise ourselves from the dead. We made the power of separation to separate from God. The Holy Spirit, however, uses this same power to separate ourselves from all the thoughts in our mind that claim we are separate from God. He beats all of our swords into plowshares.

> 6.   ¹You who speak in dark and devious symbols do not understand the language you have made. ²It has no meaning, for its purpose is not communication, but rather the disruption of communication. ³If the purpose of language is communication, how can this tongue mean anything? ⁴Yet even this strange and twisted effort to communicate through not communicating holds enough of love to make it meaningful if its Interpreter is not its maker. ⁵You who made it are but expressing conflict, from which the Holy Spirit would release you. ⁶Leave what you would communicate to Him. ⁷He will interpret it to you with perfect clarity, for He knows with Whom you are in perfect communication.

Language is yet another thing we made to break communication. This, of course, is deeply ironic, since language exists expressly *for* communication. This renders our language nonsensical, a contradiction. It's as if all we are ever saying is, "I'm not talking to you."

Jesus can sound like he's off his rocker here, because we use language to communicate every day. Yet are we really communicating? To communicate is to extend what is in my mind to your mind, so that both minds hold the exact same thing. Now our minds are joined in this single idea, this single experience. Is this what our language does—join minds? If so, it would be very hard to explain all the lonely, isolated people in the world.

Here again, however, the Holy Spirit can use what we made for His holy purpose. He can take our language and use it for the sake of real joining, if we'll let Him.

7. ¹You know not what you say, and so you know not what is said to you. ²Yet your Interpreter perceives the meaning in your alien language. ³He will not attempt to communicate the meaningless. ⁴But He <u>will</u> separate out all that <u>has</u> meaning, dropping off the rest and offering your true communication to those who would communicate as truly <u>with</u> you. ⁵<u>You speak two languages at once,</u> and this <u>must</u> lead to unintelligibility. ⁶Yet if one means nothing and the other <u>everything</u>, only that one is possible for purposes of communication. ⁷The other but <u>interferes</u> with it.

Our language does have a spark of love in it, a glimmer of an attempt to communicate. Thus, it is as if we have two languages, and we are saying opposite things at once. We are saying, "I want to kill you," and, "Can I be your friend?" all at the same time. I recently saw a movie set at a prep school. The main character was a colorful character who was constantly putting on plays, and was also constantly at odds with a much bigger student from Scotland. The animosity between them was intense, and at one point they got into a fight. At the end, the main character wrote another play that was designed to heal all of the relationships he had wrecked. He went to the Scottish student and (after shooting him in the ear with a BB gun!) offered him a part in the play, a part he said was specially designed for him. The Scottish kid said, "I always wanted to be in one of your f***ing plays." The main character responded, "I know."

The Course says that everything that lives, underneath each call to death and murder, is softly calling to us: "Nothing but calls to you in soft appeal to be your friend, and let it join with you" (T-31.I.8:2). These, I believe, are the two languages Jesus is talking about here: the call for death and the call for love.

Application: Think of someone in your life and ask the Holy Spirit to separate out what your ego has been saying to this person from the loving call that you really want to give to this person. Say,

> *Holy Spirit, if I separate out what my ego wants to say, what do I really want to say to [name]?*

8. ¹The Holy Spirit's function is <u>entirely</u> communication. ²He

therefore <u>must</u> remove whatever <u>interferes</u> with communication in order to <u>restore</u> it. ³Therefore, keep no source of interference from His sight, for He will <u>not</u> attack your sentinels. ⁴But bring them <u>to</u> Him and let His gentleness teach you that, in the light, they are not fearful, and <u>cannot</u> serve to guard the dark doors behind which nothing at all is carefully concealed. ⁵We must open all doors and let the light come streaming through. ⁶There are no hidden chambers in God's temple. ⁷Its gates are open wide to greet His Son. ⁸No one can fail to come where God has called him, if he close not the door himself upon his Father's welcome.

The Holy Spirit, as we've seen, wants to speak for us to our brothers. He wants to strip away all the hate and separation in our communication, leaving only the love and joining.

To let Him do this, though, we need to stop hiding the darkness in us that interferes with real communication, the darkness that is guarded by those dark sentinels. We need to bring the sentinels to Him, and let Him show us that they are nothing, and that the darkness in us that they guard is nothing. If we will open up all the doors in our mind and let His light come streaming through, we will realize that our mind is God's open temple, whose gates are open wide to welcome us. Closing the doors in our mind to the Holy Spirit's light makes it appear that the doors of God's temple are closed to us.

Application: Say to the Holy Spirit as sincerely as you can:

Holy Spirit, I don't want to hide my darkness from You anymore.
I will throw open the doors that conceal my darkness and let Your
light come streaming in.
For thus will I recognize that my mind is God's temple, whose
doors are open wide to welcome me.

VII. Sharing Perception with the Holy Spirit
Commentary by Robert Perry

1. ¹<u>What do you want</u>? ²Light or darkness, knowledge or ignorance are yours, but not both. ³Opposites must be brought together, not kept apart. ⁴For their separation is only in your mind, and they are reconciled by union, as <u>you</u> are. ⁵In union, everything that is not real <u>must</u> disappear, for truth *is* union. ⁶As darkness disappears in light, so ignorance fades away when knowledge dawns. ⁷Perception is the medium by which ignorance is <u>brought</u> to knowledge. ⁸Yet the perception must be without deceit, for otherwise it becomes the messenger of ignorance rather than a helper in the search for truth.

That opening emphatic question—"*What do you want?*"—only becomes truly meaningful when we realize that we can have light *or* darkness, knowledge *or* ignorance, not both. Notice how it feels when you ask yourself, "Do I want knowledge *or* ignorance, light *or* darkness?"—emphasizing the "or."

We are trying to have both. And we seem to succeed, by keeping them apart. It's as if we are a bigamist and are trying to keep two wives under the same roof. We need to make sure they stay in their separate rooms and never actually meet, or at least one is bound to leave.

In this case, though, one of the wives is *knowledge*. She lives in a room lit with a holy light deep below the house. The job of perception is to take the other wife—*ignorance*—by the hand, and lead her slowly down the long staircase to that underground room. Then, when the door is finally opened, she will disappear in the blazing light of knowledge. This is all right, because she was never that great of a wife to start with.

2. ¹The search for truth is but the honest searching out of everything that <u>interferes</u> with truth. ²<u>Truth</u> *is*. ³It can neither be lost nor sought nor found. ⁴It is there, wherever you are, being <u>within</u> you. ⁵Yet it <u>can</u> be recognized or unrecognized, real or false to <u>you</u>. ⁶If you hide it, it <u>becomes</u> unreal to you *because* you hid it and <u>surrounded it with fear</u>.

⁷Under each cornerstone of fear on which you have erected your insane system of belief, <u>the truth lies hidden</u>. ⁸Yet you cannot know this, for by <u>hiding</u> truth in fear, you see no reason to believe that the more you <u>look</u> at fear the <u>less</u> you see it, and the clearer <u>what it conceals</u> becomes.

That first line is so important. How do you search for truth? You seek out all the darkness in you that interferes with it. For truth is not distant and elusive. You carry it with you wherever you go. Without the darkness, you would instantly see this. Without the clouds, the sun is instantly apparent.

This is why we need to travel down in the house of our mind. On the way to that deepest room where knowledge dwells, we encounter the ego's foundation, its cornerstones of fear. As we look at these, in all their ugliness and insanity, we may think we are traveling away from truth. Yet the more we really *look* at the fear, the more it becomes invisible, and the more we begin to see the truth that lies beneath it.

3.   ¹It is not possible to convince the unknowing that they know. ²From their point of view <u>it is not true</u>. ³Yet it <u>is</u> true because <u>God</u> knows it. ⁴These are clearly opposite viewpoints on what the "unknowing" <u>are</u>. ⁵To God, unknowing is impossible. ⁶It is therefore not a point of view at all, but merely a belief in something that does not exist. ⁷It is only this <u>belief</u> that the unknowing have, and <u>by</u> it they are wrong about themselves. ⁸They have <u>defined</u> themselves as they were <u>not</u> created. ⁹Their creation was <u>not</u> a point of view, but rather a <u>certainty</u>. ¹⁰Uncertainty <u>brought</u> to certainty does not retain <u>any</u> conviction of reality.

The point is that we already know; we already have knowledge (in the Course sense of the word). We claim we don't know and have to go on a long search to find out. Yet God knows otherwise. His creation of us as knowing beings was an unshakable certainty.

For us to think that we have to find the truth, then, is like Bill Gates sitting around and thinking, "I wish I wasn't penniless. I wonder how I can start earning a few dollars." Would you dignify his perspective by saying, "Well, that's one point of view"? Or would you say, "Bill, open your eyes!"? If you were really wise, you would help him undo whatever resistance he must have to realizing that he is ridiculously wealthy. We are like Bill—we have all the truth in the universe, and yet think we have to go looking for it. All we need really do is get rid of our resistance to the knowledge of truth that we already possess.

> 4.   [1][Ur: You must have noticed that] Our emphasis has been on bringing what is undesirable <u>to</u> the desirable; what you do <u>not</u> want to what you <u>do</u>. [2]You will realize that salvation <u>must</u> come to you this way, if you consider what dissociation <u>is</u>. [3]Dissociation is a distorted process of thinking whereby two systems of belief which <u>cannot</u> coexist are <u>both maintained</u>. [4]If they are <u>brought together</u>, their joint acceptance becomes impossible. [5]But if one is kept in darkness <u>from the other</u>, their <u>separation</u> seems to keep them both alive and equal in their reality. [6]Their <u>joining</u> thus becomes the source of fear, for if they meet, acceptance <u>must</u> be withdrawn from one of them. [7]You <u>cannot</u> have them both, for each <u>denies</u> the other. [8]Apart, this fact is lost from sight, for each in a <u>separate</u> place <u>can</u> be endowed with firm belief. [9]<u>Bring them together</u>, and the fact of their complete incompatibility is instantly apparent. [10]One <u>will</u> go, <u>because</u> the other is seen in the <u>same</u> place.

Jesus' point about dissociation is one that we know and utilize in everyday life. I just read a story by Sam Harris (in his book, *The End of Faith*, on pages 55-58), which he calls "a bizarre partitioning of our beliefs." He and his fiancée are visiting France and while there are determined to keep clear of the American embassy, because of it being a prime terrorist target. Yet the couple had difficulty finding a hotel room. They finally located a hotel with abundant vacancies. The hotel even offered to upgrade them to a suite and offered them a choice of views—they could face the inner courtyard or face outward, overlooking the American embassy. Both Sam and his fiancée immediately agreed that they wanted the view of the embassy, thinking it would be a more peaceful view. Noting the irony of their dual stance, he says,

> On the day in question, never was there a time when we would have willingly placed ourselves near the American embassy, and never was there a time we were not eager to move to a room with a view of it.

A friend in Paris finally broke the spell for them, saying, "That hotel is directly next to the American embassy. That's why they're offering you an upgrade. Have you guys lost your minds? Do you know what day it is? It's the Fourth of July." Sam comments:

> The flimsiness of the partition was revealed by just how easily it came down. All it took for me to unify my fiancée's outlook on this subject was to turn to her—she who was still silently coveting a view of the American embassy—and say, with obvious alarm, "This hotel is ten feet from the American embassy!" The partition came down, and she was as flabbergasted as I was.

The partitioning they were doing with the American embassy is a tiny but perfect mirror of the partitioning we are doing with the two thought systems within us—the ego's and the Holy Spirit's. What will it take for *our* partition to come down?

> 5.   ¹Light cannot enter darkness when a mind <u>believes</u> in darkness, and will not let it go. ²Truth does not struggle <u>against</u> ignorance, and love does not <u>attack</u> fear. ³What needs no protection does not defend itself. ⁴Defense is [Ur: was] of <u>your</u> making. ⁵God knows it not. ⁶The Holy Spirit uses defenses <u>on behalf</u> of truth only because you made them <u>against</u> it. ⁷His perception of them, according to <u>His</u> purpose, merely changes them into a <u>call for</u> what you have <u>attacked with</u> them. ⁸Defenses, like everything you made, must be gently turned to your own good, translated by the Holy Spirit from means of self-destruction to means of preservation and release.

The partition has to come down willingly. He can't take it down; *we* must. It is not the nature of truth to go on the offensive—or the defensive, for that matter. Defense, after all, was not truth's invention; it was ours. Yet the Holy Spirit can use defenses for His purposes. We saw some of this in the previous section. There, we saw how we made separation to separate us from God, yet the Holy Spirit uses it to separate us from all our beliefs in separation. Now, the defense of separation becomes a call *to* God, rather than an attack *on* God.

> ⁹His task is mighty, but the power of God is with Him. ¹⁰Therefore, to Him it is so easy that it was accomplished the instant it was given Him for you. ¹¹Do not delay in your return to peace by wondering how He can fulfill what God has given Him to do. ¹²Leave that to Him Who

knows [Ur: !]. [13]You are not asked to do mighty tasks yourself. [14]You are merely asked to do the little He <u>suggests</u> you do, trusting Him only to the small extent of believing that, if He asks it, you can do it. [15]You will <u>see</u> how easily <u>all</u> that He asks can be accomplished.

At times we must wonder how the Holy Spirit can accomplish His mission of taking all of us egotistical, self-absorbed, sleep-walking, crazy people and turning us into holy, egoless, fully awakened Sons of God—and do so without a body, which means that very few can even hear Him. It can seem impossible. Yet this paragraph says that, since He carries the power of God, He actually accomplished this mission the *instant* it was given Him!

Therefore, we needn't delay our homecoming by sitting around wondering how He can do it. We should simply leave it all to Him. He can handle His mighty task. And because He can, we don't need to do mighty tasks ourselves. We don't need to part the Red Sea. All we need to do is the little He *suggests* we do. To do this, we need to trust that if He asks it, we *can* do it.

Notice the series of beliefs Jesus is trying to undo:

- The world is not in good hands.
- Because the world is not in good hands, I need to do some mighty deed that reverberates throughout the world, setting everything right.
- Because I really ought to fix the whole world, how can I focus on the little thing the Holy Spirit is asking me to do?
- And why should I focus on that little thing, when it is obvious that I can't do it?

6.   [1]The Holy Spirit asks of you but this; bring to Him every secret you have locked away from Him. [2]Open every door to Him [the dark doors guarded by the dark sentinels], and bid Him enter the darkness and lighten it away. [3]At <u>your</u> request He enters gladly. [4]He brings the light to darkness if you make the darkness <u>open</u> to Him. [5]But what you hide He cannot look upon. [6]He sees <u>for you,</u> and unless you look <u>with</u> Him He <u>cannot</u> see. [7]The vision of Christ is not for Him alone, but for Him <u>with you.</u> [8]Bring, therefore, all your dark and secret thoughts to Him, and look upon them <u>with</u> Him. [9]He holds the light, and you the

darkness. [10]They <u>cannot</u> coexist when Both of you <u>together</u> look on them. [11]His judgment <u>must</u> prevail, and He will <u>give</u> it to you as you join your perception to His.

Here we are told the little that He suggests, the little that we can do. It's not exactly what we were expecting.

Application:

Picture a dark door in your mind.

On this door is a sign that reads, "My dark and secret thoughts about [blank]."

Fill in the blank however you like, with the name of a person or situation or event.

You are afraid to open this door, but the Holy Spirit is with you (visualize Him however you like).

So open the door and look with Him at the dark thoughts inside.

Since there is probably more than one, it will help to write them down. (Pause to write down the dark thoughts.)

You might imagine these thoughts floating in the dim fog behind the door.

Normally, you would look away from these thoughts, or look on them (briefly) with shame.

But now you are looking on them with the Holy Spirit.

So don't shy away from them; *look.*

Look with Him beside you, with Him looking with you, even looking *through* you.

Look at each one in turn.

Look until each one slowly loses its power.

Look until you hear or sense His response to each one.

Look until they all blend together as a single blob of darkness.

This darkness, drained of all its frightening allure, is simply undesirable.

So ask His light to shine this darkness away.

Say, "Holy Spirit, shine my darkness away. I don't want it anymore. I want it replaced with Your light."

Now there is no darkened chamber; it has been filled with His light.

Silently say, "Thank you."

7.   ¹Joining with Him in seeing is the way in which you learn to share with Him the interpretation of perception that leads to knowledge [see 1:8]. ²You cannot see alone. ³Sharing perception with Him Whom God has given you teaches you how to <u>recognize</u> what you see. ⁴It is the recognition that <u>nothing</u> you see means <u>anything</u> alone. ⁵Seeing <u>with</u> Him will <u>show</u> you that all meaning, <u>including yours,</u> comes not from double vision, but from the gentle fusing of everything into *one* meaning, *one* emotion and *one* purpose. ⁶God has one Purpose which He shares with you. ⁷The single vision which the Holy Spirit offers you will bring this oneness to your mind with clarity and brightness so intense you could not wish, for all the world, not to accept what God would have you have. ⁸Behold your will, accepting it as His, with all His Love as yours. ⁹All honor to you through Him, and through Him unto God.

We all have double vision, also called diplopia. Diplopia is a condition in which you see two images of the same object. Is this not true of us? We see two images, for instance, of the people in our lives. We look at one person and simultaneously see the sinner we hate and the saint we love. This is because we are interpreting each thing we see from the standpoint of two diametrically opposed thought systems. Jesus said this about Helen in the Urtext. He told her that her mind maintained a connection to knowledge, but also suffered from the ego's intrusions. "The result," he said, "is a kind of 'double vision,' which would have produced an actual diplopia, if she had not settled for nearsightedness."

The only way to solve this double vision is to do what we just did in the previous paragraph: join with the Holy Spirit in seeing; let Him enter the abode of our dark thoughts—the source of one side of our seeing—and shine them away. The darkness and the light, as we were told at the beginning of the section, cannot coexist when brought together. Now we have one Source for our perception. Now we will see everything with one meaning, one emotion and one purpose. Just imagine that.

VIII. The Holy Meeting Place
Commentary by Robert Perry

1. ¹In the darkness you have obscured the glory God gave you, and the power He bestowed upon His guiltless Son. ²All this lies hidden in every darkened place, shrouded in guilt and in the dark denial of innocence. ³Behind the dark doors you have closed lies nothing, because nothing can obscure the gift of God. ⁴It is the closing of the doors that interferes with recognition of the power of God that shines in you. ⁵Banish not power from your mind, but let all that would hide your glory be brought to the judgment of the Holy Spirit, and there undone. ⁶Whom He would save for glory *is* saved for it. ⁷He has promised the Father that through Him you would be released from littleness to glory. ⁸To what He promised God He is wholly faithful, for He shares with God the promise that was given Him to share with you.

This paragraph's theme has also been a major theme in this chapter. We can see it in three levels:

- The dark doors, which are there to hide our darkness from awareness.
- The darkness itself, which is composed of guilt, as well as fear and death. This darkness represents the denial of the holiness underneath it.
- Our radiant holiness; the power and glory God gave us.

To hide our holiness requires *both* 1 and 2. The reason is that our darkness by itself cannot conceal our holiness, for it is nothing. Therefore, we have to conceal the *darkness* as well. We are really afraid to look at our darkness, then, because of our underlying fear of seeing, not that it is evil, but that it is *nothing*.

As an analogy, let's imagine that you are an incredibly holy person, like Mother Teresa, only you become afraid of your holiness. So you invent this idea about yourself that you have committed a horrible crime, a crime of unspeakable evil. But the crime never happened. There are no facts to support it. So to keep the crime story intact, it has to be hidden in the unconscious. Now you go around thinking that you are a well-intentioned human being, with a nagging sense of self-doubt. There is one thing, however, you do not doubt, and that is that you are anything but holy. This shows that your conscious self-image is under the control of your submerged guilt. The last thing you want to do is look at this guilt, not because you are afraid it is true, but because you know that it is *baseless.* Your "crime" was never committed. If you looked, you would discover this. And then you would be left face to face with the thing you fear: your unspeakable holiness.

This, of course, is no analogy at all. It is a literal description of our condition.

> 2.   ¹He shares it still, <u>for you</u>. ²Everything that promises otherwise, great or small, however much or little valued, He will replace with the one promise <u>given</u> unto Him to lay upon the altar to your Father and His Son. ³No altar stands to God without His Son. ⁴And <u>nothing</u> brought there that is not equally worthy of <u>Both</u>, but will be <u>replaced</u> by gifts wholly acceptable to Father <u>and</u> to Son. ⁵Can you offer guilt to God? ⁶You cannot, then, offer it to His Son. ⁷For They are <u>not</u> apart, and gifts to one <u>are</u> offered to the other. ⁸You know not God because you know not this.

We have laid our guilt on the altar to our Father and ourselves. This guilt is also a promise: "I promise never to be with God and never to accept my holiness." However unconscious that promise may be, we are in its grip. This promise is what puts lead weights on our feet on the road to God. However, another promise has been made. The Holy Spirit has promised God that He will release us "from littleness to glory" (paragraph 1). The promise we have laid on the altar is not worthy of us, because it is not worthy of God. It will therefore be replaced by the Holy Spirit's promise to bring us home. Only His promise will hold sway in the end.

> ⁹And yet you <u>do</u> know God and <u>also</u> this. ¹⁰All this is safe <u>within</u> you, where the Holy Spirit shines. ¹¹He shines not in division [between Father and Son], but in the meeting place where God, <u>united</u> with His Son, speaks to His Son <u>through</u> Him. ¹²Communication between

63

what cannot be divided <u>cannot</u> cease. ¹³The holy meeting place of the unseparated Father and His Son lies in the Holy Spirit and in <u>you</u>. ¹⁴All interference in the communication that God Himself wills with His Son is quite impossible here. ¹⁵Unbroken and uninterrupted love flows constantly between the Father and the Son, as <u>Both</u> would have it be. ¹⁶And so it <u>is</u>.

Even though we have promised to keep separate from God, to cut off all communication, there is a meeting place in us, where the Holy Spirit shines. In this meeting place, "unbroken and uninterrupted love flows constantly between" us and God. In this place, the separation has never occurred.

> 3. ¹Let your mind wander not through darkened corridors, <u>away</u> from light's center. ²You and your brother may choose to lead <u>yourselves</u> astray, but you can be <u>brought together</u> only by the Guide appointed <u>for</u> you. ³He will surely lead you to where God and His Son await your recognition. ⁴They are joined in giving you the gift of oneness, before which <u>all</u> separation vanishes. ⁵Unite with what you <u>are</u>. ⁶You <u>cannot</u> join with anything <u>except</u> reality. ⁷God's glory and His Son's <u>belong</u> to you in truth. ⁸They <u>have</u> no opposite, and nothing else <u>can</u> you bestow upon yourself.

Right now, we are wandering through darkened corridors, the corridors of our mind. And while we wander in this endless maze, we wander separate from our brother. Only if we and our brother are willing to follow the Guide given us can we truly come together. This Guide will ask us to do the last thing we want to do: Open the doors in this dark hallway and look with Him on the darkness inside, and then walk through its nothingness. This is how He leads us to the center of the building, the holy meeting place, where we at last gaze ecstatically upon God's glory, and realize we are looking upon our own.

> 4. ¹There is no substitute for truth. ²And truth will make this plain to you as you are brought into the place where you must <u>meet</u> with truth. ³And there you must be led, through gentle understanding which can lead you nowhere else. ⁴Where God is, there are <u>you</u>. ⁵Such <u>is</u> the truth. ⁶<u>Nothing</u> can change the knowledge, <u>given</u> you by God, into unknowingness [Ur: *un*knowing]. ⁷Everything God created <u>knows</u> its

Creator. [8]For this is how creation is accomplished by the Creator and by His creations. [9]In the holy meeting place are joined the Father and His creations, and the creations of His Son with Them together. [10]There is one link [the Holy Spirit] that joins them all together, holding them in the oneness out of which creation happens.

Only once we reach that center of the building, and gaze on that glory, will we finally realize that there is no substitute for truth. Our promise to stay away from God and stay in our guilt must pass away. It is a promise we cannot keep. When we reach the holy meeting place, we will realize that we can never change our unity with God and our knowledge of God.

> 5. [1]The link with which the Father joins Himself to those He gives the power to create can <u>never</u> be dissolved. [2]Heaven itself is union with <u>all</u> of creation, and with its one Creator. [3]And Heaven remains the Will of God for <u>you</u>. [4]Lay no gifts other than this upon your altars, for nothing can coexist with [Ur: *beside*] it. [5]Here your little offerings are <u>brought together</u> with the gift of God, and only what is worthy of the Father will be accepted by the Son, for whom it is intended. [6]To whom God gives Himself, He *is* given. [7]Your little gifts will vanish on the altar, where He has placed His Own.

Application: A visualization:

Think of guilt that you hold over something you have thought or done.
Now picture yourself walking up to a holy altar, the altar to God and
    to yourself.
See yourself laying your guilt on this altar as a gift (visualizing this
    "gift" in whatever form seems appropriate).
Say, "This is the gift that I deserve.
This is also my gift to You, Father. For what I give myself, I give to
    You.
This is my promise to stay apart from You forever."
Now see Jesus walk up and lay on the altar another gift—his promise,
    which is really the Holy Spirit's promise. (Visualize this gift
    however you like.)
See written on it this promise: "I *will* release [see your name written
    here] from littleness to glory. This I promise You, Father."

See the two gifts lying side by side.

The Holy Spirit's gift begins to shine. It shines brighter and brighter.

The light is blinding.

Once the light subsides, you see that your gift of guilt is gone.

Now you decide to lay a different gift upon the altar.

It is your promise that, whatever happens, you *will* make it home.

This gift says, "Father, I promise You and I promise myself that I will
awaken to You."

As you lay the gift on the altar, speak this line, with sincerity, to God
and yourself.

IX. The Reflection of Holiness
Commentary by Robert Perry

1.   ¹The Atonement does not <u>make</u> holy. ²You were <u>created</u> holy. ³It merely brings <u>un</u>holiness <u>to</u> holiness; or what you <u>made</u> to what you <u>are</u>. ⁴Bringing illusion to truth, or the ego to God [Ur: The bringing together of truth and illusion, *of the ego and God*], is the Holy Spirit's only function. ⁵Keep not your making from your Father, for hiding it has cost you knowledge of Him and of yourself. ⁶The knowledge is safe, but where is <u>your</u> safety <u>apart</u> from it? ⁷The making of time to <u>take the place</u> of timelessness lay in the decision to <u>be not</u> as you are [Ur: *were*]. ⁸Thus truth was made past, and the present was dedicated to illusion. ⁹And the past, too, was changed and <u>interposed</u> between what <u>always</u> was and <u>now</u>. ¹⁰The past that <u>you</u> remember <u>never</u> was, and represents only the denial of what <u>always</u> was.

Traditionally, the Atonement has the power to transform us from unholy to holy. Yet in the Course, all Atonement does is bring the lie of our unholiness to the truth of our holiness, where that lie is laid bare, and disappears.

The latter half of the paragraph is about the making of time. We made time, it says, by deciding to not be who we are, to be unholy. Consequently, the truth of our existence in Heaven became a thing of the past. The present then became dedicated to illusions. And as this new present rolled on, its past moments became the only past we could remember.

Application: Think of your past and how it seems to define you and your existence. Then say,

> *The past that I remember never was, and represents my denial of what always was.*

2.   ¹Bringing the ego to God is but to bring error to truth, where it stands corrected because it is the <u>opposite</u> of what it meets. ²It is

undone because the <u>contradiction</u> can no longer stand. ³How long can contradiction stand when its impossible nature is clearly revealed? ⁴What disappears in light is <u>not</u> attacked. ⁵It merely vanishes because it is not true. ⁶<u>Different</u> realities <u>are</u> meaningless, for reality <u>must</u> be one. ⁷It <u>cannot</u> change with time or mood or chance. ⁸Its changelessness is <u>what makes it real</u>. ⁹This <u>cannot</u> be undone. ¹⁰Undoing is for <u>un</u>reality. ¹¹And this reality <u>will</u> do for you.

3.   ¹Merely by <u>being what it is</u>, does truth release you from everything that it is <u>not</u>. ²The Atonement is so gentle you need but whisper to it, and all its power will rush to your assistance and support. ³You are not frail with God beside you. ⁴Yet <u>without</u> Him you are nothing. ⁵The Atonement <u>offers you God</u>. ⁶The gift that you refused is held by Him in you. ⁷The Holy Spirit holds it there <u>for</u> you.

Bringing error to truth is something we do all the time on a more mundane level. Let's say that you had an accident and believed that it was your fault. But then let's say that there was a videotape of the accident, showing that you were not at fault. You could go on maintaining your belief for years, until the belief meets the videotape. Then "it merely vanishes because it is not true." The videotape is fact; it is unalterable. It is the belief that must go.

The same is true with our ego and God. The image we hold of ourselves is so deeply convincing to us and so sacred. One word of disrespect toward it, and we go into a tailspin. This image can remain real and sacred, however, only until it is exposed to the truth. Then it will be revealed as nothing more than a false claim about reality.

Part of what keeps this meeting of truth and falsity from happening is that truth seems so distant, so inaccessible. Yet, in fact, all we need do is whisper to it, and "all its power will rush" to our assistance and support. It will undermine our illusions, but it will strengthen us. It will restore to us the power and glory that God gave us. We threw away this gift, but the Holy Spirit dug it out of the trash and has kept it safe and inviolate for us for billions of years.

⁸God has not left His altar, though His worshippers placed other gods upon it. ⁹The temple still is holy, for the Presence that dwells within it *is* holiness.

4.   ¹In the temple, holiness waits quietly for the return of them that

love it. ²The Presence knows they will return to purity and to grace. ³The graciousness of God will take them gently in, and cover all their sense of pain and loss with the immortal assurance of their Father's Love. ⁴There, fear of death will be replaced with joy of life. ⁵For God is Life, and they abide <u>in</u> Life. ⁶Life is as holy as the Holiness by Which it was created. ⁷The Presence of holiness lives in everything that lives, for holiness <u>created</u> life, and leaves not what it created holy as itself.

This poetic passage really tells a whole story, which I will attempt to draw out. Imagine a beautiful temple in a green valley. In this temple dwells a Presence of holiness that is so palpable that when you walk into the temple doors you feel as if you have stepped into a field of grace. You feel that you are in the Presence of God. For time beyond measure worshippers have faithfully gathered here, to sit in this Presence, to sing Its praises and to silently commune with It. It has been the center of their lives and the center of their ancestors' lives for as long as anyone can remember.

Then, one day, things begins to change. The worshippers begin to bring in other gods and place them on the altar, and worship them. Each worshipper brings in his own grotesque stone idol—an image from his private fantasies of what he himself is. Worship of the holy Presence is lost sight of in the people's fervent prayers to these images. Eventually, the people abandon the temple altogether. After eons of being the center of life, it now sits empty, a collection of stone idols still scattered across its altar, covered by dust and cobwebs.

But the Presence remains in the temple. Even though It has been abandoned, It does not abandon. Even though Its worshippers have left and seemingly turned themselves into sinners, It knows the truth is otherwise. It knows they have not lost their purity, nor their single desire to abide in the Presence of holiness. It knows that while they seek so greedily in other lands, their primary experience is of loss—the loss of the Presence that meant everything to them. It knows they will return. And so It waits in serene patience and calm confidence. Its only concern is to be there for Its children when they come back.

And finally they do. One day they begin to drag themselves in, one by one. Their wanderings have left them traumatized and have stripped them of everything. For years they have walked bearing a deep sense of loss, always looking over their shoulders, waiting for death to catch up with them. The Presence doesn't ask them where they have been or what they have been doing. It just takes them in as a mother would. It just enfolds them in Its pure Love. And in Its all-encompassing embrace they forget everything else, all the anguish, all the grief. The years of homeless wandering drop away from them and they are miraculously restored to their former selves. It is as if they never left. Within a short time of walking through the temple doors, they are celebrating again, caught up in the joy of life. "For God is Life, and they abide in Life," as they did in the beginning, as they will forevermore.

This is not just a story. It is *our* story. We are the worshippers who placed other gods on our altar, and who left the Presence that meant everything to us. And we are the ones who will inevitably return.

> 5.   ¹In this world you can become a spotless mirror, in which the holiness of your Creator shines forth from you to all around you. ²You can <u>reflect Heaven</u> here. ³Yet no reflections of the images of other gods must dim the mirror that would hold God's reflection in it. ⁴Earth can reflect Heaven or hell; God or the ego. ⁵You need but leave the mirror clean and clear of all the images of hidden darkness you have drawn upon it. ⁶God will shine upon it of Himself. ⁷Only the clear reflection <u>of</u> Himself can <u>be</u> perceived upon it.

Application: Please repeat these lines, with feeling:

> *In this world I can become a spotless mirror,*
> *in which the holiness of my Creator shines forth from me to all*
>   *around me.*
> *I can reflect Heaven here.*

The problem with your mirror now is that you've been finger-painting on it with grease. You've painted on it horrifying "images of hidden darkness," images of your sinfulness. Then you've obscured these images by painting nice, respectable images over them. By the time you're done, it is hard indeed to see anything reflecting in this grimy mirror. However, all you need to do is wash it off, and your job is done. Its function as mirror will be restored. And then "God will shine upon it of Himself."

Try, therefore, to imagine your mind as a "spotless mirror," with no dark images, not even a speck of dust on it. Purely spotless. Being spotless it automatically reflects the holiness of God to everyone around you. Picture yourself in a group of people or out somewhere in public, reflecting the holiness of God to everyone around you. Watch the effect you have on particular people in this scene. What happens?

6. ¹Reflections are seen in light. ²In darkness they are obscure, and their meaning seems to lie only in shifting interpretations, rather than in themselves. ³The reflection of God <u>needs</u> no interpretation. ⁴<u>It is clear</u>. ⁵Clean but the mirror, and the message that shines forth from what the mirror holds out for everyone to see, <u>no one</u> can [Ur: will] fail to understand. ⁶It is the message that the Holy Spirit is holding to the mirror that is in <u>him</u>. ⁷He recognizes it because he has been taught his <u>need</u> for it, but knows not where to look to <u>find</u> it. ⁸Let him, then, see it in <u>you</u> and share it <u>with</u> you.

Imagine that you are looking at a reflection in a still pond as darkness is gathering. Imagine further that you can only see the pond, not the actual objects it is reflecting. In the darkness, it is very hard to make out what you see. You may think at one moment that you are seeing a tree's reflection, at another moment that you are seeing a person's.

Right now, your mind—with its dark, greasy mirror—is like the pond. This makes it hard for observers—the people in your life—to interpret the dark and obscure patterns they see on the mirror of your mind. They're not sure what they see, and each has his own interpretations.

If you clean the mirror, though, everything changes. No one has trouble making out the reflections in a still pond in bright daylight. Thus, when God's light is reflecting off the clean mirror of your mind, no one actually needs to interpret that. They see it as plain as day.

What they see reflected in your mirror is the message that God's light has been shining on their own mirror. They know they need this message; they just haven't been able to see it in their grimy mirror. Now they recognize that this is what they have been looking for, and they are automatically drawn to you.

7. ¹Could you but realize for a single instant the power of healing that the reflection of God, shining in <u>you</u>, can bring to all the world,

you <u>could</u> not wait to make the mirror of your mind clean to receive the image of the holiness that heals the world. ²The image of holiness that shines in <u>your</u> mind is <u>not</u> obscure, and will <u>not</u> change. ³Its meaning to those who look upon it is not obscure, for everyone perceives it <u>as the same</u>. ⁴All bring their <u>different</u> problems to its healing light, and <u>all</u> their problems find but [Ur: *only*] healing there.

8.   ¹The response of holiness to <u>any</u> form of error is <u>always</u> the same. ²There is no contradiction in what holiness <u>calls forth</u>. ³Its <u>one</u> response is healing, without regard for what is brought <u>to</u> it.

If you realized how much healing the reflection of God, shining in the mirror of your mind, could bring to your family, your friends, your world, you would clean your mind in an instant! We hesitate to clean it only because we don't realize how much good it would do around us, in lives we care about and in lives we *would* care about if we knew them.

"Its meaning to those who look upon it is not obscure, for everyone perceives it as the same." As we already saw, people do not actually interpret the reflection of God shining from our mirror. They see it as plainly as they see our face. They powerfully sense the holiness shining from us without having to figure it out. And since they see it without the filter of interpretation, everyone sees the same meaning there. That meaning is *healing*. No matter who they are and what their problem is, when they look in that mirror, they all find the exact same healing. This reminds one of Helen's priestess vision:

> I was a priestess again….[The priestess] was hidden from the world in a small white marble temple, set in a broad and very green valley…. [She] never came further into the world than the doorway of a little room containing a plain wooden altar against the far wall….The priestess stayed close to the altar, sitting on a low wooden stool, praying with closed eyes for those who came to her for help….
>
> I was also sure that people came to her for help from all over; some, in fact, from very far away. They did not, however, speak to the priestess directly. They knelt one by one at the ledge that ran around a low wall separating the inner and outer parts of the temple, stating their needs to a man who seemed like a sort of intermediary between the priestess and the world. He stayed in the enclosed space between the priestess and those who came for help. The man conveyed their needs to her….

When people told him what they needed, he went to the door of her room and said: "Priestess, a brother has come to your shrine. Heal him for me." *She never asked anyone's name, nor for the details of their request.* She merely prayed for him, sitting very quietly beside the flame on the altar. It never occurred to her that help would not be granted. *She prayed for everyone in the same way,* and never really left God's side, remaining peacefully certain of His presence there in the room with her. (*Absence from Felicity*, pp. 103-104; italics mine)

We are being asked to be this priestess, even if we do live lives out in the world. We are being asked to greet everyone with exactly the same response of holiness, no matter what their problem, no matter how they feel about us, perfectly confident that they will find their healing by seeing God's light in our mirror.

⁴Those who have learned to offer <u>only</u> healing, because of the reflection of holiness in them, are ready at last for Heaven. ⁵There, holiness is not a reflection, but rather the <u>actual condition</u> of what was but reflected <u>to</u> them here. ⁶God is no image, and His creations, as part of Him, hold Him in them in truth. ⁷They do not merely <u>reflect</u> truth, for <u>they</u> *are* truth.

When all your mind does is reflect holiness, with a perfectly clean and spotless mirror, then you are ready to go beyond the reflection to that which it reflected. To rephrase St. Paul, "For now we see in a mirror brightly, but then face to face." What would it be like to go beyond all reflections and know holiness itself, indeed, *be* holiness itself? As Jesus says elsewhere, "I cannot tell you what this will be like, for your heart is not yet ready" (T-11.III.3:6).

An aside about Helen's priestess vision and this section

As a sort of scholarly aside, I really think that Jesus had Helen's priestess vision in his mind while dictating this section (as he also did when dictating Lesson 109, paragraph 8). There are just too many parallels with both of our key images: the temple image and the mirror image. I'll go ahead and list those parallels:

Helen's vision	this section
a temple with an altar	a temple with an altar
the Presence of God within the temple: "certain of His presence there in the room with her"	the Presence of God within the temple: "the Presence that dwells within it *is* holiness"
the issue of leaving the temple: the priestess never leaves	the issue of leaving the temple: the worshippers leave
the Presence in the temple heals those who come: "people came to her for help from all over…. It never occurred to her that help would not be granted"	the Presence in the temple heals those who come: "The graciousness of God will take them gently in, and cover all their sense of pain and loss"
a person who, through her purity, is a clear conduit for God's healing power	a person who, because of his pure mind, is a clear reflector of God's healing light
a person who responds with the same response of holiness and healing totally irrespective of the different problems brought to her	a person who responds with the same response of holiness and healing totally irrespective of the different problems brought to him

I find it truly fascinating that Jesus managed to weave all these elements of Helen's vision into this section in the way he did. It just underscores the point that he is calling us to this priestess role. He is calling us to be someone whose mind is so pure that it becomes a spotless mirror, so that God's holiness can shine out for everyone to see, healing anyone who comes before our clean and spotless mirror.

X. The Equality of Miracles
Commentary by Robert Perry

This is a real powerhouse of a section, covering such seemingly diverse topics as order of difficulty in miracles, the ordering of our thoughts, evaluating the behavior of others, love and calls for love, how the ego's judgments work, form vs. content, modern psychology, joining with others, and the traditional individual quest for oneness with God. Amazingly, all of these topics are revealed to be intimately intertwined.

1. ¹When no perception stands between God and His creations, or between His children and their own, the knowledge of creation must continue forever. ²The reflections you accept into the mirror of your mind in time but bring eternity nearer or farther. ³But eternity itself is beyond all time. ⁴Reach out of time and touch it, with the help of its reflection in you. ⁵And you will turn from time to holiness, as surely as the reflection of holiness calls everyone to lay all guilt aside. ⁶Reflect the peace of Heaven here, and bring this world to Heaven. ⁷For the reflection of truth draws everyone to truth, and as they enter into it they leave all reflections behind.

This section continues the previous section's image of the mirror of our mind. Our task is to use this mirror to reflect only the holiness of Heaven, not the dark images of the ego. When that mirror reflects only holiness, then we will pass beyond all reflections into that which is reflected. We will pass beyond all perception into knowledge. We will pass beyond all time into eternity. And we will pass beyond all guilt into holiness itself (which lies only in eternity).

Yet we will not do this alone, for just as our spotless mirror draws our own mind toward truth, so it draws the entire world toward truth as well. Our task on earth, therefore, is not reaching eternity; it is having that pure mirror. To what extent do we awaken each day saying, "Today I will keep the mirror of my mind totally pure and spotless"?

2. ¹In Heaven reality is shared and not reflected. ²By sharing its

reflection <u>here</u>, its truth becomes the only perception the Son of God accepts. ³And thus, remembrance of his Father dawns on him, and he can no longer be satisfied with anything but his own reality. ⁴You on earth have no conception of limitlessness, for the world you seem to live in <u>is</u> a world of limits. ⁵In this world, it is <u>not</u> true that anything without order of difficulty can occur. ⁶The miracle, therefore, has a unique function, and is motivated by a unique Teacher Who brings the laws of another world to this one. ⁷The miracle is the one thing you can do that <u>transcends</u> order, being based <u>not</u> on differences but on equality. [Since all Sons of God are equally deserving, the miracle gives them equal deliverance, regardless of the size of their problems.]

If we can share only the reflection of reality with our brothers, then that reflection will become the only thing that is real to us. And when that happens, we will remember reality itself, and will never be content with anything else again.

Right now, though, reality is beyond our conception. How could we conceive of it, when we have known only a world of limits, and yet reality has no limits? This is why it is so hard for us to conceive that miracles have no order of difficulty. A miracle that can overcome any problem with absolute ease carries unlimited power, and that is outside anything in our experience. In this world, every power is limited; every force can lift some things and not others. Can we even imagine a power that can lift a planet as easily as a pebble?

That is one reason that miracles are so important. They bring us an experience of a power that transcends order of difficulty. They bring us evidence of another world.

3. ¹Miracles are <u>not</u> in competition, and the number of them that you can do is <u>limitless</u>. ²They can be simultaneous and legion. ³This is not difficult to understand, once you conceive of them as possible at all. ⁴What is more difficult to grasp is the lack of order of difficulty that stamps the miracle as something that <u>must</u> come from elsewhere, <u>not</u> from here. ⁵From the world's viewpoint, this is [Ur: quite] impossible.

If you can do miracles with your thoughts, then the number of miracles that can flow from you is numberless. If, as various Workbook lessons say, in a single practice period you do can heal "many brothers far across the world" (W-pI.132.16:1), then imagine how many miracles you can do. This is not hard to understand. But the idea that miracles can raise someone from the dead as easily as they can cure a headache—that is obviously far more difficult to grasp. That violates our whole notion of how energy works.

> 4. [1]Perhaps you have been aware of [Ur: You have experienced the] lack of competition among your thoughts, which even though they may conflict, can occur together and in great numbers. [2]You may indeed be so used to this that it causes you little surprise. [3]Yet you are also used to classifying some of your thoughts as more important, larger or better, wiser, or more productive and valuable than others. [4]This is true of the thoughts that cross the mind of those who think they live apart. [5]For some are reflections of Heaven, while others are motivated by the ego, which but <u>seems</u> to think.

We return here to the mirror of the mind, which now clearly parallels the discussion about miracles. Just as we can understand the possibility of doing "simultaneous and legion" miracles, so we have experienced the fact that our *thoughts* can be simultaneous and legion. At any given second, if we really watch our mind, we are having a whole host of reactions to various things in our immediate environment and in our life. All of these reactions, however subtle, are evaluations and therefore thoughts.

And just as we would naturally assume that miracles have an order, going from bigger to smaller, so we are accustomed to seeing our thoughts as having an order, from bigger to smaller, wise to foolish, productive to useless, valuable to worthless. Jesus says that this *is* true of our current thoughts—some are reflections of Heaven, while some reflect the ego's darkness, its lack of true thought. But he'll explain later that we aren't the right one to sort them out.

> 5. [1]The result is a weaving, changing pattern that never rests and is never still. [2]It shifts unceasingly across the mirror of your mind, and the reflections of Heaven last but a moment and grow dim, as darkness blots them out. [3]Where there was light, darkness removes it in an instant, and alternating patterns of light and darkness sweep constantly across your mind. [4]The little sanity that still remains is held together by a sense of order that <u>you</u> establish. [5]Yet the very fact that you can <u>do</u> this, and bring <u>any</u> order into chaos shows you that you are <u>not</u> an ego,

and that <u>more</u> than an ego <u>must</u> be in you. ⁶For the ego *is* chaos, and if it were <u>all</u> of you, no order at all would be possible. ⁷Yet though the order you impose upon your mind limits the ego, <u>it also limits you</u>. ⁸To order is to judge, and to arrange <u>by</u> judgment. ⁹Therefore it is <u>not</u> your function, but the Holy Spirit's.

What an interesting, and *accurate*, description of our mind. It is as if we put a mirror on the ground below an unbelievably tumultuous sky, with storm clouds racing across, blotting out the sun, the sun peeking momentarily out, night falling, only to be followed seconds later by a sun rise, followed immediately by a solar eclipse.

It is insanity, chaos. So we step into this chaos and try to bring a semblance of order. We think, "That angry thought I just had—that was bad. I shouldn't have such bad thoughts. I should feel guilty." And we think, "That thought of love—that was good. That was a much better thought than some of the others." And, "That thought about that weird-shaped piece of bark on that tree—that was really worthless. Definite waste of time." The thoughts still sweep across our mind like bats wheeling overhead, but now by classifying them differently, we impose some semblance of order and sanity. If all thoughts were given equal weight and approval, we would be insane indeed.

This act of bringing order into the chaos shows that we are more than an ego, "for the ego is chaos." However, though this limits the ego's chaos, it also limits us, for it makes us the judge. We spend all day pounding the gavel in our head, rather than unleashing our true will to love.

6.   ¹It will seem difficult for you to learn that <u>you have no basis at all</u> for ordering your thoughts. ²This lesson the Holy Spirit teaches by giving you the shining examples of miracles [Ur: by giving you shining examples,] to show you that your way of ordering is wrong, but that a better way is <u>offered</u> you. ³The miracle offers <u>exactly</u> the same response to <u>every</u> call for help. ⁴<u>It does not judge the call</u>. ⁵It merely recognizes what it <u>is,</u> and answers accordingly. ⁶It does <u>not</u> consider which call is louder or greater or more important. ⁷You may wonder how you who are still bound to judgment can be asked to do that which requires no judgment of your own. ⁸The answer is very simple. ⁹The power of God, and <u>not</u> of you, engenders miracles. ¹⁰The miracle <u>itself</u> is but the witness that you <u>have</u> the power of God in you. ¹¹That is the

reason why the miracle gives <u>equal</u> blessing to <u>all</u> who share in it, and that is also why <u>everyone</u> shares in it. ¹²The power of God <u>is</u> limitless. ¹³And being always maximal, it offers <u>everything</u> to <u>every</u> call from <u>anyone</u>. ¹⁴There is no order of difficulty here. ¹⁵A call for help is <u>given</u> help.

This paragraph makes important points about the ordering of miracles and the ordering of thought. First, the ordering of miracles: It says, "The miracle offers exactly the same response to every call for help." It doesn't say, "This problem is only a headache. We'll just release a small amount of power." Or, "This call is from a really bad person. We'll release only a tiny bit of healing for this guy." Or, "This person is good-looking and really unfairly treated by life. We'll reach into the power reserves for this one." Instead, the miracle gives God's maximal power to each and every call for help. A call for help is not given a carefully measured, proportional amount of help; it is given *help*, period.

It can do this because it is not based on our judgment, which would chronically make endless distinctions between different calls for help. Rather, the miracle happens *through* us, from a Power that sees only one thing: An infinitely deserving brother has come to us for help.

We need to realize, however, that this is offered as an example. How the Holy Spirit would respond through us to the calls of others is an *example* of how He would respond inside of us to our own thoughts. Imagine the Holy Spirit in your mind evaluating your thoughts for you. Where you would say, "Oh God, that was such a judgmental thought," He would say, "That was simply a call for help." Where you would say, "What a waste of time that trivial thought was," He would again say, "That was simply a call for help."

7. ¹The only judgment involved [Ur: at all] is the Holy Spirit's one division into two categories; one of love, and the other the call for love. ²You cannot safely make this division, for you are much too confused either to recognize love, or to believe that <u>everything</u> else is nothing but a call [Ur: *need*] for love. ³You are too bound to form, and <u>not</u> to content. ⁴What you <u>consider</u> content is not content at all. ⁵It is merely form, and nothing else. ⁶For you do <u>not</u> respond to what a brother <u>really</u> offers you, but only to the particular perception of his offering by which the <u>ego</u> judges it.

8.   ¹The ego is incapable of understanding content, and is totally unconcerned with it. ²To the ego, if the form is acceptable the content must be. ³Otherwise it will attack the form.

When the Holy Spirit in you is responding to others around you, He responds to every call for help as essentially the same thing. But He does make one division into two categories (or two orders): He divides calls for help from extensions of love. He prompts you to give miracles to those issuing the former and simply rejoice with those giving the latter (see M-5.III).

It is imperative that He make this division for us, for we often don't recognize love, and we definitely don't believe that everything else is simply a need for love. This is because we don't judge by what was really in a brother's mind, by the real *content* behind a particular behavior of his. We only judge by whether our ego likes the *form* of what he did. How often have we discovered—sometimes too late—that we were wrong about what someone was really offering us? We are like gorillas—it doesn't matter how much love was in your heart; my only question is whether or not you gave me a banana.

Application: Think of a recent behavior performed by someone in your presence. Then ask:

Holy Spirit, what was displayed in this behavior?
Was it love or was it the need for love?

Then look inside at your own reaction to that behavior, and say:

Holy Spirit, classify this thought for me.
Was it love or was it the need for love?

⁴If you [Ur: You who] believe you understand something of the "dynamics" of the ego [Ur: mind], let me assure you that you understand nothing of it [Ur: that you know *nothing* of it at all]. ⁵For of yourself you could not understand [Ur: know of] it. ⁶The study of the ego is not the study of the mind. ⁷In fact, the ego enjoys studying [Ur: the study of] itself, and thoroughly approves the undertakings of students

who would "analyze" it, thus approving its importance. [8]Yet they but study form with meaningless content. [9]For their teacher is senseless, though careful to conceal this fact behind impressive sounding words [Ur: behind a lot of words that sound impressive], but which lack <u>any</u> consistent sense when they are put together.

This is a searing criticism of modern psychology, given to two working psychologists. What is Jesus saying about psychology? He is saying that it is really the study of the ego, not the mind, as its name labels it. Psychologists are studying a malicious parasite in the mind, thinking they are studying the mind itself. The parasite loves this. It actually loves being "analyzed" (a reference to Freudian analysis), which makes it feel really important. He further says that this parasite is actually the teacher, the guiding presence behind modern psychology, and that our learned psychologists are its eager students. He says that in studying the parasite, however, psychologists are actually studying nothing, since the ego is not real. It is merely form that contains chaotic, senseless, *empty* content. Finally, Jesus says that psychological jargon is actually an attempt to hide this underlying emptiness of content. This jargon (like all jargon) uses elaborate, fancy *form* to substitute for and draw attention away from vacuous *content*. In other words, psychology's big words are designed to mask the fact that behind those words is pure nonsense. They are thus an expression of psychologists' underlying insecurity about their whole endeavor.

9. [1]This is characteristic of the ego's judgments. [2]<u>Separately</u>, they seem to hold, but <u>put them together</u> and the system of thought that arises from <u>joining</u> them is incoherent and utterly chaotic. [3]For form is not enough for meaning, and the underlying <u>lack</u> of content makes a cohesive system impossible. [4]<u>Separation</u> therefore remains the ego's chosen condition. [5]For no one <u>alone</u> can judge the ego truly. [6]Yet when two or more <u>join together</u> in searching for truth, the ego can no longer defend its lack of content. [7]The fact of union tells them it is not true.

Fancy psychological terms look impressive, but when you string them together, you get nonsense. This is true of all the ego's judgments. By themselves they seem to make sense, but they don't really. You discover this when you try to assemble them into a cohesive system—and instead get total chaos.

It is very hard to see this on our own. As long as we are separate pieces, we will *see* only separate pieces. We will see only the trees, and won't realize that they don't come together to produce a real forest. In fact, it's only when we truly join with others that we can see this. Then we will see that the ego's content is truly empty, for we will have directly violated the ego's core principle: that the pieces must be separate. By joining two brothers and seeing the underlying reality, we will also join the ego's separate judgments and see their underlying nothingness. Our union, therefore, will automatically show that the ego is just a pipe dream, just a puff of smoke. In later chapters, this will become the core principle of holy relationships.

> 10. ¹It is impossible to remember God in secret and alone. ²For remembering Him means you are <u>not</u> alone, and are willing to remember it. ³Take no thought <u>for yourself</u>, for no thought you hold *is* for yourself. ⁴If you would remember your Father, let the Holy Spirit order your thoughts [Ur: thoughts,] and give [to others] only the answer with which He answers you. ⁵Everyone seeks for love as you do, but knows it not unless he joins <u>with</u> you in seeking it. ⁶If you undertake the search <u>together</u>, you bring with you a light so powerful that what you see is <u>given</u> meaning. ⁷The lonely journey fails because it has <u>excluded</u> what it would <u>find</u>.

This paragraph weaves all the major themes of the this section into one, giving us a taste of the cohesiveness of *this* thought system.

If you would remember God, let the Holy Spirit order your thoughts, classing all loving thoughts as holy, and classing all dark thoughts as mere calls for help. He will respond to these not by instilling guilt, but by extending His loving help.

If you would remember God, respond to your brothers in the same way the Holy Spirit responds to you: give only help to their calls for help. Respond with only love to their need for love.

If you would remember God, join with your brothers in searching for love. Only this can fulfill our universal need for love, for only joined minds can see the real forest instead of just separate trees.

If you do all this, you signify your willingness to no longer be alone, and then you will remember that you are not alone, that you are one with God.

However, if you take the lonely way, in which you exclude your brothers, in which your spiritual search takes thought only of yourself, then you exclude oneness itself, the very thing you are looking for. How different would our religious and mystical traditions be if they understood this one thing!

Application: What kind of search are you on? Are you on the lonely journey in which you seek for God by yourself, or have you joined with another or others in this search? Or is it something in between?

> 11. ¹As God communicates to the Holy Spirit in you, so does the Holy Spirit <u>translate</u> His communications <u>through</u> you, so <u>you</u> can understand them. ²God has no secret communications, for everything of Him is perfectly open and freely accessible to all, being <u>for</u> all. ³Nothing lives in secret, and what you would hide from the Holy Spirit <u>is</u> nothing. ⁴Every interpretation you would lay upon a brother is senseless [see paragraph 7]. ⁵Let the Holy Spirit <u>show him to you</u>, and teach you both his love and his call [Ur: and *need*] for love. ⁶Neither his mind <u>nor yours</u> holds more than these two orders of thought.

God doesn't deal in secrets. What He tells us is not just for us. Thus, we will only truly understand what He tells us when we extend it to our brothers, when we allow the Holy Spirit to translate it through us to them. We, therefore, must not deal in secrets, either. Rather than keeping our dark thoughts secret from the Holy Spirit, we must let Him judge those thoughts, let Him order them. He will show us that they are not sins, but nothing.

He will also show us who our brothers really are. If we are unable to evaluate our brother's behavior and know what he is really calling for, how can we possibly evaluate our brother's being? We need help. The Holy Spirit will show us that our brother's mind, like our own mind, contains only two orders of thought: love and the need for love.

> 12. ¹The miracle is the recognition that this is true. ²Where there is love, your brother <u>must</u> give it to you because of what it <u>is</u>. ³But where there is a call [Ur: is *need*] for love, <u>you</u> must give it because of what <u>you</u> are. ⁴Earlier I [Ur: Long ago we] said this course will teach you

83

how to remember [Ur: will teach you] what you are, restoring to you your Identity. ⁵We have already learned that this Identity is shared. ⁶The miracle becomes the means of sharing It. ⁷By supplying your Identity wherever It is not recognized, you will recognize It. ⁸And God Himself, Who wills to be with His Son forever, will bless each recognition of His Son with all the Love He holds for him. ⁹Nor will the power of all His Love be absent from any miracle you offer to His Son. ¹⁰How, then, can there be any order of difficulty among them?

The miracle is the recognition that only these two orders of thought exist. When your brother's mind is filled with love, he will naturally give it in the form of miracles, for it is love's nature to give. But when his mind is filled with need for love, you will naturally answer this need with love, with miracles, for it is *your* nature to give.

This is how you remember your Identity. Since your Identity is shared, you recognize it by sharing it with others. You supply It where it is not recognized, in minds that think they lack love. God will give all of His power to every act of supplying your Identity, to every miracle that you give. And He will give all of His Love to each recognition that results from this miracle, the recognition in the miracle receiver and in the miracle worker—*you*. If He really does that, then how can there be any order of difficulty among miracles?

XI. The Test of Truth
Commentary by Robert Perry

1.   ¹Yet the essential thing is learning that *you do not know.* ²Knowledge is power [as the saying goes], and all power is of God. ³You who have tried to keep power for yourself have "lost" it. ⁴You still <u>have</u> the power, but you have interposed so much between it and your <u>awareness</u> of it that you cannot use it. ⁵<u>Everything</u> you have taught yourself has made your power more and more obscure to you. ⁶You know not <u>what</u> it is, nor <u>where</u>. ⁷You have made a <u>semblance</u> of power and a <u>show</u> of strength so pitiful that it <u>must</u> fail you. ⁸For power is not a seeming strength, and truth is beyond semblance of any kind. ⁹Yet all that stands between you and the power of God in you is but your learning of the false, and of [the "of" crept in somewhere after the Urtext] your attempts to <u>undo the true</u>.

This paragraph tells a poignant story. We threw away the knowledge of God. We detached from Him, apparently because we didn't want to share power with Him. We wanted to keep it all to ourselves. But this attempt backfired. We lost our power, for it was one with our knowledge. The more we tried to recapture it, the further away it got. So we put on a *show* of strength. We puffed ourselves up with a *semblance* of power. Yet this pseudo-power is so flimsy that it always fails us. We are weak, and we know it.

There is good news, however. We still have all the power we possessed with God in the beginning. We simply need to undo the clouds of deception we have placed between it and our awareness. These clouds are all those false lessons we taught ourselves during our long fall from power.

2.   ¹Be willing, then, for <u>all</u> of it to be undone, and be glad that you are not bound to it forever. ²For you have taught yourself <u>how to imprison the Son of God</u>, a lesson so unthinkable that only the insane, in deepest sleep, could even <u>dream</u> of it. ³Can God learn how <u>not</u> to be God? ⁴And can His Son, <u>given</u> all power <u>by</u> Him, learn to be <u>powerless</u>? ⁵What have you taught yourself that you can possibly prefer to keep, in place of what you *have* and what you *are*?

85

We have to *want* the lessons we taught ourselves to be undone. We have every reason to want this, for these lessons haven't simply obscured our power; they have driven us insane. For they have taught us how to imprison ourselves, yet we are the omnipotent Son of God. How can God's all-powerful Son be imprisoned? We are like a mad scientist cackling, "I have wrapped several strands of spider web around Superman and have thus rendered him completely bound. He is totally under my power. Hoo hoo hoo ha ha ha!" Underneath all our feelings of being weak and powerless, at the mercy of money issues and traffic and insects, this mad cackling is constantly echoing. Is this insanity really what we want?

Application: Think of a situation in which you feel imprisoned by the situation, at the mercy of its undesirable circumstances. Then say,

> *I really believe I have managed to imprison the omnipotent Son of God.*
> *Is this sane?*

3. ¹Atonement teaches you how to escape forever from everything that you have taught yourself in the past, by showing you <u>only</u> what you <u>are</u> *now*. ²Learning <u>has been</u> accomplished <u>before</u> its effects are manifest. ³Learning is therefore <u>in the past,</u> but its influence <u>determines</u> the present by giving it whatever meaning it holds for you. ⁴*Your* learning gives the present <u>no meaning at all</u>. ⁵Nothing you have ever learned can help you understand the present, or teach you how to undo the past. ⁶Your past <u>is</u> what you have taught yourself. ⁷*Let* <u>it all</u> <u>go</u>. ⁸Do <u>not</u> attempt to understand <u>any</u> event or <u>anything</u> or <u>anyone</u> in its "light," for the [Ur: light of] darkness in which you <u>try</u> to see can <u>only</u> obscure. ⁹Put no confidence at all in darkness to illuminate your understanding, for if you do you <u>contradict</u> the light, and thereby <u>think</u> you see the darkness. ¹⁰Yet darkness cannot <u>be</u> seen, for it is nothing more than a condition in which seeing becomes impossible.

The purpose of past learning is to illuminate what is in front of us right now. For instance, I've seen stories where people see the water at a beach suddenly recede, so that fish are flapping on sand that used to be ocean bottom. They go out to inspect this curiosity, not realizing that the receding water means that a tsunami is coming. This is a mistake that you only make once. If you manage to survive, you've learned exactly what to do if the water recedes again.

Our learning may tell us a great deal about the forms of this world, but it is hopeless when it comes to content—*meaning*. On the content level, our learning doesn't illuminate the present, it completely obscures it. Our learning is like a reverse flashlight that shines darkness onto things, making them utterly invisible. In this darkness, we start imagining shapes and images, making us believe that we are seeing when we're not.

I was once in a cave and turned my (non-reverse) flashlight off. To my surprise, I could make out walls on either side and things in front of me. However, when I put my hand in front of my face, I couldn't see it at all. I was obviously imagining the walls. I thought I was seeing when I wasn't. As you look at the scene in front of you, that's what is happening now. You may see the forms accurately, but the *meaning* you think you see in those forms is not really there. You're really in the dark, imagining that you are seeing.

This is why we need to let our learning go. We need to let the Atonement undo it, and then show us what is really there now, show us the meaning that is right in front of us yet which we have been blind to.

> 4. ¹You who have not yet brought all of the darkness you have taught yourself into the light in you, can hardly judge the truth and value of this course. ²Yet God did not abandon you. ³And so you have another lesson sent from Him, already learned for every child of light by Him to Whom God gave it [the Holy Spirit]. ⁴This lesson shines with God's glory, for in it lies His power, which He shares so gladly with His Son. ⁵Learn of His happiness, which is yours. ⁶But to accomplish this, all your dark lessons must be brought willingly to truth, and joyously laid down by hands open to receive, not closed to take. ⁷Every dark lesson that you bring to Him Who teaches light He will accept from you, because you do not want it. ⁸And He will gladly exchange each one for the bright lesson He has learned for you. ⁹Never believe that any lesson you have learned apart from Him means anything.

The opening lines suggest that our dark lessons make the Course seem untrue and not very valuable. This, of course, makes learning the Course extremely difficult for us. Thankfully, though, God has sent us another lesson, one that the Holy Spirit has *already* learned for us. This is called the "bright lesson," and learning it reclaims for us the power and joy that we threw away. Yet there is a catch. In order to realize that this bright lesson is already learned (somewhere deep inside us), we need to willingly bring to the Holy Spirit all the dark lessons we have taught ourselves.

Application: Think of a lesson that is very ingrained in you, yet which is causing you difficulty in your life, such as "people can't be trusted," or "there's never enough time," or "I will never succeed on the spiritual path," or "I am guilty." Picture this lesson as written on the side of a reverse flashlight, which you are using all the time to shine darkness onto present situations and make their meaning invisible. Now imagine yourself walking up to the Holy Spirit and humbly laying this reverse flashlight before Him, with your hands open to receive. Say,

> *I joyously lay this dark lesson down, because I do not want it.*
> *My hands are open to receive the bright lesson You have learned*
> *for me.*

5.   ¹You have one test, as sure as God, by which to recognize if what you learned is true. ²If you are <u>wholly</u> free of fear of any kind, and if all those who meet or even <u>think</u> of you <u>share</u> in your perfect peace, then you can be sure that you have learned <u>God's</u> lesson, and <u>not</u> your own [Ur: *not* yours]. ³Unless all this is true, there <u>are</u> dark lessons in your mind that hurt and hinder you, <u>and everyone around you</u>. ⁴The <u>absence</u> of <u>perfect</u> peace means but one thing: You <u>think</u> you do not will for God's Son what his Father wills for him. ⁵Every dark lesson teaches this, in one form or another. ⁶And each bright lesson with which the Holy Spirit will <u>replace</u> the dark ones you do <u>not</u> accept [Ur: and hide], teaches you that you will <u>with</u> the Father and His Son.

Now we have the test from the section title. To have learned God's lesson, you must be wholly free of fear and all its forms—anxiety, worry, nervousness, tension, apprehension, etc.—which means you are wholly at peace. Further, everyone who meets or even *thinks* about you must share in your peace. Who has passed this test? You can (maybe) fool yourself about the first part, but not about the second. That you haven't passed this test means there are still dark lessons in your mind "that hurt and hinder you, *and everyone around you.*"

Did even Jesus pass this test? After all, why would they have killed him if they were sharing in his perfect peace? I believe, however, that somewhere inside they *were*, and their egos found this so threatening that that is why they had to kill him.

How do the dark lessons rob us of peace? They cause guilt. They teach us that we want pain and suffering for God's Son—our brothers—rather than what God wants for them. Guilt is simply the result of not wishing others well, isn't it? The bright lesson releases us from guilt by teaching us that we not only wish others well, but that we *will* them the perfect happiness that God wills for them. If we really knew that, could we feel guilty?

> 6. ¹Do not be concerned about how you can learn a lesson so <u>completely</u> different from everything that you have taught yourself. ²How would you know? ³Your part is very simple. ⁴You need only recognize that everything <u>you</u> learned you <u>do not want</u>. ⁵Ask to <u>be</u> taught, and do <u>not</u> use your experiences to confirm what <u>you</u> have learned. ⁶When your peace is threatened or disturbed in <u>any</u> way, say to yourself:
>
> > ⁷*I do not know what anything, <u>including this</u>, means.*
> > ⁸*And so I do <u>not</u> know <u>how to respond to it</u>.*
> > ⁹*And I will not use my own past learning as the light to guide me now.*
>
> ¹⁰By this refusal to attempt to teach yourself what you do not know, the Guide Whom God has given you will speak to you. ¹¹<u>He</u> will take His rightful place in your awareness the instant <u>you</u> abandon it, and offer it to Him.

The practice in this paragraph is a beloved one among Course students. If you think about it, it is exactly like what we find in the Workbook. First, we have several paragraphs of teaching. That teaching is then funneled into a practice. This practice takes the form of selecting a specific situation, one that threatens or disturbs our peace, and then repeating words to ourselves that are designed to dispel our current perception of that situation. I find this practice extremely helpful. The reason it works so well is that my negative emotions are the direct result of what I think a situation *means*. If, by using this practice, I can honestly admit that I don't know what it means, then the negative emotions have to go. If they stay, it is only because I couldn't say the words sincerely to myself.

Notice that this is how we learn the bright lesson. Rather than trying to squeeze into our head something that is totally different from everything we have learned, we need to focus on giving up our dark lessons, the lessons that have been serving as our reverse flashlights. Admitting that we really don't know is the most sincere way to invite the Holy Spirit into our mind, more sincere than flowery prayers. If you say to someone, "Please, you amazing driver, take over the wheel for me," but you don't get out of the driver's seat, how sincere is your request?

Application: We should, of course, do this practice. Pick a current situation that seems to be threatening or disturbing your peace, and say the words provided, as honestly and sincerely as you can.

> 7. ¹You cannot be your guide to miracles, for it is you who made them necessary. ²And because you did, the means on which you can depend for miracles has been provided for you. ³God's Son can make no needs His Father will not meet, if he but turn to Him ever so little. ⁴Yet He cannot compel His Son to turn to Him and remain Himself [God is not a compeller]. ⁵It is impossible that God lose His Identity, for if He did, you would lose yours. ⁶And being yours He cannot change Himself, for your Identity is changeless. ⁷The miracle acknowledges His changelessness by seeing His Son as he always was, and not as he would make himself. ⁸The miracle brings the effects that only guiltlessness can bring, and thus establishes the fact that guiltlessness must be.

Asking us to be our own guide to miracles is like asking the learning disabled child to design his own educational curriculum (the example from 12.V). Thankfully, our Father sees our need and meets it. We can lay hold of this if we just turn to Him ever so slightly. But He will not compel us to do so, for overpowering us would mean changing His eternally gentle nature. And He cannot change Himself, for this would automatically change us, and we are changeless.

Giving miracles shows us that we are changeless. How? Our miracle brings to the receiver effects that could only have come from the heart of a guiltless being. This teaches us that, despite all our judgmental thoughts, all our ignoring of others' needs, we haven't changed our original purity. Purity is still in there. Otherwise, how could we have given to our brother the beautiful gift that we did?

> 8.   ¹How can you, so firmly bound to guilt and committed so to remain, establish <u>for yourself</u> your guiltlessness? ²That is impossible. ³But be sure that you are willing to acknowledge that it *is* impossible. ⁴It is only because you think that you can run some little part, or deal with certain aspects of your life alone, that the guidance of the Holy Spirit is limited. ⁵Thus would you make <u>Him</u> undependable, and <u>use</u> this fancied undependability as an excuse for keeping certain dark lessons <u>from</u> Him. ⁶And by so limiting the guidance that you would <u>accept,</u> <u>you</u> are unable to <u>depend</u> on miracles to answer <u>all</u> your problems <u>for</u> you.

He knows us so well. First, we decide that we want to run some part of our life alone, or deal with some problem alone. We want to stay in the driver's seat. Then, in some other area of our life, we ask the Holy Spirit to take the wheel. Now we are giving Him a double message: Take the wheel; no, don't take the wheel. It's like we are sitting halfway in the driver's seat. This obviously limits how much He can really take over. This is why we can't consistently hear His guidance—we are constantly saying to Him, "Please speak/shut up." So now we think, "You know, I can't always depend on this Holy Spirit. And if I can't depend on Him, why would I hand over to Him my deepest and most cherished beliefs, along with my darkest secrets?" Because we won't hand over our dark lessons to Him, He is unable to give us a miracle to solve *all* our problems.

This mindset of "I'll handle it myself" gets us into trouble. Why, then, would we think we can establish our guiltlessness for ourselves? Our efforts to become guiltless are secretly based on the fact that we are "firmly bound to guilt and committed so to remain"? What else could those efforts result in but the accumulation of more guilt?

> 9.   ¹Do you think that what the Holy Spirit would have you <u>give</u> He

would withhold from you? ²You have no problems that He cannot solve by offering you a miracle. ³Miracles are for you. ⁴And every fear or pain or trial you have has been undone. ⁵He has brought all of them to light, having accepted them instead of you, and recognized they never were. ⁶There are no dark lessons He has not already lightened for you. ⁷The lessons you would teach yourself He has corrected already. ⁸They do not exist in His Mind at all. ⁹For the past binds Him not, and therefore binds not you. ¹⁰He does not see time as you do. ¹¹And each miracle He offers you corrects your use of time, and makes it His.

The Holy Spirit is constantly asking us to give miracles. Why, then, would He withhold them from *us*? He not only *can* solve "every fear or pain or trial" we face, He has already done so. He has so fully solved and undone them that they don't even exist in His Mind anymore.

Application: Think of some trial that you face right now. Repeat to yourself the following:

> *The Holy Spirit can solve this.*
> *The Holy Spirit has already solved this.*
> *It is so completely over that it doesn't even exist in His Mind anymore.*
> *I want His solution, not my own.*
> *Holy Spirit, what is Your solution to this problem?*

10. ¹He Who has freed you from the past would teach you are free of it. ²He would but have you accept His accomplishments as yours, because He did them for you. ³And because He did, they *are* yours. ⁴He has made you free of what you made. ⁵You can deny Him, but you cannot call on Him in vain. ⁶He always gives His gifts in place of yours [Ur: He *always* gives what *He* has made, *in place* of you]. ⁷He would establish His bright teaching so firmly in your mind, that no dark lesson of guilt can abide in what He has established as holy by His Presence. ⁸Thank God that He is there and works through you. ⁹And all His works are yours. ¹⁰He offers you a miracle with every one you let Him do through you.

Application: Think of something you carry from your past that you wish was undone. Perhaps it is a belief you carry. Perhaps it is something you did that you regret. Then, with this past thing in mind, read the paragraph again in first person (I have put in the emphases from the Urtext version).

He Who has freed me from the past would teach I *am* free of it.

He would but have me accept His accomplishments *as mine*, because
He did them *for* me.

And because He did, they *are* mine.

He has *made* me free of what I made.

I can deny Him, but I *cannot* call on Him in vain.

He *always* gives what *He* has made, *in place* of what I made.

He would establish His bright teaching so firmly in my mind that no
dark lesson of guilt can abide in what He has established as holy
by His Presence.

I thank God that He is there and works through me.

And all His works are mine.

He offers *me* a miracle with every one I *let* Him do through me.

11. ¹God's Son will <u>always</u> be indivisible. ²As we are held as one in God, so do we learn as one in Him. ³God's Teacher is as like to His Creator as is His Son, and through His Teacher does God proclaim His Oneness <u>and</u> His Son's. ⁴Listen in silence, and do <u>not</u> raise your voice against Him. ⁵For He teaches the miracle of oneness, and before <u>His</u> lesson division disappears. ⁶Teach <u>like</u> Him here, and you <u>will</u> remember that you have <u>always</u> created like your Father. ⁷The miracle of creation has never ceased, having the holy stamp of immortality upon it. ⁸This is the Will of God for all creation, and all creation joins in willing this.

Just as we are all one in Heaven, so do we learn as one on earth. We can teach this oneness here, but only if we listen to the Holy Spirit and let Him teach through us. This teaching is an act of extending on earth, a reflection of extension in Heaven. And if we enter fully into this reflection, we will awaken to the light it reflects. We will remember our eternal function of creation in God.

12. ¹Those who remember always that they know nothing, and who have become willing to learn everything, will learn it. ²But whenever they trust themselves, they will not learn. ³They have destroyed their motivation for learning by thinking they already know. ⁴Think not you understand ["understand" and "know" are synonyms in this section] anything until you pass the test of perfect peace, for peace and understanding go together and never can be found alone. ⁵Each brings the other with it, for it is the law of God they be not separate. ⁶They are cause and effect, each to the other, so where one is absent the other cannot be.

13. ¹Only those who recognize they cannot know unless the effects of understanding [peace] are with them, can really learn at all. ²For this it must be peace they want, and nothing else. ³Whenever you think you know, peace will depart from you, because you have abandoned the Teacher of peace. ⁴Whenever you fully realize that you know not, peace will return, for you will have invited Him to do so by abandoning the ego on behalf of Him. ⁵Call not upon the ego for anything; it is only this that you need do. ⁶The Holy Spirit will, of Himself, fill every mind that so makes room for Him.

If you think you know, you will not learn. Obviously, you have no reason for learning if you already know everything. You also have no reason for listening to God's Teacher. However, if you admit that you know nothing, you are in a position to learn everything. The key to this is that you have to refuse to think you know anything until you pass the test of perfect peace, until you are perfectly peaceful and everyone who meets or thinks of you shares your peace. Peace is the test of understanding. If you understand, you are at peace. If you are at peace, you understand.

Application: Say to yourself,

> *I am not perfectly at peace.*
> *And so I do not understand anything.*
> *But I am willing to learn everything,*
> *And I will,*
> *Because I want peace more than anything.*

14. ¹If you want peace you <u>must</u> abandon the teacher of attack. ²The Teacher of peace will <u>never</u> abandon <u>you</u>. ³<u>You</u> can desert <u>Him</u> but He will never reciprocate, for His faith in you <u>is</u> His understanding. ⁴It is as firm as is His faith in His Creator, and He knows that faith in His Creator <u>must</u> encompass faith in His creation. ⁵In this consistency lies His holiness which He <u>cannot</u> abandon, for it is not His will to do so. ⁶With your perfection ever in His sight, He gives the gift of peace to everyone who perceives the <u>need</u> for peace, and who would have it. ⁷Make way for peace, and it will come. ⁸For understanding <u>is</u> in you, and from it peace <u>must</u> come.

If I really want peace, I have to abandon the teacher of war—the ego. Yet even while I follow this teacher around like a duckling follows its mother, the Teacher of peace will never abandon me. Since He is the Teacher, He possesses real knowledge, the knowledge I don't have. And what does He know? He knows that faith in me is justified. He never, ever doubts that I will come to understand everything. Indeed, His faith in me is so certain that it's every bit as firm as His faith in God. This consistency of faith—the same faith in me that He has in God—is what makes Him holy, and He will never abandon His holiness, any more than He will abandon me. All I need do, then, is leave room for peace by admitting that I simply don't understand. Then understanding will dawn on me, for it is already within me.

15. ¹The power of God, from which they both arise, is yours as surely as it is His. ²You think you know Him not, only because, alone, it is impossible to know Him [see X.10:1]. ³Yet see the mighty works [see VII.5:13] that He will do through you, and you <u>must</u> be convinced you did them through Him. ⁴It is impossible to deny the Source of effects so powerful they <u>could</u> not be of you. ⁵Leave room for Him, and you will find yourself so filled with power that <u>nothing</u> will prevail against your peace. ⁶And this will be the test by which you recognize that you <u>have</u> understood.

Peace and understanding both arise from God's power. This power, amazingly, is just as much yours as it is the Holy Spirit's. You think that you don't know God, only because (as we saw in X.10), you can't know Him by yourself. And thus you think you lack His power and His peace as well. However, you will become convinced that you have all three—

power, peace, and understanding—once you see the mighty works God will do through you.

How does this work? Here again we see the Course describing a psychological process that occurs when we extend miracles to our brothers—miracles being the "mighty works" here. Section VII said that we are not asked to do mighty works ourselves. But God will do mighty works through us. As we witness these mighty works, playing the role of observer to our own acts, our thought process will go something like this: "The works I have seen myself do are quite simply beyond me to do. They must have been the power of God working through me, a power that is also peace, for peace is what it brings. This power is so great that it has brought peace to my brothers when the barriers to this peace seemed insurmountable. In fact, it seems that nothing can stand against my peace. Regardless of the obstacles, it spreads out and is shared by everyone who meets me or thinks of me.

"This means that I have finally passed the test of perfect peace. Thus, I can at last be sure that I *have* understood. Peace is not delusional; it is clarity. It is understanding. The peace I have given must have come from a true understanding in me. Now I know that God's power, God's peace, and God's understanding all reside in me. How else could I have given them?"

Commentaries on Chapter 15

THE HOLY INSTANT

I. The Two Uses of Time
Commentary by Robert Perry

1.   ¹Can you imagine what it means to have no cares, no worries, no anxieties, but merely to be perfectly calm and quiet all the time? ²Yet that is what time is for; to learn just that and nothing more. ³God's Teacher cannot be satisfied with His teaching until it constitutes all your learning. ⁴He has not fulfilled His teaching function until you have become such a consistent learner that you learn only of Him. ⁵When this has happened, you will no longer need a teacher or time in which to learn.

Application: Try to imagine what it would be like to:

- have no cares
- have no worries
- have no anxieties
- but merely to be perfectly calm
- and perfectly quiet
- all the time.

This is what you are here to learn, not how to juggle all the balls, but how to be totally at peace even while juggling. Correction: to be totally at peace *all the time*. The Holy Spirit is only done with us when we possess *only* what He taught us, when we abide in His learning all the time.

2.   ¹One source of perceived discouragement from which you may suffer [Ur: from which you suffer] is your belief that this takes time, and that the results of the Holy Spirit's teaching are far in the future. ²This is not so. ³For the Holy Spirit uses time in His Own way, and is not bound by it. ⁴Time is His friend in teaching. ⁵It does not waste Him, as it does you. ⁶And all the waste that time seems to bring with it is due but to your identification with the ego, which uses time to support its belief in destruction. ⁷The ego, like the Holy Spirit, uses time to convince you of the inevitability of the goal and end of teaching. ⁸To

99

the ego the goal is death, which *is* its end. ⁹But to the Holy Spirit the goal is life, which *has* no end.

In contemplating the goal of being totally carefree all the time, we get discouraged. We think it will take forever. The Holy Spirit seems to be taking His sweet time with us. He seems to be wasting a lot of time in moving us to this goal. "Why doesn't He hurry up?" we wonder.

The fact is, however, that *we* are the time wasters. We are sitting like a mule on the trail, refusing to move. If our willingness were really present, the Holy Spirit would carry us to the end in an instant. And what is the end? It is life without end and without limit.

The ego, on the other hand, is trying to keep us caught up in time so that, lashed to time's revolving wheel, it wears us out. It grinds us down. It wastes us, until we die.

> 3.   ¹The ego is an ally of time, but not a friend. ²For it is as mistrustful of death as it is of life, and what it wants for you it cannot tolerate. ³The ego wants *you* dead, but not itself. ⁴The outcome of its strange religion must therefore be the conviction that it can pursue you beyond the grave. ⁵And out of its unwillingness for you to find peace even in death [Ur: even in the death it *wants* for you], it offers you immortality in hell. ⁶It speaks to you of Heaven, but assures you that Heaven is not for you. ⁷How can the guilty hope for Heaven?

Back in Chapter 12, we were told that the ego is trying to kill us, that its goal for us is death. Now, however, that teaching is expanded. The ego wants us dead but not entirely annihilated, for that would mean its own annihilation, which it definitely does not want. It wants us first dead, and then it wants to pursue us beyond the grave, in the living-death of hell, where all hope is gone, where the ego will punish us forever for our sins.

It is easy to distance ourselves from such a paragraph. It seems so extreme and macabre. Yet we need to resist this temptation. The ego that wants to torment us forever in hell is the same ego that appears today to be our friend, constantly advising us on what to do and how to be happy. This ego *does* tell us that hell awaits us. How else do we explain why hell is such a widespread belief in this world?

> 4.   ¹The belief in hell is inescapable to those who identify with the

ego. ²Their nightmares and their fears are all associated with it. ³The ego teaches that hell is <u>in the future</u>, for this is what <u>all</u> its teaching is directed to. ⁴<u>Hell is its goal</u>. ⁵For although the ego aims at death and dissolution as an end, <u>it</u> does not believe it. ⁶The goal of death, which it craves for you, leaves <u>it</u> unsatisfied. ⁷No one who follows the ego's teaching is without the <u>fear</u> of death. ⁸Yet if death were thought of merely as an end to pain, would it be <u>feared</u>? ⁹We have seen this strange paradox in the ego's thought system before, but never so clearly as here. ¹⁰For the ego must <u>seem</u> to <u>keep fear from you</u> to hold your allegiance. ¹¹Yet it must <u>engender</u> fear in order to maintain <u>itself</u>. ¹²Again the ego tries, and all too frequently succeeds, in doing both, by using dissociation for holding its contradictory aims together so that they <u>seem</u> to be reconciled. ¹³The ego teaches thus: Death is the end as far as hope of Heaven goes. ¹⁴Yet because you and the ego [Ur: *itself*] cannot be separated, and because it cannot conceive of its <u>own</u> death, it will pursue you still, because guilt is eternal [Ur: *because your guilt is eternal*]. ¹⁵Such is the ego's version of immortality. ¹⁶And it is <u>this</u> the ego's version of time supports.

The first line bears re-reading: *Everyone* who identifies with the ego is afraid of hell. Each nightmare and each fear ultimately traces back to the fear of hell. It doesn't matter if you are an atheist who doesn't believe in an afterlife or a New Ager who believes in reincarnation. Somewhere in your mind is the fear that your sins are so bad they will consign you to a shadow existence in a gloomy place of everlasting punishment.

This, Jesus says, is the real reason we fear death. Think about it: If death were simply passing into nonexistence, an end to the pain of this life, it would be like going to sleep after a really bad day and never waking up. At that point, it wouldn't be reasonable to fear your own death (although it would still be reasonable for those still living who would grieve for you to fear your death). So why do we fear death? Because of the unconscious fear of hell.

Here we see the ego doing its characteristic juggling act. It says, "Don't be afraid. Death is a welcome end to this painful life that is so full of struggle." Then it whispers very quietly, "But then you'll spend forever in hell." It just makes sure that it speaks these messages on different levels of your mind, so that they never meet and the contradiction never becomes apparent.

This, then, is the real message the ego is telling you, even now: "You know that mistake you just made, the one that made you afraid? It *should* make you afraid, because that mistake is a deposit in your account. This account is always growing and the interest is compounding daily. Someday, after you die, it will all catch up with you, and you will spend forever paying it off. Forever."

> 5. ¹The ego teaches that Heaven is here and now because the <u>future</u> is hell. ²Even when it attacks so savagely that it tries to take the life of someone who thinks its is the only voice [Ur: someone who hears it temporarily as the *only* voice], it speaks of hell even to him. ³For it tells him hell is <u>here</u> as well [Ur: hell is *here*], and bids him leap from hell into oblivion. ⁴The only time the ego allows anyone to look upon with [Ur: some amount of] equanimity is the <u>past</u>. ⁵And even there, its only value is that it is no more.

Not all appreciation of the present is spiritually enlightened. Even the ego says, "Enjoy the present. This is heaven." Then it adds, "You better enjoy it, for the future is hell." This sounds a great deal like "Eat, drink and be merry, for tomorrow we shall die" (Ecclesiastes).

Unfortunately, after enough eating, drinking, and being merry, it all starts to turn sour. It all begins to fall down on your head. Then your wonderful counselor, who has been waiting for this moment, steps back in and says, "That hellish future I was telling you about—it has arrived. Your only choice is to leap from this into nonexistence. Yes, you understand me; it's time to kill yourself."

So at different points, the ego will tell you that the future is hell and the present is hell. What about the past? It says, "Thank God *that's* over!"

> 6. ¹How bleak and despairing is the ego's use of time! ²And how <u>terrifying</u>! ³For underneath its fanatical insistence that the past and future be the same is hidden a far more insidious threat to peace. ⁴The ego does not advertise its final threat, for it would have its worshippers still believe that <u>it</u> can offer them <u>escape</u> [Ur: that *it* can offer the *escape* from it]. ⁵But the belief in guilt <u>must</u> lead to the <u>belief in hell</u>, and <u>always does</u>. ⁶The only way in which the ego allows the fear of hell to be experienced is to <u>bring hell here</u>, but <u>always</u> as a foretaste of the future. ⁷For no one who considers himself as <u>deserving</u> of hell can believe that punishment will end in peace.

As we've seen, the ego's view of time can be summarized in this way: the past *was* hell, the present *is* hell, and the future *will be* hell. The ego may fanatically insist that the future will be like the past, yet this is a definite case of the lady doth protest too much. For what it refuses to tell you—for fear of you abandoning it—is that its whole plan leads to the future being immeasurably *worse* than the past. Its plan is all about you accumulating guilt, and what does guilt lead to but hell? That's the future it has planned for you. How can you believe you are guilty yet think you'll magically never have to pay your debt?

Yet again, the ego doesn't let this fear of hell surface to consciousness. The closest it comes is when the present seems like hell. Haven't there been times in all of our lives when it felt like we were in hell, when it seemed that all our sins had come down upon us and there was no way out? That was just a tiny surfacing of the state we unconsciously believe we'll spend eternity in.

> 7. ¹The Holy Spirit teaches thus: There <u>is</u> no hell. ²Hell is only what the ego has made <u>of the present</u>. ³The <u>belief</u> in hell is what <u>prevents</u> you from <u>understanding</u> the present, because <u>you are afraid of it</u>. ⁴The Holy Spirit leads as steadily to Heaven as the ego drives to hell. ⁵For the Holy Spirit, Who knows <u>only</u> the present, uses it to <u>undo</u> the fear by which the ego would make the present useless. ⁶There is <u>no escape</u> from fear in the ego's use of time. ⁷For time, according to its teaching, is nothing but a teaching device for <u>compounding</u> guilt until it becomes all-encompassing, demanding [Ur: and demands] vengeance forever.

Despite all this talk about hell, the fact is that hell is a myth. It may be a myth that has been perpetuated for thousands of years by many traditions, but it is still a myth. The only "reality" to hell is that hell is what the ego makes of our present. The ego makes the present so hellish, so fearful, that we become afraid of the present, and so do not understand it nor really use it. We *could* use it to undo fear. We could use it to enter more and more deeply into the present until we realize that the present is eternity. Under the ego, however, we just use it to compound our guilt, "until it becomes all-encompassing, and demands vengeance forever."

> 8. ¹The Holy Spirit would undo <u>all</u> of this *now*. ²Fear is <u>not</u> of the present, but <u>only</u> of the past and future, which do not exist. ³There is

no fear in the present when each instant stands clear and separated from the past, without its [the past's] shadow reaching out into the future. ⁴Each instant is a clean, untarnished birth, in which the Son of God emerges <u>from</u> the past into the present. ⁵And the present <u>extends forever</u>. ⁶It is so beautiful and so clean and free of guilt that nothing but happiness is there. ⁷No darkness is remembered, and immortality and joy are <u>now</u>.

The Holy Spirit wants to undo the ego's whole terrifying approach to time. You can't really fear the present. You can only fear the past catching up with you in the future. When you fear the present, then, you are really slapping onto it the remembered past or the anticipated future. You aren't seeing it for what it is. And what is it? Each present moment is a "clean, untarnished birth." Think of those three words: clean, untarnished, birth. All three of these words say the same thing: new, fresh, not conditioned by the past, not stained by the past. The real present moment is free of the past. The forms in this moment may be the product of the past. But the moment itself is one hundred percent free of the past. How can we fear that?

9. ¹This lesson takes <u>no</u> time. ²For what <u>is</u> time <u>without</u> a past and future? ³It <u>has</u> taken time to misguide you so completely, but it takes no time at all to <u>be</u> what you <u>are</u>. ⁴Begin to practice the Holy Spirit's <u>use</u> of time as a teaching aid to happiness and peace. ⁵Take this very instant, <u>now</u>, and think of it as <u>all there is</u> of time. ⁶Nothing can reach you here out of the past, and it is here that you are <u>completely</u> absolved, <u>completely</u> free and <u>wholly</u> without condemnation. ⁷From this holy instant wherein holiness was born again you will go forth in time without fear, and with no sense of change <u>with</u> time.

Application: This is an extremely important paragraph. It is actual instruction in how to enter the holy instant (in fact, the term "holy instant" occurs here for the first time in the Course). I have filled this exercise out with some material (slightly reworded) from the previous paragraph, a couple of lines from the following section, and a line from the Workbook. All the italics, by the way, are from the Urtext. Take your time with these lines. Don't just read them; enter the space of which they speak. Use them to actually enter the present, to have a holy instant.

There is no fear in the present when this instant stands clear and
    separated from the past,
    without the past's shadow reaching out into the future.
This instant is a clean, untarnished birth,
    in which the Son of God emerges *from* the past into the present.
And the present *extends forever*.
It is so beautiful
    and so clean
    and free of guilt
    that nothing but happiness is there.
No darkness is remembered,
    and immortality and joy are *now*. (adapted from paragraph 8)

Take this very instant, *now*,
    and think of it as *all there is* of time.
Nothing can reach you here out of the past,
    and it is here that you are *completely* absolved,
    completely free
    and *wholly* without condemnation [not under condemnation].

Look straight into the present. (W-pI.18.9:5)

Learn to separate out this single second,
    and to experience it as timeless. (T-15.II.6:3)

From this holy instant wherein holiness was born again
    you will go forth in time without fear,
    and with no sense of change *with* time.

> 10. ¹Time is inconceivable without change, yet [Ur: and] holiness does <u>not</u> change. ²Learn from this instant more than merely that hell does not exist. ³<u>In this redeeming instant lies Heaven</u>. ⁴And Heaven will <u>not</u> change, for the birth into the holy present is <u>salvation</u> from change. ⁵Change is an illusion, taught by those who cannot see themselves as guiltless. ⁶There is no change in Heaven because <u>there is no change in God</u>. ⁷In the holy instant, in which you see yourself as bright with freedom, you <u>will</u> remember God. ⁸For remembering Him *is* to remember freedom.

If you truly enter the present and find holiness reborn in you, you will go beyond change, for holiness doesn't change. Time will flow by, but your state will stay the same. You will become the eye of the storm.

Getting in touch with your changeless holiness will accomplish at least three things. First, it will show you that hell does not exist. Hell is not for the holy. Second, it will carry you beyond change, for change itself is a form of punishment for guilt. Thus, without guilt there is no change. Third, it will give you Heaven, where there is no change. It will give you God. All of this comes from the simple act of realizing that here, in the present, you are free of the sins of the past. For the present is unconditioned by the past. It is a clean, untarnished birth.

> 11. ¹If [Ur: Whenever] you are tempted to be dispirited by thinking <u>how long</u> it would take to change your mind so completely, ask yourself, "How long is an instant?" ²Could you not give so <u>short</u> a time to the Holy Spirit for your salvation? ³He asks no more, for He has no need of more. ⁴It takes far longer to teach you to be willing to <u>give</u> Him this than for Him to use this tiny instant to offer you the whole of Heaven. ⁵In exchange for this instant He stands ready to give you the remembrance of eternity.

We are easily discouraged when we contemplate the Course's goals. They entail such a profound transformation of the whole way we see everything—self, others, world, God. We assume that that kind of change must take nearly forever. Yet Jesus tells us that the Holy Spirit can take us the whole way in a single instant. Imagine that—you could become as advanced as Jesus in just one instant! But here's the catch: You first need to go through a learning process in which you become willing to *fully* give the Holy Spirit this one instant.

> 12. ¹You will never give this holy instant to the Holy Spirit on behalf of <u>your</u> release while you are unwilling to give it to your brothers on behalf of <u>theirs</u>. ²For the instant of holiness is <u>shared</u>, and <u>cannot</u> be yours alone. ³Remember, then, when you are tempted to attack a brother, that <u>his</u> instant of release is <u>yours</u>. ⁴Miracles <u>are</u> the instants of release you offer, and will <u>receive</u>. ⁵They attest to <u>your</u> willingness to *be* released, and to offer time to the Holy Spirit for <u>His</u> use of it.

How do we become willing to fully offer the Holy Spirit a single instant? We learn to give an instant to our brother. This doesn't mean that for a minute we give him our full attention. It means we give him the message that he is fully released from his past sins. We give him the message that, in this instant, he is completely absolved, completely free, and wholly uncondemned. We give him the message that he is born again. Only when we have granted this right to our brother will we feel that we have this right ourselves—the right to leave our past sins fully behind us.

> 13. ¹How long is an instant? ²It is as short for your brother as it is for you. ³Practice <u>giving</u> this blessed instant of freedom to all who are <u>enslaved</u> by time, and thus make time their friend <u>for</u> them. ⁴The Holy Spirit gives their blessed instant <u>to</u> you through your giving it. ⁵As you <u>give</u> it, He offers it to <u>you</u>. ⁶Be not unwilling to give what you would receive of Him, for you join <u>with</u> Him in giving. ⁷In the crystal cleanness of the release you <u>give</u> is <u>your instantaneous</u> escape from guilt. ⁸You <u>must</u> be holy if you <u>offer</u> holiness.

Now we are told a second thing we must practice. The first thing was to practice entering the present free of the past. The second thing is to practice giving this gift to our brother. This releases *us* from guilt and allows us to enter the present. We look at our gift of release and think, "If I offer holiness to my brother, I guess I must be holy." Thus our past sins drop away and we step into the clean, untarnished present.

Application: Choose someone who you see as compromised, sullied, dirtied by the sins of his or her past. Then say these lines to this person as a true gift of release:

> *In this instant, nothing can reach you out of the past.*
> *It is here that you are completely absolved,*
>   *completely free,*
>   *and wholly uncondemned.*
> *This instant is a clean, untarnished birth,*
>   *in which you emerge from the past and are born again.*
> *This is your holy instant of release.*

14. ¹How long is an instant? ²As long as it takes to re-establish perfect sanity, perfect peace and perfect love for everyone, for God and for <u>yourself</u>. ³As long as it takes to remember immortality, and your immortal creations who share it with you. ⁴As long as it takes to exchange hell for Heaven. ⁵Long enough to transcend <u>all</u> of the ego's making, and ascend unto your Father.

Notice the refrain: "How long is an instant?" This was the first sentence of paragraphs 11, 13, and 14. He really wants us to ask ourselves this question. So let's do that.

Application: Try to get in touch with any sense of being discouraged or dispirited by how long it will take you to change your mind so completely. Then ask yourself several times:

How long is an instant?

Realize that the Holy Spirit can do it all in just one instant, if you will give that one instant wholly to Him. Then say:

How long is an instant?
As long as it takes to re-establish perfect sanity, perfect peace
  and perfect love for everyone, for God and for myself.
How long is an instant?
As long as it takes for me to remember immortality, and my
  immortal creations who share it with me.
How long is an instant?
As long as it takes for me to exchange hell for Heaven.
How long is an instant?
*Long enough for me to transcend **all** of the ego's making, and*
  ascend unto my Father.

15. ¹Time is your friend, if you leave it to the Holy Spirit to use. ²He needs but very little to restore God's whole power to you. ³He Who transcends time <u>for</u> you understands what time is <u>for</u>. ⁴Holiness lies not in time, but in eternity. ⁵There never <u>was</u> an instant in which God's Son could lose his purity. ⁶His changeless state is <u>beyond</u> time, for

his purity remains forever beyond attack and without variability. ⁷Time stands still in his holiness, and changes not. ⁸And so it is no longer time at all. ⁹For caught in the single instant of the eternal sanctity of God's creation, it is <u>transformed</u> into forever. ¹⁰<u>Give</u> the eternal instant, that eternity may be remembered <u>for</u> you, in that shining instant of perfect release. ¹¹Offer the miracle of the holy instant <u>through</u> the Holy Spirit, and leave His giving it to you to Him.

We generally have the sense that time is not on our side. But it *is* on our side, if we let the Holy Spirit use it the way He wants. He only needs a little bit of time to restore to us all the power and purity we have thrown away. Why can our holiness be recovered so quickly? Because it is not a thing of time, not something that could be torn and trampled on our march through time. It stands outside of time, outside of change. Caught in its light, time stands still and changes not. "And so it is no longer time at all." It has become eternity.

The final lines capture the whole point of the section: "*Give* the eternal instant [to your brother], that eternity may be remembered *for* you, in that shining instant of perfect release [that you give]. Offer [to your brother] the miracle of the holy instant *through* the Holy Spirit, and leave His giving it to you to Him."

II. The End of Doubt
Commentary by Robert Perry

1. ¹The Atonement is *in* time, but not *for* time. ²Being in [Ur: Being for] you, it is eternal. ³What holds remembrance of God <u>cannot</u> be bound by time. ⁴No more are you. ⁵For unless <u>God</u> is bound, you <u>cannot</u> be. ⁶An instant offered to the Holy Spirit is offered to God on your behalf, and in that instant you will awaken gently in Him. ⁷In the blessed instant you will let go <u>all</u> your past learning, and the Holy Spirit will quickly offer you the <u>whole</u> lesson of peace. ⁸What can take time, when <u>all</u> the obstacles to learning it have been removed? ⁹Truth is so far beyond time that <u>all</u> of it happens at once. ¹⁰For as it was created one, so its oneness depends not on time at all.

The Atonement may operate in time, but it's not for the sake of time. It's for the sake of an eternal being: you. It brings you the memory of God, the memory of the Timeless. It therefore can't be bound by time and neither can you. You can only be bound if *God* is bound, and that, of course, is a ridiculous notion.

If you really offer the Holy Spirit just one instant (as we saw in the previous section), then the Holy Spirit will offer you the whole lesson of peace. It can be that instantaneous. Only your obstacles make the process take time. Beyond your obstacles is truth, which "happens all at once."

Application: Think of something in your life you feel bound by. Then say,

Can God be bound by this?
Then I cannot be bound by this.

2. ¹Do not be [Ur: Be not] concerned with time, and fear not the instant of holiness that will remove <u>all</u> fear. ²For the instant of peace is eternal *because* it is <u>without</u> fear. ³It <u>will</u> come, being the lesson God gives you, through the Teacher <u>He</u> has appointed to translate time into eternity. ⁴Blessed is God's Teacher, Whose joy it is to teach God's holy

110

Son his holiness. [5]His joy is not contained in time. [6]His teaching is for you <u>because</u> His joy is yours. [7]Through Him <u>you</u> stand before God's altar, where He gently translates [Ur: translated] hell into Heaven. [8]For it is only in Heaven that God would have you be.

We are so concerned with how long this journey will take, but we don't need to be. Time is in our hands, and when we fully hand it over to the Holy Spirit, it will be over. The big holy instant in which our learning is complete (which is what this section seems to be talking about) *will* come. In it, we will stand before God's altar, and the hell of our passage through time will be translated into the Heaven of eternity. There, all our fear will pass away in the revelation of our holiness. How can we fear an experience that is the *removal* of all fear?

3. [1]How long can it take to be where God would have you? [2]For you <u>are</u> where you have forever been and will forever be. [3]All that you have, you have forever. [4]The blessed instant reaches out to <u>encompass</u> time, as God extends Himself to encompass <u>you</u>. [5]You who have spent days, hours and even years in chaining your brothers <u>to</u> your ego in an attempt to support it and uphold its <u>weakness,</u> do not perceive the Source of strength. [6]In this holy instant you will unchain <u>all</u> your brothers, and refuse to support either <u>their</u> weakness <u>or your own</u>.

How long can it take for us to get to where we are now and have always been? We are in God right now, simply dreaming that we are on planet Earth. To go from here to eternity takes as long as to go from a dream to the bed we're sleeping in.

Are we willing to admit that we have been spending our time chaining our brothers to our ego, in an attempt to prop up its dilapidated house? Our egos are so insecure that they need constant shoring up from our brothers. Without their continual encouragement and reassurance, we tell ourselves, our insecurity and self-doubt would swallow us up.

Application: Think of various people in your life and, to each one, say,

In the holy instant, [name], I will unchain you from my ego.
I will release you from supporting its failing house.

4. ¹You do not realize how much you have <u>misused</u> your brothers by seeing them as sources of <u>ego</u> support. ²As a result, they witness <u>to</u> the ego in your perception, and <u>seem</u> to provide reasons for <u>not</u> letting it go. ³Yet they are far stronger and <u>much</u> more compelling witnesses for the Holy Spirit. ⁴And they support His <u>strength</u>. ⁵It is, therefore, your choice whether they support the ego or the Holy Spirit <u>in you</u>.

One of the things that make the spiritual path so difficult is other people. To modify an Al Pacino line from *The Godfather III*, just when I try to get out of the ego, they *pull* me back in! While I bravely attempt to leave the ego's compound, a hundred hands are grabbing at me, making my escape impossible.

Not so, says Jesus. The problem is not the egos of our brothers but our own *misuse* of our brothers. We are trying to use our brothers to shore up our ego. This turns them into witnesses for its reality. We could just as easily use them to support the Holy Spirit's strength in us. And they are actually much better suited to doing *that*!

Application: Think of someone in your life whose ego seems to be holding you back on your spiritual path. Now ask two questions of yourself:

How do I see this person's ego pulling me back into my ego?
How do I look to this person to boost my ego, shore up my ego, or stroke my ego?

Now realize that the latter, not the former, is what's really reinforcing your ego and holding you back.

⁶And you will recognize [Ur: know] which you have chosen by *their* reactions. ⁷A Son of God [your brother] who has been released through the Holy Spirit in a brother [Ur: *if the release is complete*] is <u>always</u> recognized. ⁸He cannot <u>be</u> denied. ⁹If <u>you</u> remain uncertain, it is <u>only</u> because you have not given <u>complete</u> release. ¹⁰And because of this, you have not given a single instant <u>completely</u> to the Holy Spirit. ¹¹For when you <u>have</u>, you will be <u>sure</u> you have. ¹²You will be sure because the witness [your brother] <u>to</u> Him will speak so clearly <u>of</u> Him that you

will hear and <u>understand</u>. [13]You <u>will</u> doubt until you hear <u>one</u> witness [your brother] whom you have <u>wholly</u> released through the Holy Spirit. [14]And then you will doubt no more.

It is in our hands whether a brother supports the ego's weakness in us or the Holy Spirit's strength in us. How do we know which we have chosen? By *his* reactions. If we release him from his past sins *completely*, he will turn into such a clear and undeniable witness to the Holy Spirit in us that all our doubts will vanish. We will enter our own holy instant, in which we are certain that we chose to support the Holy Spirit in us, and we are certain that the Holy Spirit *is* in us.

Here again we see the Course's method of salvation: We release our brother, and he then becomes an active witness—through his "reactions"—to the presence of holiness in us.

> 5. [1]The holy instant has not yet happened to you. [2]Yet it will, and you will recognize it with perfect certainty. [3]No gift of God is recognized in any other way. [4]You can practice the mechanics of the holy instant, and will learn much from doing so. [5]Yet its shining and glittering brilliance, which will literally blind you to this world by its <u>own</u> vision, you ca<u>nnot</u> supply. [6]And here it is, <u>all</u> in this instant, complete, accomplished and <u>given wholly</u>.

The holy instant spoken of here is, you could say, *the* holy instant, the big one, in which you reach the end of the road. Later, the Course will speak of the holy instant in less exalted and final terms, as any instant in which you momentarily step out of the ego. In fact, in 17.V it will say "You *have* received the holy instant"—referring to Helen and Bill's joining, which had already happened by this point in the dictation (where we are now), since it happened before *any* of the dictation.

I love this paragraph, because it captures so much of what the Course is about. Our job is to practice the mechanics of the holy instant, and keep practicing, all the while waiting for the Holy Spirit to give us the actual experience of the holy instant.

> 6. [1]Start <u>now</u> to practice your little part in <u>separating out</u> the holy instant. [2]You will receive very specific instructions as you go along [in the subsequent sections]. [3]To learn to separate out this single second,

and to experience it as timeless, is to begin to experience yourself as not separate. ⁴Fear not that you will not be given help in this. ⁵God's Teacher and His lesson will support your strength. ⁶It is only your weakness that will depart from you in this practice, for it is the practice of the power of God in you. ⁷Use it but for one instant, and you will never deny it again. ⁸Who can deny the Presence of what the universe bows to, in appreciation and gladness? ⁹Before the recognition of the universe that [Ur: the universe, which] witnesses to It, your doubts must disappear.

He wants us to start now to practice the holy instant. We do so by separating out this single second and imagining that it is all of time—the practice we were given in paragraph 9 of the last section. To separate out this second convinces us that we ourselves *aren't* separate. This is the Course's practice of the power of now. Indeed, this is the Course's practice of the Presence of God. (*The Practice of the Presence of God* is a seventeenth-century spiritual classic from a monk named Brother Lawrence.) For if we really enter the present and release the past, we will give this release to the universe (our brothers). Having been released by the divine in us, they will recognize God's Presence in us, bow to it, and witness to it. And only then will we be convinced that the Presence of God really is in us. Only then will all our doubts disappear.

III. Littleness versus Magnitude
Commentary by Robert Perry

1. ¹Be not content with littleness. ²But be sure you understand what littleness is, and why you could never <u>be</u> content with it. ³Littleness is the offering you give [Ur: gave] <u>yourself</u>. ⁴You offer [Ur: offered] this in place of magnitude, and you accept it [Ur: *and accepted it*]. ⁵Everything in this world is little because it is a world made out of littleness, in the strange belief that littleness <u>can</u> content you. ⁶When you strive for anything in this world in [Ur: *with*] <u>the belief that it will bring you peace</u>, you are belittling yourself and blinding yourself to glory. ⁷Littleness and glory are the choices open to your striving and your vigilance. ⁸You will <u>always</u> choose one <u>at the expense</u> of the other.

Who wants to be little? The opening line, "Be not content with littleness," would meet with approval from nearly anyone. What we could not all agree on, however, is what littleness means. We think that littleness means not amounting to much on the level of this world, not being an important person, lacking things like pride, control, status, influence. Those things are what we see as making us big. Yet this paragraph says that *everything* in this world is little, and so being a big person in this world is still being little. It is just littleness blown up into a false sense of greatness. The alternative to littleness is not trying to be a big fish in the little pond of this world. It is being aware of our inherent glory, of the magnitude God gave us. We are always choosing one of those at the expense of the other.

2. ¹Yet what you do not realize, each time you choose, is that your choice is your evaluation <u>of yourself</u>. ²Choose littleness and you will <u>not</u> have peace, for you will have judged yourself <u>unworthy</u> of it. ³And whatever you offer as a substitute is much too poor a gift to satisfy you. ⁴It is essential that you accept the fact, and accept it gladly, that there is <u>no</u> form of littleness that can <u>ever</u> content you. ⁵You are free to try as many as you wish, but all you will be doing is to delay your homecoming. ⁶For you will be content <u>only</u> in magnitude, which <u>is</u> your home.

115

Let's say I get a big-screen TV in the belief it will bring me peace. I don't realize it, but this choice is really an evaluation of myself. It says, "You are so small, so needy and lacking, that you think you need some hunk of wires and metal to make you whole." Then it adds, "You are so little that you don't even *deserve* peace." At that point, I have the TV, but I don't have peace. The TV has become my substitute for peace.

Application: Think of something in your life that you think is needed for your happiness.

My attachment to this is an evaluation of myself.

Then ask yourself, "What picture of myself and my value is implied in this attachment?" Then say,

It affirms that I am little, so little that I don't deserve peace.
Yet this thing cannot content me.
There is no form of littleness that can ever content me.
I will be content only in magnitude, which is my home.

3. ¹There is a deep responsibility you owe yourself, and one you must learn to remember all the time. ²The lesson may seem hard at first, but you will learn to love it when you realize that it is true and is but [Ur: and constitutes] a tribute to your power. ³You who have sought and found littleness, remember this: Every decision you make stems from what you think you are, and represents the value that you put upon yourself. ⁴Believe the little can content you, and by limiting yourself you will not be satisfied. ⁵For your function is not little, and it is only by finding your function and fulfilling it that you can escape from littleness.

Application: Think about decisions you have made in the last few minutes, decisions to perform seemingly trivial behaviors, decisions to think certain thoughts. Try to find three or four decisions, and with each one say to yourself,

III. Littleness versus Magnitude

This decision stemmed from what I think I am,
and represented the value that I put upon myself.

Then realize this is true of *every* decision you make. Tell yourself that remembering this with every decision is a deep responsibility you owe yourself. Tell yourself that, however hard this seems right now, you will learn to love it when you realize it is true and is actually a tribute to your power.

If we believe that the little things of this world can content us, we define ourselves as little. The solution is to assume our function (of extending to others), which is not little and which teaches us that *we* are not little.

4. ¹There is no doubt about what your function is, for the Holy Spirit <u>knows</u> what it is. ²There is no doubt about its magnitude, for it reaches you through Him *from* Magnitude. ³You do not have to strive for it [your function], because you <u>have</u> it. ⁴All your striving must be directed <u>against littleness,</u> for it <u>does</u> require vigilance to protect your magnitude in this world. ⁵To hold your magnitude in perfect awareness in a world of littleness is a task the little cannot undertake. ⁶Yet it is asked of you, in tribute to your magnitude and <u>not</u> your littleness. ⁷Nor is it asked of you alone. ⁸The power of God will support every effort you make on behalf of His dear Son. ⁹Search for the little, and you <u>deny</u> yourself His power. ¹⁰God is not willing that His Son be content with less than everything. ¹¹For He is not content without His Son, and His Son cannot be content with less than His Father has given him.

Our function of healing our brothers is a real thing (in this-world terms). The Holy Spirit has designed a special form of this function for each one of us. My experience is that before people find out what their function is, they think in terms of striving for it. But then after they find out what it is, they often find it threatening, as if it is too big for them.

Jesus seems to be speaking to this very state of affairs. In the previous paragraph, he said that your function will teach you your magnitude. Now he says that, rather than striving for it, you should direct all your striving against your belief in littleness, and you will find that your function is yours.

Then he asks you to learn to hold your magnitude in perfect awareness, even in a world that surrounds you with littleness. This may seem impossible, and it is impossible for the little. But you can do this, because you are not little, and because the power of God will support you.

Application: Do you find the thought of discovering your magnitude to be vaguely threatening? If so, repeat these words,

> *I will never be content with less than everything.*
> *Yet God has already given me everything.*
> *And He is not willing that I, His dear Son, be content without it.*
> *For He is not content without me.*

5.   ¹I asked you earlier [Ur: We asked you once before], "Would you be hostage to the ego or host to God?" ²Let this question be asked you by the Holy Spirit <u>every</u> time you make a decision. ³For every decision you make <u>does</u> answer this, and invites sorrow or joy accordingly. ⁴When God <u>gave</u> Himself to you in your creation, He <u>established</u> you as host to Him forever. ⁵He has <u>not</u> left you, and <u>you</u> have not left <u>Him</u>. ⁶All your attempts to deny His magnitude, and make His Son hostage to the ego, <u>cannot</u> make little whom God has joined with Him. ⁷Every decision you make is for Heaven or for hell, and brings you the <u>awareness</u> of what you decided <u>for</u>.

The question, "Would I affirm my littleness or accept my magnitude?" is really the same question we were asked before: "Would I be hostage to the ego or host to God?" It doesn't take a genius to see that being hostage to the ego means extreme littleness, while being host to God means a state of honor and grandeur.

And both of those are really the question, "Would I withdraw into my own fantasies or accept the eternal truth?" For we cannot make ourselves little. God gave Himself to us in our creation. Such a gift cannot be returned. We will therefore forever be His host. And as His host, we can never be truly hostage to the ego.

Application: Think of a recent decision you made that was fairly substantial. Then say,

III. Littleness versus Magnitude

This decision answers this question: Would I be hostage to the ego or host to God?

And then ask yourself,

What answer does this decision give to that question?

6.   ¹The Holy Spirit can hold your magnitude, clean of <u>all</u> littleness, clearly and in perfect safety in your mind, untouched by every little gift the world of littleness would offer you. ²But for this, you cannot side <u>against</u> Him in what He wills for you. ³Decide for God through Him. ⁴For littleness, and the belief that you can be <u>content</u> with littleness, are decisions <u>you</u> make [Ur: have made] about yourself. ⁵The power and the glory that lie in you from God are for all who, like you, perceive themselves as little, and believe [Ur: have deceived themselves into believing] that littleness can be blown up [Ur: *by them*] into a sense of magnitude that can content them. ⁶Neither <u>give</u> littleness, nor <u>accept</u> it. ⁷All honor is due the host of God. ⁸Your littleness deceives you, but your magnitude is of Him Who dwells in you, and in Whom you dwell. ⁹Touch no one, then, with littleness in the Name of Christ, eternal Host unto His Father.

In paragraph 4, Jesus asked us to hold our magnitude in perfect awareness in this world of littleness. If this struck you as impossible, you were not alone. Here we are told how it is possible: The Holy Spirit will hold it in our minds for us, perfectly clear and clean of all littleness. Given that, it suddenly seems doable. There is, however, one catch: We have to consistently side against the belief that we are little and that littleness can content us. The decisions that contain that belief push the Holy Spirit out of our mind.

It is crucial that we realize that we are doing no one a favor with our littleness. We think being small is an act of kindness to others, so that we make them feel secure. Yet the power and glory God gave us is not for us alone. If we accept that power and glory, we can give it to our brothers. They are lost in their love affair with littleness, in their vain fantasy that littleness can be inflated into real magnitude. We can free them of this *if* we accept our magnitude. If we accept littleness, we give them littleness. We reinforce their sickness. But if we accept magnitude, we can set them free. Let us accept it, then, for *their* sake, as well as our own.

> 7. ¹In this season (Christmas) which celebrates the birth of holiness into this world, join with me who decided for holiness for <u>you</u>. ²It is our task <u>together</u> to restore the awareness of magnitude to the host whom God appointed for Himself. ³It is beyond <u>all</u> your littleness to give the gift of God, but <u>not</u> beyond <u>you</u>. ⁴For God would give Himself *through* you. ⁵He reaches from you to everyone and beyond everyone to His Son's creations, but <u>without</u> leaving you. ⁶Far beyond your little world but still in you, He extends forever. ⁷Yet He brings all His extensions to you, as host to Him.

The first sentence contains a whole picture of what Christmas was about. Jesus was born into this world to decide for holiness for himself *and* for everyone else, so that holiness itself could be born into this world. He, in other words, came to make us all aware of our magnitude, by being aware of it himself. It is our task now to join with him in his mission. Together, we can restore the awareness of magnitude to the entire Sonship. This is not just Jesus' mission; it is God's, too. God does not want to be the Guest of a sleeping host. He wants to awaken His host, and to do so through *us*. He wants to reach out to everyone through us, to extend to infinity, yet without leaving us, bringing all His extensions to us, since, after all, we are His host.

> 8. ¹Is it a sacrifice to leave littleness behind, and wander not in vain? ²It is not sacrifice to wake to glory. ³But it <u>is</u> sacrifice to accept anything <u>less</u> than glory. ⁴Learn that you <u>must</u> be worthy of the Prince of Peace, born in you in honor of Him Whose host you are. ⁵You know not what love means because you have sought to purchase it with little gifts, thus <u>valuing</u> it too little to understand its magnitude. ⁶<u>Love is not little</u> and love dwells in you, for you are host to Him. ⁷Before the greatness that lives in you, your poor appreciation of yourself and all the little offerings you give slip into nothingness.

We feel like it is a sacrifice to stop seeking after the rewards of the world. We act like it is a sacrifice to awaken to a whole different self than we thought we were. Yet we have it completely backwards. "It is not sacrifice to wake to glory." Rather, "it is sacrifice to accept anything less than glory."

The fact is that we are not on the side of our happiness, nor on the side of our worth. All of our bold assertions that we *deserve* the gifts of the world add up to affirmations that we are little and unworthy. All of our attempts to purchase love from our brothers with the world's little gifts add up to affirmations that love is little and that we are lacking it.

We don't need to make ourselves worthy; we need to acknowledge that we are already worthy. Jesus is already born in us. Love in all its magnitude already dwells in us. And God is already the eternal Guest of our being.

> 9.   ¹Holy child of God, when will you learn that <u>only</u> holiness can content you and give you peace? ²Remember that you learn not for yourself alone, no more than I did. ³It is <u>because</u> I learned for <u>you</u> that you can learn of <u>me</u>. ⁴I would but teach you what is yours, so that together we can replace the shabby littleness that binds the host of God to guilt and weakness with the glad awareness of the glory that is in him. ⁵My birth in you is your awakening to grandeur. ⁶Welcome me not into a manger, but into the altar to holiness, where holiness abides in perfect peace. ⁷My Kingdom is not of this world because it is in <u>you</u>. ⁸And <u>you</u> are of your Father. ⁹Let us join in honoring you, who <u>must</u> remain forever <u>beyond</u> littleness.

If we were to make a list of the things that, if we had them, would content us, where would holiness be on that list? Would it even *be* on the list? Yet here we are told that *only* holiness can content us. That is because in our holiness we are pure, we are clean, we are glorious, and we are powerful. We possess the magnitude of God. Just as Jesus came to learn this lesson for us, so we are here to learn it for others, so that we can join Jesus in his Great Crusade.

Application: Speak these words to Jesus, as sincerely as you can:

> *Jesus, I must be worthy of you being born in me.*
> *You are born in me in honor of my divine Guest—my Father.*
> *Your birth in me is my awakening to grandeur.*
> *I will welcome you not into a manger; I will not confine your*
>   *welcome to my external Christmas celebrations.*
> *I welcome you into the altar to holiness within me.*

121

I welcome you into the altar to holiness within me.
Your Kingdom is not of this world, because it is in me.
And I am of my Father.
I will join you in honoring me,
I who must remain forever beyond littleness.
Your birth in me is my awakening to grandeur.
Be born in me today.

10. ¹Decide with me, who has decided to abide with you. ²I will as my Father wills, knowing His Will is constant and at peace forever with itself. ³You will be content with nothing <u>but</u> His Will. ⁴Accept no less, remembering that everything I learned is yours. ⁵What my Father loves I love as He does, and I can no more accept it as what it is <u>not</u>, than He can. ⁶And no more can <u>you</u>. ⁷When you have learned to accept what you are, you will make no more gifts to offer to yourself, for you will know you are <u>complete</u>, in need of nothing, and unable to accept <u>anything</u> for yourself. ⁸But you will gladly give, <u>having</u> received. ⁹The host of God needs not seek to find <u>anything</u>.

Why shouldn't we decide with Jesus? After all, he has decided to abide with us. He loves us exactly as God loves us. Furthermore, everything he learned is ours. What a thought! You might want to repeat to yourself, *"Everything Jesus learned is mine. All I need do is decide with him."* He holds out to us the infinite magnitude that God gave us in the beginning. Our job is to put all our strength into *refusing* to settle for anything less.

When we finally do this and accept who we are, we won't give any more gifts to ourselves. Why? Because we will realize that God has already given us everything. At that point, having received so much, the only logical thing will be to give.

Application: See yourself filled with the Love of God, feeling so complete that you are in need of nothing. Then see yourself encountering someone you know. Say silently to this person,

My needs are taken care of.
*How can I help **you** along the way?*

11. ¹If you are wholly willing to leave salvation to the plan of God and <u>un</u>willing to attempt to grasp for peace <u>yourself</u>, salvation will be <u>given</u> you. ²Yet think not you can substitute <u>your</u> plan for His. ³Rather, join with me in <u>His</u>, that we may release all those who would be bound, proclaiming together that the Son of God is host to Him. ⁴Thus will we let no one forget what <u>you</u> would remember. ⁵And thus <u>will</u> you remember it.

What a fascinating thought: If I don't try to make myself happy, if I don't try to acquire peace for myself, if I just work on clearing my mind of the belief in littleness, God will simply *give* me happiness, peace, and glory. And then I can stand shoulder to shoulder with Jesus, working with him to release everyone from the bonds of littleness. And finally, through this work, I will really get it. I will fully and completely remember to Whom I am host.

12. ¹Call forth in everyone <u>only</u> the remembrance of God, and of the Heaven that is in him. ²For where you would have your brother be, there will you think <u>you</u> are. ³Hear not his appeal to [Ur: call for] hell and littleness, but only his call for Heaven and greatness. ⁴Forget not that his call is yours, and answer him with me. ⁵God's power is forever on the side of His host, for it protects <u>only</u> the peace in which He dwells. ⁶Lay not littleness before His holy altar, which rises above the stars and reaches even to Heaven, because of what is given it.

Application: Think of someone who is really irritating you these days. Notice how you see this person being petty and just "asking for it." Then tell this person silently:

[Name], I will not hear your call for hell and littleness.
I will hear only your call for Heaven and greatness.
For whatever call I acknowledge in you, I acknowledge in me.
Therefore, I join with Jesus in answering your true call.
Like him, I call forth in you only the remembrance of the Heaven
*   that is in you.*
*For where I would have **you** be, there will I think **I** am.*

IV. Practicing the Holy Instant
Commentary by Robert Perry

Two sections ago, we were encouraged to "practice the mechanics of the holy instant" (T-15.II.5:4). Here we are given a number of practical ways to do exactly that, all of which aim to give us the one thing we need to make the holy instant ours: *willingness* to receive it.

> 1.   ¹This course is not beyond <u>immediate</u> learning, unless you [Ur: prefer to] believe that <u>what God wills takes time</u>. ²And this means <u>only</u> that you would rather <u>delay</u> the recognition that His Will <u>is</u> so. ³The holy instant is <u>this</u> instant and <u>every</u> instant [Ur: *this* one and *every* one]. ⁴The one you <u>want</u> it to be it <u>is</u>. ⁵The one you would <u>not</u> have it be is lost to you. ⁶<u>You</u> must decide <u>when</u> it is. ⁷Delay it not. ⁸For beyond the past and future, where you will <u>not</u> find it, it stands in shimmering readiness for your acceptance. ⁹Yet you cannot bring it into glad awareness while you do not want it, for it holds the whole <u>release</u> from littleness.

We think the Course must take a very long time to learn, that "the results of the Holy Spirit's teaching are far in the future" (T-15.I.2:1). Surely, we say, it will take a lot of time to purify ourselves, to sufficiently evolve, to burn off our karma, to fully forgive Hitler (or slow drivers).

But in fact, this Course could be learned *immediately*. Why? First, because it is God's Will that we learn it, and God's Will takes no time at all. Second, because the only thing standing in the way of learning it immediately is our decision to put God's Will off, and we can change that decision at any time. The holy instant is here *right now*, standing "in shimmering readiness for your acceptance."

The spiritual path is thus not a journey toward a goal that will become available only in the distant future, but a journey toward full willingness to accept what is already so. This may indeed take a long time, but only because our *un*willingness is so strong (see T-15.I.11:4). Why not accept the holy instant now and save ourselves all this trouble?

> ¹Your practice <u>must</u> therefore rest upon your willingness to let all littleness go. ²The instant in which magnitude dawns upon you is but as

far away as your <u>desire</u> for it. [3]As long as you desire it not and cherish littleness instead, by so much is it far from you. [4]By so much as you want it will you bring it nearer. [5]Think not that you can find salvation in your own way and <u>have</u> it. [6]Give over <u>every</u> plan you have made for your salvation in exchange for God's. [7]<u>His</u> will content you, and [Ur: for there *is*] nothing else [Ur: that] can bring you peace. [8]For peace is of God, and no one beside Him.

All that blocks the holy instant, as the last section said, is our desire for littleness—our insistence that the littleness of our ego-identification can satisfy us more than the magnitude of who we really are. The second we let go of our littleness and all the futile plans for happiness that come with it, the holy instant will be ours.

Application: Here is an important aspect of our holy instant practice: our "willingness to let all littleness go." Let's affirm our willingness to do this and embrace our magnitude:

I will no longer cherish littleness instead of magnitude.
I am willing to let all littleness go.
*I give over **every** plan I have made for my salvation in exchange for God's.*
*Only His plan will content me, for there **is** nothing else that can bring me peace.*
I choose the holy instant.
I choose to let my magnitude dawn upon me.

3. [1]Be humble before Him, and yet great *in* Him. [2]And value <u>no</u> plan of the ego <u>before</u> the plan of God. [3]For you leave empty your place in His plan, which you <u>must</u> fill if you would join with me, by your decision to join in any plan <u>but</u> His. [4]I call you to fulfill your holy part in the plan that He has given to the world for its release from littleness. [5]God would have His host abide in perfect freedom. [6]Every allegiance to a plan of salvation [Ur: that is] <u>apart</u> from Him diminishes the value of His Will for you in your own mind [Ur: minds]. [7]And yet it is your mind that <u>is</u> the host to Him.

I love the first sentence, because it captures so well the attitude the

Course would have us hold toward God. On the one hand, we should be "humble before Him." He is our Creator, and "Awe is proper in the Presence of your Creator" (T-1.VII.5:3). Yet this is not a groveling sort of awe that makes us pitiful worms in comparison to Him. On the contrary, we should be (and are) "great *in* Him," because we are part of Him.

Cherishing the ego's plans for salvation violates both parts of this injunction. We are being arrogant before Him because we are rejecting His Will, devaluing His Will in our own minds. We are also refusing to be great *in* Him, because we are deciding to be apart from Him and therefore deciding for littleness.

The only way to be free of this is to give up every plan for salvation but His—to answer Jesus' call and fulfill our holy part in God's plan to free *everyone* from littleness. Doing this is both a humble acknowledgement of His Will and an affirmation of our greatness as part of His Will.

> 4. ¹Would you learn how perfect and immaculate is the holy altar on which your Father has placed <u>Himself</u> [your mind]? ²This you <u>will</u> recognize in the holy instant, in which you willingly and gladly give over <u>every</u> plan but His. ³For there lies peace, <u>perfectly</u> clear because you have been willing to meet its conditions. ⁴You can claim the holy instant <u>any</u> time and <u>anywhere</u> you want it. ⁵In your practice, try to give over <u>every</u> plan you have accepted for finding magnitude in littleness. ⁶*It is not there.* ⁷<u>Use</u> the holy instant <u>only</u> to recognize that you alone <u>cannot</u> know where it [magnitude] is, and can only <u>deceive</u> yourself.

Jesus is really hammering the message home, isn't he? Do we want to know how holy our minds are? Then we need to be humble enough to set aside our own plans for salvation, which are desperate attempts to make our littleness look magnificent, and enter the holy instant, in which we will recognize our true magnitude. By ourselves we can never discover this—we will inevitably continue to seek magnitude in mansions, Hummers, washboard abs, or "collect[ing] bodies to worship at [our] shrine" (P-3.II.9:8). But in the holy instant, we will find the true magnitude that has always been ours and is available to us *right now*.

> 5. ¹I stand within the holy instant, as clear as you would have me. ²And the extent to which you learn to [Ur: be willing to] <u>accept</u> me <u>is</u> the measure of the time in which the holy instant will be yours. ³I

call to you to make the holy instant yours <u>at once</u>, for the release from littleness in the mind of the host of God depends on willingness, and <u>not</u> on time.

Jesus has already accepted the holy instant himself and yearns to share it with us. Therefore, one important measure of our willingness for the holy instant is our willingness to join with Jesus. The more we truly accept him as our elder brother and teacher, the quicker the holy instant in which he stands will come to us.

Application: Another important aspect of our holy instant practice is bolstering our willingness to join with Jesus. To do this, reread the paragraph as a personal message to you from Jesus, inserting your name at appropriate points.

6.   ¹The reason this course is simple is that <u>truth</u> is simple. ²Complexity is of the ego, and is nothing more than the ego's attempt to obscure the obvious. ³You could live forever in the holy instant, <u>beginning now</u> and reaching to eternity, but for a very simple reason. ⁴Do not obscure the simplicity of this reason, for if you do, it will be <u>only</u> because you prefer <u>not</u> to recognize it and <u>not</u> to let it go. ⁵The simple reason, simply stated, is this [Ur: stated simply as what it is]: The holy instant is a time in which you receive <u>and give</u> perfect communication. ⁶This means, however, that it is a time in which your mind is <u>open</u>, both to receive <u>and</u> give. ⁷It is the recognition that all minds <u>are</u> in communication. ⁸It therefore seeks to <u>change</u> nothing, but merely to <u>accept</u> everything.

We can concoct all sorts of elaborate theories to explain why we don't experience the holy instant all the time. But the real reason we don't is both very simple and has probably never occurred to us: In the holy instant there is *perfect communication* between minds. The next paragraph will explain why this is a problem for us.

7.   ¹How can you do this when you would prefer to have <u>private</u> thoughts <u>and keep them</u>? ²The <u>only</u> way you <u>could</u> do that would be to <u>deny</u> the perfect communication that makes the holy instant <u>what it is</u>. ³You <u>believe</u> you can [Ur: You believe that it is possible to] harbor thoughts you would <u>not</u> share, and that salvation lies in keeping

thoughts <u>to yourself alone</u>. ⁴For in private thoughts, <u>known only to yourself</u>, you think you find a way to keep what you would <u>have</u> alone, and share what *you* would share. ⁵And then you wonder why it is that you are not in full communication with those around you, and with God Who surrounds <u>all</u> of you together.

Here's the problem: We don't *want* perfect communication. We would much rather keep certain things to ourselves, thank you very much. In the holy instant we share absolutely everything in our minds, receiving and giving without limit. But we would rather have private thoughts and share only what *we* want to share. This is why we don't experience the holy instant all the time: our preference for private thoughts causes us to push it away.

Think about it: Doesn't the idea of completely open minds sound scary? A lot of people are nervous these days about the US government wiretapping their phones; how do you feel about the prospect of every single mind in the universe tapping your mind? Having private thoughts feels like a sacred right to us—indeed, we think that "salvation lies in keeping thoughts to yourself alone." But it doesn't take a rocket scientist to figure out that harboring private thoughts interferes with perfect communication. If you've ever wondered why human beings have so much trouble communicating with each other and God seems so inaccessible, look no further. This is the reason: our *unwillingness* to communicate.

> 8. ¹Every thought you would keep hidden shuts communication off, <u>because you would have it so</u>. ²It is impossible to <u>recognize</u> perfect communication while <u>breaking</u> communication holds value to you. ³Ask yourself honestly, "Would I <u>want</u> to have perfect communication, and am I <u>wholly</u> willing to let <u>everything</u> that <u>interferes with it</u> go forever?" ⁴If the answer is no, then the Holy Spirit's readiness to <u>give</u> it to you is not enough to make it yours, for you are <u>not</u> ready to share it <u>with</u> Him. ⁵And it cannot come into a mind that has decided to <u>oppose</u> it. ⁶For the holy instant is given and received with <u>equal</u> willingness, being the acceptance of the <u>single</u> Will that governs <u>all</u> thought.

Here, then, is another aspect of practicing the holy instant: becoming willing to give up our desire to hold onto private thoughts and break communication. As long as we keep thoughts hidden, the Holy Spirit cannot give us the holy instant because we're not truly willing to receive it. In order to receive it, we must be just as willing to receive it as He is to give it.

Application: To apply this teaching, we are given a question to ask ourselves. Ask yourself this question now, answering it as honestly as you can (even if the honest answer is no):

"Would I want to have perfect communication, and am I wholly willing to let everything that interferes with it go forever?"

Whatever your answer, whether it be no or a less than fully committed yes (I think virtually all of us will fall into this range), bolster your willingness by saying the following:

The holy instant is given and received with equal willingness.
I must be as willing to receive it as the Holy Spirit is to give it.
Holy Spirit, help me to become wholly willing
   to have perfect communication
   and to let everything that interferes with it go forever.
This is God's Will, which I share,
   the single Will that governs all thought, including mine.

9.   ¹The necessary condition for the holy instant does <u>not</u> require that you have no thoughts that are not pure. ²But it <u>does</u> require that you have none that you would <u>keep</u>. ³Innocence is not of your making. ⁴It is <u>given</u> you the instant you would <u>have</u> it. ⁵Atonement would not <u>be</u> if there were no <u>need</u> for it. [Ur: But it would not *be* Atonement, if there were no *need* for Atonement.] ⁶You will not be able to <u>accept</u> perfect communication as long as you would <u>hide</u> it from yourself. ⁷For what you would hide *is* hidden from you. ⁸In your practice, then, try only to be vigilant <u>against deception,</u> and seek not to <u>protect</u> the thoughts you would keep to yourself. ⁹Let the Holy Spirit's purity shine them away, and bring all your awareness to the <u>readiness</u> [Ur: *readiness*]for purity He offers you. ¹⁰Thus will He make you ready to acknowledge that you <u>are</u> host to God, and hostage to no one and to nothing.

A question may arise in our minds as we read this material: Does giving up all private thoughts and embracing perfect communication mean that we must verbally share whatever enters our minds with everyone? Must we now air all of our dirty laundry? Is Jesus telling us to "let it all hang out"?

In a word, no. In this paragraph, it becomes clear that the "private thoughts" Jesus is talking about here are ego thoughts, "thoughts that are not pure," thoughts that produce guilt. Jesus is using the word "communication" in the strict Course sense: the direct joining of minds in the sharing of God's Love. Our private thoughts here are unloving thoughts that by their very nature cannot be truly shared and actually *break* communication (see T-6.V(A).5:6-10).

The way to restore perfect communication, then, is not to share our "dirty laundry" thoughts with everyone, but to give them over to the Holy Spirit to be washed out. This is the condition for receiving the holy instant. (Thank God we don't have to be fully free of impure thoughts!) If we stop trying to protect our private thoughts from His purity and allow Him to shine them away, we will come to recognize our own purity—we will accept the Atonement. Restored to the perfect communication that is given and received in the holy instant, we will recognize that we are host to God.

Application: Here is one more aspect of our holy instant practice. We must be willing to turn over our impure, private thoughts to the Holy Spirit so He can shine them away. Part of this willingness is being vigilant against deception, vigilant against our tendency to hide those thoughts from Him. So, look within your mind right now for "private thoughts": impure thoughts, thoughts you would rather keep to yourself, ego thoughts that break communication with your brothers. As you hold each one in your mind, say the following:

> *This is not a thought that is pure.*
> *Therefore, it is not a thought that I would keep.*
> *I will not protect this thought by keeping it to myself.*
> *Holy Spirit, I am ready for the purity You offer me.*
> *I let your purity shine this thought away,*
>   *so I can recognize that I am host to God*
>   *and hostage to no one and nothing.*

V. The Holy Instant and Special Relationships
Commentary by Robert Perry

1. ¹The holy instant is the Holy Spirit's most useful learning device for teaching you love's meaning. ²For its purpose is to suspend judgment entirely. ³Judgment always rests on the past, for past experience is the basis on which you judge. ⁴Judgment becomes impossible without the past, for without it you do not understand anything. ⁵You would make no attempt to judge, because it would be quite apparent to you that you do not understand [Ur: know] what anything means. ⁶You are afraid of this because you believe that without the ego, all would be chaos. ⁷Yet I assure you that without the ego, all would be love.

We don't know the meaning of love because we judge, and judgment is the antithesis of love. We look at everything from the perspective of our past experience and on this basis decide what everything means and what it is for. Through our past learning we order our lives.

The holy instant changes everything, because it lifts us out of the past and thus removes the basis on which we judge. We realize how utterly clueless we are about what things mean, which is exactly what the Holy Spirit wants us to see: "The essential thing is learning that *you do not know*" (T-14.XI.1:1). To the ego, this is terrifying. It whispers in our ears, "What will become of you if the entire basis I gave you for ordering your life is pulled out from under you? This crazy course you're taking is a recipe for *utter chaos*!" But if we really let in the holy instant, we are in for a pleasant surprise: life without judgment is not chaos but *love*.

2. ¹The past is the ego's chief learning device, for it is in the past that you learned to define your own needs and acquired methods for meeting them on your own terms. ²We have said that to limit love to part of the Sonship is to bring guilt into your relationships, and thus make them unreal. ³If you seek to separate out certain aspects of the totality [particular people] and look to them to meet your imagined needs, you are attempting to use separation to save you. ⁴How, then, could guilt

131

<u>not</u> enter? ⁵For separation <u>is</u> the source of guilt, and to <u>appeal</u> to it for salvation <u>is to believe you are alone</u>. ⁶To be alone *is* to be guilty. ⁷For to experience yourself *as* alone is to deny the Oneness of the Father and His Son, and thus to <u>attack reality</u>.

In the past, we determined our own needs and devised methods for meeting them. And of course, one primary method we use is to enter into "love" relationships with particular people who, in our eyes, are especially good at meeting our needs. This is such a basic part of daily life that most of us never even question it. It seems perfectly natural to turn to our "loved ones" to get our needs met—especially our need for love, which seems to be in such short supply.

As natural as this sounds, though, it carries a heavy price: guilt. When we turn to particular people to meet our imagined needs, we are separating out aspects of totality and limiting our love to those aspects. Limiting love in this way is separation, an attack on the oneness of reality, so how could we *not* feel guilty? This leads to a disturbing conclusion: *all* of our relationships are permeated with this guilt, so they are not real relationships at all.

> 3.   ¹You cannot love <u>parts</u> of reality and understand what love <u>means</u>. ²If you would love <u>un</u>like to God, Who <u>knows</u> no special love, how <u>can</u> you understand it? ³To believe that *special* relationships, with *special* love, can offer you salvation <u>is</u> the belief that separation is salvation. ⁴For it is the <u>complete equality</u> of the Atonement in which salvation lies. ⁵How can <u>you</u> decide that special aspects of the Sonship can <u>give you more than others</u>? ⁶The past <u>has</u> taught you this. ⁷Yet the holy instant teaches you <u>it is not so</u>.

The relationships we're discussing are, of course, special relationships. In the past, we decided that "*special* relationships, with *special* love" could meet our needs, but they really can't. Our real needs can be met only through union, and special relationships are based on separation. Our real needs can be met only through the equality of the Atonement, and special relationships are based on inequality—the belief that some people can give us more than others. Our real needs can be met only through love, and special relationships are based on ignorance of love's meaning, because they are attempts to love unlike God. Only the holy instant can teach us this, because it undoes the past upon which special relationships are based.

> 4. ¹Because of guilt, <u>all</u> special relationships have [Ur: some] elements of fear in them. ²This is why they shift and change so frequently. ³They are <u>not</u> based on changeless love alone. ⁴And love, where fear has entered, <u>cannot</u> be depended on because it is <u>not</u> perfect. ⁵In His function as Interpreter of what you made, the Holy Spirit <u>uses</u> special relationships, which you have chosen to support the ego, as learning experiences that point to truth. ⁶Under His teaching, <u>every</u> relationship becomes a lesson in love.

Our special relationships are such unstable things. Why? The underlying reason is *guilt*—the guilt that stems from using our partners to meet our imagined needs. This guilt over our lack of love brings fear into our relationships. We're always looking over our shoulder, waiting for the other shoe to drop, anticipating the tongue lashing we're sure is coming, dreading the day when our partner will wise up, pack her bags, and leave for good. Because of this fear, whatever real love may be in our relationships seems undependable. Fasten your seatbelts—it's going to be a bumpy ride.

Fortunately, the Holy Spirit has reinterpreted these crazy relationships for us. We didn't base them on changeless love alone; on the contrary, we formed them to support our egos (see T-15.II.3-4). But as He uses them, they become true lessons in changeless love.

> 5. ¹The Holy Spirit knows <u>no one is special</u>. ²Yet He also perceives that you have <u>made</u> special relationships, which He would purify and <u>not</u> let <u>you</u> destroy. ³However <u>unholy</u> the reason you made them may be, He can <u>translate</u> them into holiness by removing <u>as much fear as you will let Him</u>. ⁴You can place <u>any</u> relationship under His care and be sure that it will <u>not</u> result in pain, if you offer Him your willingness <u>to have it serve no need but His</u>. ⁵All the guilt in it arises from <u>your</u> use of it. ⁶All the love from His. ⁷Do not, then, be <u>afraid</u> to let go your <u>imagined</u> needs, which would <u>destroy</u> the relationship. ⁸Your <u>only</u> need <u>is</u> His.

After reading Jesus' withering indictment of special relationships, we may wonder if he wants us to become hermits in the desert. Fortunately, the Holy Spirit can turn all our relationship lemons into lemonade. Our job in this transformation is to place our relationships under His care, to let go of our imagined needs and let our relationships serve His need instead. Our unholy use of them brings guilt, fear, and pain; His holy use of them brings true love**Application:** Bring to mind a special relationship in your life and place it under the Holy Spirit's care with the following words:

> *All the guilt in this relationship comes from my using it to meet*
> *my imagined needs.*
> *All the love in it comes from Your use of it to meet Your need.*
> *Therefore, I am willing to let it serve no need but Yours.*
> *I place this relationship under Your care,*
> *trusting that You will remove all guilt, fear, and pain from it,*
> *and translate it from specialness into holiness, a lesson in love.*

6.   ¹Any relationship you would <u>substitute for another</u> has not been offered to the Holy Spirit for His use. ²There *is* no substitute for love. ³If you would attempt to substitute <u>one</u> aspect of love [one person] for <u>another</u>, you have placed <u>less</u> value on one and <u>more</u> on the other. ⁴You have not only <u>separated</u> them, but you have also <u>judged against both</u>. ⁵Yet you had judged against yourself <u>first</u>, or you would never have imagined that you needed your brothers <u>as they were not</u>. ⁶Unless you had seen yourself as <u>without</u> love, you <u>could</u> not have judged them so <u>like</u> you in lack.

A whole process is sketched out here. First, we see ourselves as lacking, without love. This is a judgment on ourselves. It reduces us from holy Sons of God to limited creatures full of imagined needs. Lacking love, we now must find a substitute for love. The substitute for love is the special relationship.

When we choose a particular special relationship partner, we carry the process of substitution one step further: we substitute one person for another. We say, "This person meets my needs better than that one, and is therefore more valuable." The most obvious example of this is when we leave one romantic partner for another, but this dynamic of substitution permeates all of our special relationships. This is a judgment on other people that mirrors our judgment on ourselves. It reduces our brothers from holy Sons of God to limited creatures who in our eyes exist only to meet our imagined needs.

> 7.   [1]The ego's use of relationships is so fragmented that it frequently goes even farther [Ur: further]; one <u>part</u> of one aspect suits its purposes, while it prefers <u>different</u> parts of another aspect. [2]Thus does it <u>assemble</u> reality to its own capricious liking, offering for <u>your</u> seeking a picture whose likeness <u>does not exist</u>. [3]For there is nothing in Heaven <u>or</u> earth that it resembles, and so, however much you seek for its reality, you <u>cannot</u> find it because it is <u>not</u> real.

Now we carry the process of substitution yet one step further: we substitute *parts* of one person for *parts* of another. In other words, we say, "These parts of one person meet some needs of mine better, but those parts of another person meet other needs of mine better." My wife's lips serve one need, my furniture mover's strong back another need, my massage therapist's hands yet another. When we look at people this way, we're seeing them as little more than particular body parts. Not only are we not aware of their heavenly reality, but even from a strictly earthly perspective we are not seeing them as whole persons. Our ego has simply constructed a fantasy picture of them based on how well certain parts fulfill its needs.

Application: Bring to mind a particular special relationship partner and ask yourself the following questions:

> *What needs of mine led me to choose [name] over others? What needs does (s)he meet?*

> *What particular parts of [name] meet my needs?*

The answers to these questions have made an entire picture of this person in your mind, a fantasy picture based only on your imagined needs. Now, offer your willingness to give up this fantasy picture with the following words:

> *My picture of [name] is a picture whose likeness does not exist.*

There is nothing in Heaven or earth that it resembles, and so,
   however much I seek for its reality,
I cannot find it because it is not real.
Holy Spirit, I offer you my willingness to let it go.

8.   ¹Everyone on earth has formed special relationships, and although this is not so in Heaven, the Holy Spirit knows how to bring a touch of Heaven to them here. ²In the holy instant no one is special, for your <u>personal</u> needs <u>intrude</u> on no one to <u>make</u> your brothers seem different. ³Without the values from the past, you <u>would</u> see them all the same and <u>like yourself</u>. ⁴Nor would you see <u>any</u> separation between yourself and them. ⁵In the holy instant, you see in each relationship what it <u>will</u> be when you perceive <u>only</u> the present.

Jesus has already told us that special relationships can be made holy under the Holy Spirit's care. How does He "bring a touch of Heaven to them here"? Through the holy instant. Remember, we choose our special relationship partners on the basis of our "values from the past": we use our past experience to determine how well these particular people will meet our perceived personal needs. The holy instant undoes all this because it undoes the past. Without our values from the past, we will see our brothers as they really are: not special, not different, not separate, but "all the same and like yourself."

Application: Bring to mind the same person you used in the previous exercise and use the following words to replace your fantasy picture:

[Name] is not special,
*for my **personal** needs do not intrude on him to make him seem*
   different.
Without my values from the past, I see him as the same as everyone
   else and like myself.
There is no separation between myself and him.
In the holy instant, I see in my relationship with him what it will
   be when I perceive only the present.

9. ¹God knows you *now*. ²He remembers <u>nothing</u>, having <u>always</u> known you exactly as He knows you now. ³The holy instant reflects [Ur: *parallels*] His knowing by bringing <u>all</u> perception <u>out</u> of the past, thus removing the frame of reference you have built by which to <u>judge</u> your brothers. ⁴Once this is gone, the Holy Spirit substitutes His frame of reference <u>for</u> it. ⁵His frame of reference is simply God. ⁶The Holy Spirit's timelessness lies only [Ur: lies simply] here. ⁷For in the holy instant, <u>free</u> of the past, you see that <u>love is in you</u>, and you <u>have</u> no need to look <u>without</u> and snatch love guiltily from where you <u>thought</u> it was.

As we've seen, the past has given us an entire frame of reference from which we view reality. In the past we saw ourselves as lacking love, and thus as needy creatures. We defined our own needs and devised ways to get them. Based on this, we now judge which brothers will best meet the needs we've established, and we form special relationships with the lucky winners.

The Holy Spirit undoes all of this by offering the holy instant. The holy instant brings us from the past to the present, and thus completely removes the past frame of reference on which the entire special relationship game is based. With that frame of reference out of the way, the Holy Spirit can substitute His frame of reference: the timelessness of God. Basking in the timelessness of God, we see that we are *not* lacking love, so we no longer see a need to steal a substitute for love from "special" people.

10. ¹All your relationships are blessed in the holy instant, <u>because the blessing is not limited</u>. ²In the holy instant the Sonship gains <u>as one</u>, and <u>united</u> in your blessing it <u>becomes</u> one <u>to you</u>. ³The meaning of love is the meaning God <u>gave</u> to it. ⁴Give to it <u>any</u> meaning <u>apart</u> from His, and it is <u>impossible</u> to understand it. ⁵God loves every brother as He loves you; neither less nor more. ⁶<u>He needs them all equally</u>, and so do you. ⁷In time, you have been told to offer miracles as I direct [Ur: Christ directs], and let the Holy Spirit bring to you those who are seeking you. ⁸Yet in the holy instant you unite <u>directly</u> with God, and <u>all</u> your brothers join in Christ. ⁹Those who are joined in Christ are in no way separate. ¹⁰For Christ is the Self the Sonship shares, as God shares His Self with Christ.

Way back in paragraph 1, Jesus said, "The holy instant is the Holy

Spirit's most useful learning device for teaching you love's meaning." Here we get a real sense of what we learn of "love's meaning" in that instant. Unlike the selective and limited love of the special relationship, God's Love is *equal* and *total*. He showers everyone and everything with unlimited blessing. He loves all His Sons equally with a limitless Love. He *needs* all His Sons equally; all are essential aspects of His Wholeness. Our job on earth is to love all of our brothers as He does. There is a kind of selectivity in the *form* of this love: we are to offer specific miracles to specific brothers as Jesus directs. But the *content* is the limitless love we experience in the holy instant, where we unite directly with God and with all of our brothers in Christ, the Self the entire Sonship shares.

> 11. ¹Think you that you can judge the Self of God? ²God has created It <u>beyond</u> judgment, out of <u>His</u> need to extend His Love. ³With love in you, you <u>have</u> no need <u>except to extend it</u>. ⁴In the holy instant there is no conflict of needs, for there is <u>only one</u>. ⁵For the holy instant reaches to eternity, and to the Mind of God. ⁶And it is only there love <u>has</u> meaning, and <u>only</u> there <u>can</u> it be understood.

We are not lacking in love, so we have no need to judge our brothers on the basis of how well they meet our needs. We have no need for the substitute for love we seek in special relationships. To judge ourselves and our brothers as lacking is to judge the very Self of God. *We* are the Self of God, and He created us out of His need to extend His Love. Therefore, our only need is to extend love as He does. Through this extension, which happens in the holy instant, we will learn the meaning of love.

VI. The Holy Instant and the Laws of God
Commentary by Robert Perry

1. ¹It is impossible to use one relationship <u>at the expense</u> of another and <u>not</u> to suffer guilt. ²And it is equally impossible to condemn <u>part</u> of a relationship and find peace <u>within</u> it. ³Under the Holy Spirit's teaching <u>all</u> relationships are seen as <u>total</u> commitments, yet they do not conflict with one another in <u>any</u> way. ⁴Perfect faith in each one, for its ability to satisfy you <u>completely</u>, arises only from perfect faith <u>in yourself</u>. ⁵And this you cannot have while guilt remains. ⁶And there <u>will</u> be guilt as long as you accept the possibility, <u>and cherish it</u>, that you can make a brother into <u>what he is not</u>, because you would have him so.

Our relationships seem to be rife with conflict. We have conflict *within* a relationship, which causes us to condemn parts of it: "I love him, but I sure hate it when he leaves his dirty socks on the floor." And we have conflict *between* relationships, which causes us to constantly juggle them and value some more than others. My relationship with my wife feels a lot more important to me than my relationship with my barber. This inability to make a wholehearted commitment to any relationship naturally makes us feel guilty.

To the Holy Spirit, though, all relationships are *total commitments*. What an amazing idea! There is no conflict within them or between them. Each one is perfectly satisfying in every way, even if there are dirty socks on the floor. Of course, on a form level we will spend more time with some people than others. But on a content level, my encounter with my barber can be an experience of total love every bit as satisfying as an encounter with my wife. This will only happen, though, when we have perfect faith in ourselves, which comes only when we stop making our brothers into delivery devices for our imagined needs.

Application: Bring to mind a series of your relationships, both ones you regard as very important and ones you regard as of little importance. As you hold each one in mind, say:

139

This relationship is a total commitment
  which does not conflict with my other relationships in any way.
It can satisfy me completely.
I will have perfect faith in this relationship
  when I have perfect faith in myself.
And I will have perfect faith in myself
  when I stop using this relationship to meet my imagined needs.

2.   ¹You have so little faith in yourself because you are unwilling to accept the fact that perfect love is <u>in</u> you. ²And so you seek <u>without</u> for what you <u>cannot</u> find without. ³I offer you <u>my</u> perfect faith in you, <u>in place</u> of all <u>your</u> doubts. ⁴But forget not that my faith <u>must</u> be as perfect in <u>all</u> your brothers as it is in you, or it would be a limited gift to <u>you</u>. ⁵In the holy instant we <u>share</u> our faith in God's Son because we recognize, together, that he is wholly worthy <u>of</u> it, and in our appreciation of his worth we <u>cannot</u> doubt his holiness. ⁶And so we love him.

We lack perfect faith in ourselves because we don't believe perfect love is in us. This leads us to desperately seek love outside ourselves to fill the lack of love within us. But we can't find it there. What we find instead is the conflicted, guilt-infested, and uncommitted relationships described in the last paragraph. This "proves" to us all the more that perfect love is not in us.

Instead of seeking outside ourselves, we need to join Jesus in a holy instant, where we will receive his gift of perfect faith in us and all those people with whom we have those conflicted relationships. In the holy instant, we share Jesus' vision of the infinite worth and holiness of God's Son in everyone. Seeing this, we naturally love our brothers and ourselves with perfect love, which proves to us that perfect love is in us.

3.   ¹All separation vanishes as holiness is shared. ²For holiness is power, and by <u>sharing</u> it, it <u>gains</u> in strength. ³If you seek for satisfaction in gratifying your needs as <u>you</u> perceive them, you <u>must</u> believe that strength comes from <u>another</u>, and <u>what you gain he loses</u>. ⁴Someone must <u>always</u> lose if you perceive yourself as weak. ⁵Yet there is another interpretation of relationships that <u>transcends</u> the concept of <u>loss</u> of power completely.

Sharing Jesus' vision of the infinite worth and holiness of God's Son is sharing holiness with our brothers, which totally reverses the dynamics of our relationships. Normally, our relationships are based on lack: we see ourselves as needy and weak, so we seek another person to gratify our needs and shore up our strength. Because the other person is seen as separate from us, we think that whatever we manage to extract from her she loses. Isn't this why relationships so often become power struggles? True power, though, comes not from extracting strength from others, but from sharing the power of holiness *with* them. This sharing affirms that we are not separate, and because sharing holiness strengthens it, *everyone* gains in strength.

> 4.   ¹You do not find it difficult to believe that when another calls on God for love, your call remains as strong. ²Nor do you think that when God answers him, your hope of answer is diminished. ³On the contrary, you are more inclined to regard his success as witness to the possibility of yours. ⁴That is because you recognize, however dimly, that God is an idea, and so your faith in Him is strengthened by sharing. ⁵What you find difficult to accept is the fact that, like your Father, *you* are an idea. ⁶And like Him, you can give yourself completely, wholly without loss and only with gain. ⁷Herein lies peace, for here there *is* no conflict.

This paragraph presents the other interpretation of relationships referred to in the previous paragraph. It is an application of the logic presented to us back in Chapter 5:

> *Thoughts increase by being given away.*
> *The more who believe in them the stronger they become.*
> *Everything is an idea.*
> *How, then, can giving and losing be associated? (T-5.I.2:2-5)*

God is an idea, so He increases by giving Himself away. Moreover, the more who believe in Him—by calling on Him and receiving His answer—the stronger everyone's faith in Him becomes. Now, here's the part we have difficulty believing: like God, *we* are ideas. Therefore, like Him, we can give ourselves away "completely, wholly without loss and only with gain." If this is so, how can giving and losing be associated?

This interpretation of relationships transcends the concept of *loss* of power completely. Instead of sucking power from others to jump-start our dead batteries, we share the power of holiness with them completely and thus increase it. This is another way of saying that all relationships are total commitments. This is how we end the conflict in our relationships and find peace.

> 5. ¹In the world of scarcity, love <u>has</u> no meaning and peace is impossible. ²For gain and loss are <u>both</u> accepted, and so no one is aware that perfect love is <u>in</u> him. ³In the holy instant you recognize the <u>idea</u> of love in you, and <u>unite</u> this idea with the Mind that thought it, <u>and could not relinquish it</u>. ⁴By <u>holding</u> it within itself [Ur: Itself], <u>there</u> *is* [Ur: *was*] no loss. ⁵The holy instant thus becomes a lesson in how to hold <u>all</u> of your brothers in <u>your</u> mind, experiencing not loss but <u>completion</u>. ⁶From this it follows you can <u>only</u> give. ⁷And this *is* love, for this alone is natural under the laws of God. ⁸In the holy instant the laws of God prevail, and only <u>they</u> have meaning. ⁹The laws of this world cease to hold any meaning at all. ¹⁰When the Son of God <u>accepts</u> the laws of God as what he gladly wills, it is impossible that he be bound, or limited in <u>any</u> way. ¹¹In that [Ur: this] instant he <u>is</u> as free as God would have him be. ¹²For the instant he refuses to <u>be</u> bound, he is <u>not</u> bound.

We seem to live in a world where everyone is lacking and relationships are feeding frenzies in which everyone leeches off of everyone else. We seem stuck in a zero-sum game of give and take, in which all gains happen at the expense of someone's loss. In this state of war, how can we experience peace? If we believe loss is possible, how can we believe perfect love is in us?

In the holy instant, though, we recognize the idea of love in us and join with God's Mind in holding this idea. As a result, we align our mind with the laws of God. Just as God holds all our brothers in His Mind, so we hold them in *our* mind. Just as this completes Him, so it completes *us*. And just as God's completion means He never needs to take and can only give, so our completion means *we* never need to take and can only give. We become perfect channels for God's laws of love, laws that "forever give and never take" (W-pI.76.9:6). In this state, we are perfectly free from the laws of this world, the whole zero-sum game that prevails in the world of scarcity. Freed from all that seems to limit us, we learn that perfect love is in us.

6.   ¹In the holy instant nothing happens that has not always been. ²Only the veil that has been drawn <u>across</u> reality is lifted. ³Nothing has changed. ⁴Yet the <u>awareness</u> of changelessness comes swiftly as the veil of time is pushed aside. ⁵No one who has not yet experienced the lifting of the veil, and felt himself drawn irresistibly into the light behind it, can have faith in love <u>without</u> fear. ⁶Yet the Holy Spirit <u>gives</u> you this faith, because He offered it to me and <u>I accepted</u> it. ⁷Fear not the holy instant will be denied you, for I denied <u>it</u> not. ⁸And through me the Holy Spirit gives [Ur: *gave*] it unto you, as <u>you</u> will give it. ⁹Let no need <u>you</u> perceive obscure your need of <u>this</u> [your need for the holy instant]. ¹⁰For in the holy instant you will recognize the <u>only</u> need the Sons of God share equally, and <u>by</u> this recognition you will join with me in <u>offering</u> what is needed.

In the holy instant, the veil of time is drawn aside to reveal what has always been. Only the experience of having this veil lifted and being "drawn irresistibly into the light behind it" will give us faith that perfect love is in us. Those of us (like me) who belong to the spiritual "non-experiencers club" may wonder if we'll ever experience the holy instant the way Jesus describes it here, and discover the unwavering faith in our own loving nature such a holy instant brings. But he assures us that these things are absolutely guaranteed, because the Holy Spirit gave them to him, and through him the Holy Spirit has already given them to us. What's more, we ourselves will give the holy instant to others. Once we let go of our imagined needs, we will join Jesus in giving the only thing the Sonship really needs.**Application:** Bring to mind some worldly thing you think you need and say the following:

> *Let me not allow this need I perceive to obscure my need for the holy instant.*
> *Let me recognize that all the Sons of God share equally the need for the holy instant,*
> *By this recognition I will join with Jesus in offering what is needed.*

7.   ¹It is through *us* that peace will come. ²Join me in the <u>idea</u> of peace, for in ideas minds <u>can</u> communicate. ³If you would <u>give</u>

yourself as your Father gives His Self, you will learn to understand Selfhood. ⁴And therein is love's meaning understood. ⁵But remember that understanding is of the mind, and only of the mind. ⁶Knowledge is therefore of the mind, and its conditions are in the mind with it. ⁷If you were not an idea, and nothing but an idea, [Ur: If you were not *only* an idea, and *nothing else*,] you could not be in full communication with all that ever was. ⁸Yet as long as you prefer to be something else, or would attempt to be nothing else and something else together, you will not remember the language of communication [ideas], which you know perfectly.

Our special relationships are heavily focused on the body; as the Course says later, "The special relationship is a ritual of form" (T-16.V.12:2). As long as we see ourselves as bodies or as some combination of body and mind, we will not understand love's meaning, for we will not be able to speak the language of love: the language of pure *ideas*, the only language in which minds can communicate. It is only because we are formless minds, limitless ideas in the Mind of God, that we can fully communication with God and all our brothers. Only by recognizing our nature as formless minds can we give ourselves as our Father gives, come to understand Selfhood, join with Jesus in the idea of peace, and truly learn the meaning of love.

> 8. ¹In the holy instant God is remembered, and the language of communication with all your brothers [the language of ideas] is remembered with Him. ²For communication is remembered together, as is truth. ³There is no exclusion in the holy instant because the past is gone, and with it goes the whole basis for exclusion. ⁴Without its source exclusion vanishes. ⁵And this permits your Source, and That of all your brothers, to replace it in your awareness. ⁶God and the power of God will take Their rightful place in you, and you will experience the full communication of ideas with ideas. ⁷Through your ability to do this you will learn what you must be, for you will begin to understand what your Creator is, and what His creation is along with Him.

As we've seen so often in these past few sections, the holy instant brings about a complete reversal of the way we normally see things. Our lives are anchored in the past; in the holy instant, the past is gone. Our relationships are rooted in exclusion based on the past; in the holy instant, there is no exclusion because the past on which it was based is gone. We believe we are separate from God and therefore weak; in the holy instant, God and His power take their rightful place in us. We think we are imprisoned in bodies and thus struggle to communicate; in the holy instant, we recognize we are limitless ideas, in full communication with all our brothers everywhere. What an amazing thing the holy instant is! Through it, we will come to understand what God and His creation truly are, and thus learn what *we* truly are.

VII. The Needless Sacrifice
Commentary by Robert Perry

This is a key section on the nature of the special relationship. Though its language sounds extreme and bizarre, it is describing ordinary things we do every day in our "loving" relationships. It brilliantly exposes the dark underbelly of those relationships, so that we will become willing to let them be transformed by the Holy Spirit.

> 1. ¹Beyond the poor attraction of the special love relationship, and <u>always</u> obscured by it, is the powerful attraction of the Father for His Son. ²There is no <u>other</u> love that can satisfy you, because there *is* no other love. ³This is the only love that is fully given <u>and fully returned</u>. ⁴Being complete, it asks nothing. ⁵Being wholly pure, everyone joined in it <u>has</u> everything. ⁶This is <u>not</u> the basis for <u>any</u> [Ur: love] relationship in which the ego enters. ⁷For <u>every</u> relationship on which the ego embarks *is* special.

As tempting and juicy as our special love relationships seem to be, they are pale substitutes for the only love that can really satisfy us: the Love of God. Special love relationships are extremely limited versions of "love" in which, as Robert puts it, "I have a special arrangement with and receive special treatment from a very special person, so that I can feel more special." (Any "friendly" relationship can be a special relationship, but perhaps the best example is the romantic relationship.) In contrast, God's Love is a pure, limitless Love that pours itself out indiscriminately to everyone and everything. It is not only fully given; it is fully returned—His "powerful attraction" for us is mirrored by our "irresistible attraction" (Urtext) for Him. When you see special love and God's Love side by side, which sounds more attractive to you?

Application: Bring to mind a special relationship of yours that seems to attract you. With this relationship in mind, say the following:

This special relationship with [name] obscures the Love of God.

*Only the Love of God can satisfy me because there **is** no other
   love.*
The Love of God is fully given by Him and fully returned by me.
*[Name] and I are joined in this Love, which includes everyone
   and gives everything.*
Let me accept the Love of God in place of our special "love."

2.   ¹The ego establishes relationships <u>only</u> to <u>get</u> something. ²And it would keep the giver <u>bound to itself</u> through guilt. ³It is impossible for the ego to enter into any relationship without anger, for the ego believes that <u>anger makes friends</u>. ⁴This is <u>not</u> its statement, but it *is* its purpose. ⁵For the ego <u>really believes</u> that it can get and <u>keep</u> *by making guilty*. ⁶This is its <u>one</u> attraction; an attraction so weak that it would have no hold at all, except that <u>no one recognizes it</u>. ⁷For the ego always <u>seems</u> to attract through love, and has no attraction at all to anyone who perceives that <u>it attracts through guilt</u>.

When we identify with the ego, we enter into relationships only to get things for ourselves. We do this by getting angry at our partners in order to make them feel guilty, so they will feel obligated to give to us. This is how "anger makes friends": it makes our partners feel so guilty that they feel honor bound to stick around and give us what they owe us. They are bound to us through guilt.

Think about when you get angry at your partner for something he's done or neglected to do. Aren't you trying to make him feel guilty? Aren't you trying to extract something from him: correction of what he has done "wrong," some kind gesture that will make it up to you, at the very least an apology? Aren't you sending the message that it is his sacred duty to give you what you want? "You're my husband—you're *supposed* to help out around the house!" Isn't this binding him to you through guilt?

Of course, we're convinced that the real attraction in the relationship is love. Even the anger and obligation seem rooted in love: "I only get so angry because I love you so much." But guilt is what really binds the relationship together. Guilt is what each partner is really attracted to. This sounds creepy, and it is. If we really saw this without blinders, we would immediately recognize that it is nuts.

3.   ¹The sick attraction of guilt must be recognized for what it is. ²For having been made real to you, it is essential to look at it clearly, and by withdrawing your investment in it, to learn to let it go. ³No one would choose to let go what he believes has value. ⁴Yet the attraction of guilt has value to you only because you have not looked at what it is, and have judged it [Ur: as valuable] completely in the dark. ⁵As we bring it to light, your only question will be why it was you ever wanted it. ⁶You have nothing to lose by looking open-eyed [Ur: at this], for ugliness such as this belongs not in your holy mind. ⁷This host of God can have no real investment here.

We've seen in recent sections just how much importance Jesus places on looking at our darkness. Well, it doesn't get much darker than this. Our attraction to guilt is truly a "sick attraction." But we're attracted to it only because the ego has disguised it so well; as the last paragraph said, to us it looks like the attraction of love. What we need to do is peel the masks off of it and look at it clearly and dispassionately. If we do so, reason dictates only one conclusion: "This is completely wacko. How could I have ever been attracted to *this*?" Once we draw this conclusion, we will have no problem letting it go.

Application: Throughout the rest of this section, which examines the darkness of our special relationships in grim detail, I encourage you to look with calm honesty at your own special relationships and see how this material applies to them. This may seem like a drag, but "You have nothing to lose by looking open-eyed at this." It is the gateway to your release.

4.   ¹We said before [T-13.II.1-2] that the ego attempts to maintain and increase guilt, but in such a way that you do not recognize what it would do to you. ²For it is the ego's fundamental doctrine that what you do to others you have escaped. ³The ego wishes no one well. ⁴Yet its survival depends on your belief that you are exempt from its evil intentions. ⁵It counsels, therefore, that if you are host to it, it will enable you to direct its anger outward, thus protecting you. ⁶And thus it embarks on an endless, unrewarding chain of special relationships, forged out of anger and dedicated to but one insane belief; that the more anger you invest outside yourself, the safer you become.

As we've seen before, the ego has a problem: *It* wants to increase our guilt, but *we* want to be free of guilt. Its ingenious solution is to get us to project anger and guilt outward. It tells us, "Just blame that SOB special relationship partner of yours for everything, and you're in the clear." We think this frees us from guilt, but because it is an attack, it actually *increases* our guilt—exactly what the ego wants. Sadly, this ploy has been working for a long time, leading us unwittingly into "an endless, unrewarding chain of special relationships." I bet you could come up with a fairly sizable list of former friends and lovers right now.

> 5. ¹It is this chain that binds the Son of God to guilt, and it is this chain the Holy Spirit would <u>remove</u> from his holy mind. ²For the chain of savagery belongs not around the chosen host of God, who <u>cannot</u> make himself host to the ego. ³In the name of his release, and in the Name of Him Who would release him, let us look more closely at the relationships the ego contrives, and let the Holy Spirit judge them truly. ⁴For it is certain that if you will <u>look</u> at them, you will offer them gladly <u>to</u> Him. ⁵What <u>He</u> can make of them you do <u>not</u> know, but you <u>will</u> become willing to find out, if you are willing first to perceive what <u>you</u> have made of them.

Again, Jesus stresses the need to look squarely at the darkness of our special relationships. We have such a strong investment in *not* looking. In the world's eyes, the special love relationship is the crowning glory of life, celebrated in song and story, the great bastion of love in a loveless world. It's so easy to say, "Don't confuse me with the facts." But the real cost of special relationships is enormous: they bind us with a "chain of savagery" to the living hell of guilt and blind us to the glorious truth that we are the "chosen host of God." Only by looking with unflinching honesty at what we have made of our relationships will we be willing to offer them to the Holy Spirit and learn what *He* can make of them.

> 6. ¹In one way or another, every relationship the ego makes is based on the idea that by <u>sacrificing</u> itself, <u>it becomes bigger</u>. ²The "sacrifice," which it regards as purification, is actually the root of its bitter resentment. ³For it would [Ur: much] prefer to attack directly, and avoid delaying what it <u>really</u> wants. ⁴Yet the ego acknowledges "reality" as it sees it, and recognizes that <u>no one</u> could interpret <u>direct</u> attack as love. ⁵Yet to make guilty *is* direct attack, although it does not

seem to be. [6]For the guilty <u>expect</u> attack, and having <u>asked</u> for it they are <u>attracted</u> to it.

Special relationships are based on the idea that by sacrificing ourselves—by giving time, attention, material gifts, affection, sex, etc.—we become "bigger" through acquiring more specialness from our partner. Think of how we wine and dine our potential romantic partners and fawn over people we want to do a favor for us. It's like a financial transaction, using the currency of specialness.

This sacrifice feels like a "purification." When we sacrifice for others, we feel like a good person who now deserves something good in return. We can't just take without giving anything—that would be stealing. Yet secretly we feel "bitter resentment" because deep down, we would really rather steal. We would rather just take without sacrificing at all. We don't like to admit this, but have you ever caught yourself muttering under your breath, "I wish she would just give me what I want without me having to jump through all these hoops?"

Usually, though, this stays safely under our breath, because we've all been socialized well enough to recognize that we can't just steal from others without giving anything in return. We call people like that sociopaths. So, we attack "indirectly" by making "loving" sacrifices to extract special love. Yet in truth, this is just as direct an attack as trying to steal outright, because is an attempt to make our partner guilty. Our apparently loving sacrifice sends a vicious message: "I'm suffering because of you. You owe me." This increases guilt in the partner and (because it is an attack) increases our own guilt as well, which is exactly what both of us are attracted to underneath our surface attraction to "love."

> 7. [1]In such [Ur: In these] insane relationships, the attraction of what you do <u>not</u> want [guilt, sacrifice] seems to be much stronger than the attraction of what you <u>do</u> want [real love]. [2]For each one thinks that he has <u>sacrificed</u> something to the other, <u>and hates him for it</u>. [3]Yet this is what he thinks he <u>wants</u> [sacrifice]. [4]He is <u>not</u> in love with the other at all. [5]He merely believes he is <u>in love with sacrifice</u>. [6]And <u>for</u> this sacrifice, which he demands <u>of himself,</u> he demands that the other <u>accept</u> the guilt and <u>sacrifice himself</u> as well. [7]Forgiveness becomes impossible, for the ego believes that to forgive another <u>is to lose him</u>.

⁸[Ur: For] It is only by attack <u>without</u> forgiveness that the ego can ensure the guilt that holds <u>all</u> its relationships together.

Of course, both partners are playing the exact same game. Each one sacrifices to the other, overtly to acquire special love and covertly to acquire guilt. In truth, this decision to sacrifice is solely the responsibility of the one making the sacrifice. But each partner convinces himself that the other is *demanding* sacrifice of him, which he resents. (Have you ever felt that your partner was unreasonably demanding?) So, each partner makes a bargain with the other: "You're forcing me to sacrifice to you. This makes you guilty of my loss, so now you have to pay up by sacrificing to me in return." Back and forth we go. We call this reciprocity: "I scratched your back, now you have to scratch mine."

The awful conclusion: We are not really in love with our partner but with *sacrifice*. This game of sacrificing ourselves to make the other guilty (thus reinforcing our own guilt) is the real glue that "holds all [the ego's] relationships together." Forgiveness is now impossible, for if guilt is the glue that holds us together, the last thing we want is the one thing that *undoes* guilt.

8. ¹Yet they only *seem* to be together. ²For relationships, to the ego, mean <u>only</u> that <u>bodies</u> are together. ³It is always this [Ur: *physical* closeness] that the ego demands, and it does not object where the mind goes or what it thinks, for this seems unimportant. ⁴As long as the <u>body</u> is there to receive its sacrifice, it is content. ⁵To the ego <u>the mind is private</u>, and only the body <u>can</u> be shared. ⁶Ideas [the real language of communication between minds—see previous section] are basically of no concern, except as they bring the <u>body</u> of another closer or farther. ⁷And it is in these terms that it evaluates ideas as good or bad. ⁸What makes another guilty <u>and holds him through guilt</u> is "good." ⁹What releases him <u>from</u> guilt is "bad," because he would no longer believe that <u>bodies</u> communicate, and so he would be "gone."

Now we see another element of these twisted relationships: the glue of guilt only holds *bodies* together. In truth, only minds can have relationships, in which they communicate fully using the language of timeless ideas. But in the ego's view, only bodies can have relationships, and the only ideas it's interested in are the ones that keep bodies together through guilt and mutual sacrifice. Forgiveness is anathema in this view, because without guilt to bind our partner to us, what's to stop her from walking out the door?

This sounds bizarre, but haven't we all seen (or been in) relationships where bodies are together—going through the daily routine, saying the right words, keeping up appearances, having sex—while there is no real connection between the minds at all? Aren't we all familiar with relationships where two people are "in the same room and yet a world apart" (T-22.In.2:8)? This, says the Course, is the state of *all* our special relationships.

> 9. ¹Suffering and sacrifice are the gifts with which the ego would "bless" all unions. ²And those who are united at its altar <u>accept</u> suffering and sacrifice as the <u>price</u> of union. ³In their angry alliances, born of the fear of loneliness and yet dedicated to the <u>continuance</u> of loneliness, each seeks <u>relief</u> from guilt by <u>increasing</u> it in the other. ⁴For each believes that this <u>decreases</u> guilt in him. ⁵The other seems always to be attacking and wounding him, perhaps in little ways, perhaps "unconsciously," yet never without demand of sacrifice. ⁶The fury of those joined at the ego's altar far exceeds your awareness of it. ⁷For what the ego really wants [guilt] you do <u>not</u> realize.

Don't we all "accept suffering and sacrifice as the price of union"? We just assume that being in relationship means making compromises, having to give up things we like, sacrificing for the sake of the other. We take for granted that, no matter how hard we try to be the good guy and make things work, we'll have to put up with our partner's unfair demands and attacks. We tell ourselves that feeling lonely and distant even when our bodies are together is just part of the human condition.

We simply have no idea of what lies at the heart of all this: the game of trying to absolve ourselves of guilt by blaming our partner and angrily demanding restitution. We have no clue that our apparently loving interactions are designed to collect guilt and place it at the ego's altar. "The fury of those joined at the ego's altar far exceeds your awareness of it." No wonder Jesus is so intent on us looking at this.

> 10. ¹Whenever you are angry, you can be sure that you have formed a special relationship which the ego has "blessed," for anger *is* its

blessing. ²Anger takes many forms, but it cannot long deceive those who will learn that <u>love brings no guilt at all</u>, and what brings guilt <u>cannot</u> be love and *must* be anger. ³All anger is nothing more than an attempt to <u>make someone feel guilty</u>, and this attempt is the <u>only</u> basis the ego accepts for special relationships. ⁴Guilt is the only need the ego has, and as long as you identify <u>with</u> it, guilt will remain <u>attractive</u> to you. ⁵Yet remember this; to be <u>with a body</u> is <u>not</u> communication. ⁶And if you think it <u>is</u>, you will feel guilty about <u>communication</u> and will be <u>afraid</u> to hear the Holy Spirit, recognizing in His Voice your <u>own</u> need to communicate.

We would all like to think that our relationships are really not as bad as this section makes them out to be. Yet the evidence that we are indeed playing the special relationship game is all the anger and guilt we feel. If our relationships were really totally loving, we wouldn't have these feelings, for "love brings no guilt at all." Can you imagine what a relationship with no guilt and no anger at all would feel like?

To open the door to truly loving relationships, it is crucial for us to learn that just being with a body is not a real relationship, because it is not real communication. As long as we believe otherwise, we will feel guilty about communication, because our form of "communication" is an attempt to bind someone else to us through guilt. This will make us fear the Holy Spirit's communication, because we'll assume that He's using communication to attack us the same way we use our bogus "communication" to attack others.

> 11. ¹The Holy Spirit <u>cannot</u> teach through fear. ²And how can He communicate with you, while you believe that to communicate is to <u>make yourself alone</u>? ³It is <u>clearly</u> insane to believe that by communicating you will be abandoned. ⁴And yet many <u>do</u> [Ur: you *do*] believe it. ⁵For they think their minds [Ur: you think that your minds] must be kept <u>private</u> or they [Ur: you] will <u>lose</u> them, but if their [Ur: your] <u>bodies</u> are together their [Ur: your] minds remain their [Ur: your] own. ⁶The union of bodies thus becomes the way in which they [Ur: you] would <u>keep minds apart</u>. ⁷For bodies cannot forgive. ⁸They can only do as the mind directs.

The Holy Spirit will never try to force His way through our fear, and we *do* fear His communication, for several reasons. First, as we just discussed, we have projected our bogus form of "communication" onto Him and thus see His communication as an attack. Second, we think His communication, being true mind-to-mind communication, will cause our special relationship partner to abandon us. Third, we think His true mind-to-mind communication will cause us to lose our minds—our minds will no longer be the private domain of the ego.

We thus have many reasons, in our eyes, to keep the Holy Spirit out, and we cling to our special relationships to do this. We avoid joining minds by trying to join bodies through guilt instead. Thus we chain our partners to us ever tighter, maintain our grip on our private minds, avoid the forgiveness that would end this whole charade, and keep that pesky Holy Spirit out.

> 12. ¹The illusion of the autonomy of the body and <u>its</u> ability to overcome loneliness is but the working of the ego's plan to establish its <u>own</u> autonomy. ²As long as you believe that to be with a body is companionship, you will be <u>compelled</u> to attempt to keep your brother <u>in</u> his body, <u>held there by guilt</u>. ³And you will see <u>safety in guilt</u> and <u>danger in communication</u>. ⁴For the ego will <u>always</u> teach that loneliness is solved by guilt, and that communication is the <u>cause</u> of loneliness. ⁵And despite the evident insanity of this lesson, many <u>have learned it</u> [Ur: *you have learned it*].

The ego tells us that the bodies can join independently of the mind, because this reinforces our belief that the *ego itself* can work independently of the mind—the body's autonomy equals the ego's autonomy. As long as we're holding on to this belief, we will see guilt as the source of safety and companionship because it keeps our partner bound to us, and true communication as the source of danger and loneliness because it releases our partner from the guilt that keeps him bound to us. When we see the "lesson" worded this way, we may find it hard to believe that anyone could believe anything so preposterous. But before we laugh at those benighted souls who believe this nutty lesson, we should pause to consider the final words of this paragraph: "*you have learned it.*"

> 13. ¹Forgiveness lies in communication as surely as damnation lies in guilt. ²It is the Holy Spirit's teaching function to instruct those who believe communication to be damnation that communication is

salvation. ³And He will do so, for the power of God in Him and you is joined in a real relationship so holy and so strong, that it can overcome even this without fear.

Application: We may feel awfully depressed at this point in our nightmare tour through the subterranean caverns of our special love relationships. But as insane as our special relationships are and as afraid as we may be of the Holy Spirit's communication, *He will get through.* Repeat the following words of reassurance:

> *I believe that communication is damnation and guilt is salvation.*
> *The Holy Spirit knows that guilt is damnation and communication*
>   *is salvation.*
> *He **will** teach me this, for the power of God is in Him **and me**.*
> *We are joined in a real relationship so holy and so strong*
>   *that it can overcome even these insane beliefs of mine without*
>   *fear.*

14. ¹It is through the holy instant that what seems impossible is accomplished, making it evident that it is not impossible. ²In the holy instant guilt holds no attraction, since communication has been restored. ³And guilt, whose only purpose is to disrupt communication, has no function here. ⁴Here there is no concealment, and no private thoughts. ⁵The willingness to communicate attracts communication to it, and overcomes loneliness completely. ⁶There is complete forgiveness here, for there is no desire to exclude anyone from your completion, in sudden recognition of the value of his part in it. ⁷In the protection of your wholeness, all are invited and made welcome. ⁸And you understand that your completion is God's, Whose only need is to have you be complete. ⁹For your completion makes you His [completion] in your awareness. ¹⁰And here it is that you experience yourself as you were created, and as you are.

How is the seemingly impossible task of undoing our special relationships accomplished? Through the holy instant. The holy instant, as we've seen throughout this chapter, is a moment in which we are lifted out of the past—the whole basis for the special relationship—into the timeless present where communication has never been disrupted. This one glorious instant of true communication unravels the entire grimy tapestry of the special relationship. With communication restored, guilt is no longer attractive, private thoughts and loneliness are no more, forgiveness is complete, and everyone is welcome. In this glorious state, we recognize that we are complete and that our completion is God's. At last, we experience ourselves as God created us and as we still are.

VIII. The Only Real Relationship
Commentary by Robert Perry

1. ¹The holy instant does not <u>replace</u> the need for learning, for the Holy Spirit must not leave you as your Teacher until the holy instant has extended far beyond time. ²For a teaching assignment such as His, He must use <u>everything</u> in this world for your release. ³He must side with <u>every</u> sign or token of your willingness to learn of Him what the truth <u>must</u> be. ⁴He is swift to utilize <u>whatever</u> you offer Him on behalf of this. ⁵His concern and care for you are limitless. ⁶In the face of your fear of forgiveness, which He perceives as clearly as He knows forgiveness <u>is</u> release, He will teach you to remember that forgiveness is <u>not</u> loss, <u>but your salvation</u>. ⁷And that in <u>complete</u> forgiveness, in which you recognize that there is nothing to forgive, <u>you</u> are absolved completely.

At the end of the last section, we were told that in the holy instant the seemingly impossible task of forgiveness is accomplished. However, simply having a temporary experience of the holy instant is not enough; the Holy Spirit must stay with us as our Teacher until the holy instant becomes permanent. And what an amazing Teacher! His concern and care for us are limitless. He'll never force Himself on us, but will use whatever tiny opening we give Him to teach us the truth. He'll immediately put to good use anything we offer Him for this purpose. He'll use literally "everything in this world" to release us from the prison of our attraction to guilt. He sees with perfect clarity that we fear forgiveness because we think it means "losing" the people we've chained to our guilt, but He also knows how to convince us that forgiveness is salvation from every kind of loss. Where there's God's Will, there's a way.

The last line is a nice brief summary of how Course-based forgiveness works. I've sometimes heard Course students say, "I don't need to forgive that person because there's really nothing to forgive." But it doesn't work that way. We need to forgive others because forgiving others is how we *recognize* there is nothing to forgive. That recognition *is* Course-based forgiveness. Through recognizing our brothers' innocence, we ourselves are absolved completely.

2.   ¹Hear Him gladly, and learn of Him that you have need of no special relationships at all. ²You but seek in them what you have <u>thrown away</u>. ³And through <u>them</u> you will never learn the value of what you have cast aside, but still desire with all your heart [Ur: hearts]. ⁴Let us join together in making the holy instant all that there is, by desiring that it *be* all that there is. ⁵God's Son has such great need of your willingness to strive for this that you cannot conceive of need so great. ⁶Behold the only need that God and His Son share, and will to meet together. ⁷You are <u>not</u> alone in this. ⁸The will of your creations calls to you, to share your will with them. ⁹Turn, then, in peace from guilt to God and them.

Jesus passionately appeals to us to hear the Holy Spirit and accept the holy instant. We don't need special relationships, because they cannot give us what we truly want. Making the holy instant permanent is the only need that God, the Sonship, and all our creations share and will to have accomplished.

Application: Let us answer Jesus' appeal. Repeat the following words to the Holy Spirit:

> *Let me remember that I need no special relationships at all.*
> *My only need is to make the holy instant all that there is*
>   *by desiring that it* ***be*** *all that there is.*
> *This is what I really desire with all my heart.*
> *God's Son has such great need of my willingness to strive for this*
>   *that I cannot conceive of need so great.*
> *This is the only need that God, the Sonship, and all our creations*
>   *share,*
>   *and will to meet together.*
> *Let me join with them in meeting this need.*
> *Let me turn in peace from guilt to God and them.*

3.   ¹Relate only with what will never <u>leave</u> you, and what <u>you</u> can never leave. ²The loneliness of God's Son is the loneliness of his Father. ³Refuse not the awareness of your completion, and seek not to restore it to yourself [Ur: yourselves]. ⁴Fear not to give redemption over to your Redeemer's Love. ⁵He will <u>not</u> fail you, for He comes from One Who <u>cannot</u> fail. ⁶Accept <u>your</u> sense of failure as nothing more than

a mistake in who you are [Ur: *who you were*]. ⁷For the holy host of God is <u>beyond</u> failure, and <u>nothing</u> that he wills can <u>be</u> denied. ⁸You are forever in a relationship so holy that it calls to everyone to <u>escape</u> from loneliness, and join you in your love. ⁹And where <u>you</u> are must everyone seek, and <u>find</u> you there.

In our special relationships, we pick out a few special people and try to relate to their bodies. This is a recipe for loneliness: we're lonely even when those bodies are with us, and of course we're lonely when they leave us, which they inevitably do. Jesus calls us to leave the Lonely Hearts Club by relating only with what will *never* leave us and we can never leave: God and all the brothers He created one with us. Even in the midst of our apparent loneliness, we are forever in a holy relationship with God, a relationship that calls all the lonely ones to join with us in love. Our attempts to find love on our own terms have failed, but our true nature is beyond failure, and with the help of the equally unfailing Holy Spirit, we *will* be restored to awareness of the holy relationship we never really left.

4. ¹Think but an instant on this: God gave the Sonship to you, to ensure your perfect creation. ²This was His gift, for as He withheld Himself not from you, He withheld not His creation. ³Nothing that ever was created but is yours. ⁴Your relationships are with the universe. ⁵And this universe, being of God, is far beyond the petty sum of all the separate bodies <u>you</u> perceive. ⁶For all its parts are joined in God through Christ, where they become like to their Father. ⁷[Ur: For] Christ knows of no separation <u>from</u> His Father, Who is His one relationship, in which He gives as His Father gives to Him.

Again, our special relationships are so narrow and limited. We pick out a few special bodies to relate with and exclude everyone and everything else. Jesus sees the insanity of this and tries to talk some sense into us: "Think about it: God gave you Himself and everything He created. You are actually in relationship with Him, with all your brothers, with the entire *universe* of infinite spirit, a universe far greater than all the bodies in your physical universe put together. You are joined with everyone and everything in God through Christ, Who shares perfect love eternally with His Father. Do you really want to give all this up for a few hunks of meat?"

5. ¹The Holy Spirit is God's attempt to free you of what He does not understand. ²And because of the Source of the attempt, <u>it will succeed</u>. ³The Holy Spirit asks you to respond as God does, for He would teach you what <u>you</u> do not understand. ⁴God would respond to <u>every</u> need, <u>whatever</u> form it takes. ⁵And so He keeps [Ur: has kept] this channel open to receive His communication to you, <u>and yours to Him</u>. ⁶God does <u>not</u> understand your problem in communication, for He does <u>not</u> share it with you. ⁷It is only <u>you</u> who believe that it <u>is</u> understandable. ⁸The Holy Spirit <u>knows</u> that it is not understandable, and yet He <u>understands</u> it because you [Ur: have] <u>made</u> it.

God does not even understand our problem in communication, which might lead us to conclude that He wouldn't lift a finger to help us. Some Course students really do believe this, saying that He can't help us because, in their view, He doesn't even know about the separation. Fortunately, this is not the case. He *does* recognize that we are not communicating fully with Him (see T-4.VII.6 and T-6.V.1) and therefore have a communication need. As a truly loving Father, He "would respond to every need, whatever form it takes." Therefore, He responded to our need by creating a two-way communication link: the Holy Spirit.

The Holy Spirit is God's loving attempt to free us from the communication problem He doesn't understand. Since He is God, this attempt cannot fail. Now the Holy Spirit calls on us "to respond as God does." Just as God responded to the communication problem He doesn't understand by reaching out to us, so we should respond to the God *we* don't understand by reaching out to Him. Through the Holy Spirit we can do this, and we will come to understand our Father.

6. ¹In the Holy Spirit alone lies the awareness of what God <u>cannot</u> know, and what <u>you</u> do <u>not</u> understand. ²It is His holy function to <u>accept them both,</u> and by removing <u>every</u> element of <u>disagreement</u>, to join them into one. ³He will do this <u>because</u> it is His function. ⁴Leave, then, what seems to you to be impossible, to Him Who knows it <u>must</u> be possible because it is the Will of God. ⁵And let Him Whose teaching is <u>only</u> of God teach you the <u>only</u> meaning of relationships. ⁶For God created the only relationship that <u>has</u> meaning, and that is His relationship with <u>you</u>.

Since the Holy Spirit is the communication link between God and us,

He acts as a bridge between God's perspective and ours. He thus holds in His mind both the knowledge of God *we* don't understand and the awareness of our communication problem that *God* doesn't understand. His job is to take both of these and reconcile them—and therefore reconcile us with God—by finding their common elements. How does He do this? We don't have to know. It may sound impossible to us, but our job is simply to get out of the way and let Him accomplish what seems impossible to us but *can't* be impossible because it is the Will of God. If we stop trying to figure things out on our own, He will undo our special relationships and teach us that the only real relationship is God's relationship with us.

Application: It really does seem impossible to us that we and God will ever be reunited. Repeat the following words to the Holy Spirit as an affirmation of your confidence in Him to bring about what seems impossible:

> *Reconciliation between God and me seems impossible to me.*
> *But You know it must be possible because it is the Will of God.*
> *Bringing about this reconciliation is Your function.*
> *Let me, then, leave what seems impossible to You.*
> *You will teach me that not only is reconciliation with God possible,*
>   *it has already been accomplished.*
> *For God created the only relationship that has meaning,*
>   *and that is His relationship with me.*

IX. The Holy Instant and the Attraction of God
Commentary by Robert Perry

1. ¹As the ego would <u>limit</u> your perception of your brothers to the body, so would the Holy Spirit <u>release</u> your vision and let you see the Great Rays shining from them, so unlimited that they reach to God. ²It is this shift to [Ur: in] vision that is accomplished in the holy instant. ³Yet it is needful for you to learn just what this shift entails, so you will become willing to make it permanent. ⁴Given this willingness it will <u>not</u> leave you, for it *is* permanent. ⁵[Ur: For,] Once you have accepted it as the <u>only perception you want</u>, it is translated into knowledge by the part that God Himself plays in the Atonement, for it is the <u>only</u> step in it He understands. ⁶Therefore, in this there will be <u>no</u> delay when <u>you</u> are ready for it. ⁷God is ready <u>now,</u> but <u>you</u> are not.

A couple of sections ago, we learned that the ego wants us to chain our special relationship partners to their bodies through guilt. The Holy Spirit's alternative is to give us a holy instant, where we will see beyond their bodies to the Great Rays that shine eternally from their true nature. The last section told us that our greatest need is to make the holy instant permanent. To do so, we must learn just how much the shift to vision that occurs in the holy instant brings us. In this way we will become willing to make the holy instant permanent, and once we are fully willing, God *will* make it permanent by lifting us to knowledge in His final step.

2. ¹Our task is but to continue, as fast as possible, the necessary process of looking straight at <u>all</u> the interference and seeing it <u>exactly</u> as it is. ²For it is impossible to recognize as <u>wholly</u> without gratification <u>what you think you want</u>. ³The body is the symbol of the ego, as the ego is the symbol of the separation. ⁴And both are nothing more than attempts to <u>limit</u> communication, and thereby <u>to make it impossible</u>. ⁵For communication <u>must</u> be <u>un</u>limited in order to <u>have</u> meaning, and <u>deprived</u> of meaning, it will <u>not</u> satisfy <u>you</u> completely. ⁶Yet it remains the <u>only</u> means by which you <u>can</u> establish real relationships, which <u>have</u> no limits, having been established by God.

To bring about the willingness we need to make the shift to vision in the holy instant permanent, we must look without blinders at everything that gets in the way of that shift and realize how unwanted and unsatisfying it really is. The "interference" here is the body and the ego, the static on the Holy Spirit's communication channel. This static makes true communication impossible, for true communication is an all or nothing proposition: you either communicate or you don't. Only unlimited communication will really satisfy us, because only unlimited communication will restore our awareness of the real relationship we have with God and all He created.

Application: Bring to mind one of your special relationships and think of some way in which you are using this person to meet your perceived needs. When you use this person this way, you are serving the ego's goals by holding this person to his body through guilt. Now, ask for a new vision of this person with these words:

> *Holy Spirit, my way of seeing [name] interferes with what I really want.*
> *Let me look straight at the interference of the ego and the body*
>   *and see it exactly as it is.*
> *It is nothing more than an attempt to limit communication*
>   *and thereby to make it impossible.*
> *Limited communication will never satisfy me completely.*
> *Release my vision and let me look beyond [name's] body*
>   *to see the Great Rays shining from him, so unlimited that they*
>   *reach to God.*
> *This will open my mind to limitless communication,*
>   *and only limitless communication will satisfy me completely.*
> *For it will establish a real relationship with [name]*
>   *which has no limits, having been established by God.*

3. ¹In the holy instant, where the Great Rays <u>replace</u> the body in awareness, the recognition of relationships <u>without</u> limits is given you. ²But in order to <u>see</u> this, it is necessary to give up <u>every</u> use the ego has for the body, and to accept the fact that the ego has <u>no</u> purpose you would <u>share</u> with it. ³For the ego would limit everyone <u>to</u> a body for <u>its</u> own purposes, and while you think it <u>has</u> a purpose, you will

choose to utilize the means by which <u>it</u> tries to turn its purpose into accomplishment. ⁴This will never <u>be</u> accomplished. ⁵Yet you have surely recognized that the ego, whose goals are altogether <u>unattainable</u>, will strive for them with all its might, and will do so with the strength that <u>you</u> have given it.

We really need to look at all that interference, because the ego is one tough nut to crack. We have given it the strength of our minds, and it uses this strength to pursue its impossible goals with a single-mindedness the most dedicated Olympic athlete would envy. As long as we continue to identify with the ego, we will continue to use its means to pursue its goals. We will enter into special relationships in which we use our brothers' bodies to gratify our imagined needs. If we want to see beyond their bodies to the Great Rays—if we want to enter the holy instant and experience limitless relationships—we must recognize that we don't truly want what the ego wants and give up its twisted uses of the body.

> 4. ¹[Ur: Yet] It is impossible to <u>divide</u> your strength between Heaven and hell, God and the ego, and <u>release</u> your power to creation, which is the <u>only</u> purpose for which it was <u>given</u> you. ²Love would *always* give <u>increase</u> [Ur: For love would always give *increase*]. ³Limits are <u>demanded</u> by the ego, and represent its demands [Ur: Limits are *demanded*, representing the ego's demands] to make little and ineffectual. ⁴Limit your sight [Ur: vision] of a brother to his body, which you <u>will</u> do as long as you would not release him <u>from</u> it, and you have denied <u>his</u> gift to <u>you</u>. ⁵<u>His body cannot give it</u>. ⁶And seek it not through <u>yours</u>. ⁷Yet your minds are <u>already</u> continuous, and <u>their</u> union need only be accepted and the loneliness in Heaven is gone.

Our investment in the ego divides our strength between God and the ego, which makes it impossible to devote our full strength to creation in Heaven. The ego's goals, after all, are the very antithesis of creation in Heaven. Love is limitless and always gives increase, while the ego is a limit and always gives the "gift" of littleness. The prime example of this is the special relationship, in which the limitless sharing of love with God and all the Sonship is reduced to the exchange of sacrificial "gifts" between one body and another to bolster specialness and accumulate guilt. Chaining our brothers to their bodies through this sacrificial "gift" exchange keeps us from seeing their real gift, which cannot be given or received by the body at all. Their real gift is the priceless gift of freedom from all limits, which leads to the acceptance of the union of our minds in Heaven.

5.   ¹If you would but let the Holy Spirit tell you of the Love of God for you, and the need your creations have to be with you forever, you would experience the attraction of the eternal. ²No one can hear Him speak of this and long remain willing to linger here. ³For it is your will to be in Heaven, where you are complete and quiet, in such sure and loving relationships that any limit is [Ur: *any* limits are] impossible. ⁴Would you not exchange your little relationships for this? ⁵For the body *is* little and limited, and only those whom you would see without the limits the ego would impose on them can offer you the gift of freedom.

The whole time we're trying to make do with our pitiful special relationships and feeding the ego's sick attraction to guilt, the Holy Spirit is constantly reminding us of our *real* attraction: the attraction of the eternal. How could our paltry "joining" of bodies possibly compare with the pure oneness of Heaven? If we only knew what we were missing, we would be eager to free our brothers from their bodies so they could offer *us* the gift of freedom.

Application: Hear the Holy Spirit speak to you of the attraction of the eternal:

You are in Heaven this very moment,
   in the limitless embrace of God's Love.
You are surrounded by your creations,
   who want only to be with you forever.
You are complete and quiet,
   in such sure and loving relationships
   that any limit is impossible.
Are you still willing to linger here in this world?
Would you not exchange your little relationships for this?
Would you not let your brother offer you the gift of freedom?

6. ¹You have no conception of the limits you have placed on your perception, and no idea of all the loveliness that you <u>could</u> see. ²But this you must remember; the attraction of guilt <u>opposes</u> the attraction of God. ³His attraction for you remains unlimited, but because your power, <u>being</u> His, is <u>as great</u> as His, you can <u>turn away</u> from love. ⁴What you invest in guilt you withdraw from God. ⁵And your sight grows weak and dim and limited, for you have attempted to <u>separate</u> the Father from the Son, and <u>limit</u> their communication. ⁶Seek not Atonement in <u>further</u> separation. ⁷And limit not your vision of God's Son to what <u>interferes</u> with his release, and what the Holy Spirit must <u>undo</u> to set him free. ⁸For his belief in limits *has* imprisoned him.

Here's our choice, laid out plainly: the attraction of guilt or the attraction of God. The attraction of God is the only choice with *real* power, but because our holy minds are as powerful as His, we have the ability to fool ourselves into believing we prefer guilt to Him. But what a costly belief! Our attempt to separate the Father from the Son makes our sight grow "weak and dim and limited." It places painful limits on our perception and leads us to futilely seek Atonement in separation. But if we choose the attraction of God—if we choose to release our brothers from their bodies instead of limiting them to their bodies—we will see the loveliness that our attraction to guilt obscured.

7. ¹When the body ceases to attract you, and when you place no value on it as a means of <u>getting anything</u>, then there will be <u>no</u> interference in communication and your thoughts will be as free as God's. ²As you let the Holy Spirit teach you how to use the body <u>only</u> for purposes of communication, and <u>renounce</u> its use for separation and attack which the <u>ego</u> sees in it, you will learn you have no need of a body at all. ³In the holy instant there <u>are</u> no bodies, and you experience <u>only</u> the attraction of God. ⁴Accepting it as undivided you join Him wholly, in an instant, for you would place <u>no</u> limits on your union <u>with</u> Him. ⁵The reality of <u>this</u> relationship becomes the only truth that you could ever want. ⁶<u>All</u> truth *is* here.

When we let go of our attraction to bodies and stop using our body as a means of getting things through separation and attack, our communication problem will be solved. When we let the Holy Spirit use our body only *for* communication, we will eventually learn that we don't need a body at all. Wow! What would it be like to not need a body at all? This may sound impossible, but again, the holy instant makes it possible. In the holy instant, we experience a taste of what life without the body is like. In the holy instant, we experience only the attraction of God. Feeling only this attraction, we will instantly join Him completely and realize that this relationship is all we could ever want.

X. The Time of Rebirth
Commentary by Robert Perry

1.   ¹It *is* in your power, <u>in time,</u> to delay the perfect union of the Father and the Son. ²For in this world, the attraction of guilt <u>does</u> stand between them. ³Neither time nor season means anything in eternity. ⁴But here it is the Holy Spirit's function to use them both, though <u>not</u> as the ego uses them. ⁵This is the season when you would celebrate my birth into the world. ⁶Yet you know not how to do it. ⁷Let the Holy Spirit teach you, and let <u>me</u> celebrate *your* birth through Him. ⁸The only gift I can accept of you is the gift I <u>gave</u> to you. ⁹Release <u>me</u> as I choose <u>your</u> own release [Ur: as I willed *your* release]. ¹⁰The time of Christ we celebrate <u>together,</u> for it <u>has</u> no meaning if we are apart.

We have an overpowering attraction to God, and God has one to us, yet the union with Him that must result is delayed now, because we have another love: guilt. We are like a man whose true love is waiting for him, longing for him, while he is engrossed in his love for a corpse.

The Holy Spirit uses the seasons of time, even though they are meaningless in eternity. Therefore, He uses the Christmas season, but does so in a totally different way than how we do. In His use, Christmas is all about mutuality. We give Jesus the same gift of release that he gave us. If we do this, we won't just be celebrating Jesus' birth. *He* will be celebrating *ours*. When was the last time Christmas brought us a sense of rebirth that was worth celebrating?

2.   ¹The holy instant is truly the time of Christ. ²For in this liberating instant no guilt is laid upon the Son of God, and his unlimited power is thus restored to him. ³What <u>other</u> gift can you offer me, when <u>only this</u> I choose [Ur: I will] to offer <u>you</u>? ⁴And to see me is to see me in everyone, and <u>offer</u> everyone the gift you offer me. ⁵I am as incapable of receiving sacrifice as God is, and every sacrifice you ask of <u>yourself</u> you ask of me. ⁶Learn <u>now</u> that sacrifice of <u>any</u> kind is nothing but a <u>limitation imposed on giving.</u> ⁷And <u>by</u> this limitation you have limited [Ur: *your*] acceptance of the gift I offer <u>you</u>.

In this section, Jesus introduces the term "the time of Christ," which doubles both for the Christmas season and the holy instant. This implies that the Christmas season is meant to be a holy instant, in which we experience release from the past and from guilt, and restoration of our true power. This is the gift of release we are supposed to give Jesus. How do we give it to him? By seeing him in everyone and giving to everyone release from the past.

Is this how we celebrate Christmas now, by freeing everyone from the weight of their past sins? Or do we celebrate it by making sacrifices for others, sacrifices which obligate them to reciprocate? We think that by our sacrifices we are giving, but Jesus has something to tell us: Our sacrifice "is nothing but a *limitation imposed on giving*." And by limiting our giving, we limit what we can receive from Jesus.

> 3.   ¹We who are one cannot give separately. ²When you are willing to accept <u>our</u> relationship <u>as real</u>, guilt will hold <u>no</u> attraction for you. ³For in <u>our</u> union you will accept <u>all</u> of our brothers. ⁴The gift of union is the only gift that I was born to give. ⁵Give it to <u>me</u>, that <u>you</u> may have it. ⁶The time of Christ is the time appointed for the gift of freedom, offered to everyone. ⁷And by <u>your</u> acceptance of it, you offer it <u>to</u> everyone.

Now giving to Jesus what he gave to us is making more sense. He says here that he was born to give the gift of union. *That* is the gift we need to give to him. We need to unite with him. We do this by simply acknowledging that the relationship we have with him *is real*. He is not a figment of our imagination. He is real; he is there. By uniting with him, we gain everything. We unite with all our brothers, and having at last stopped withholding ourselves from them, we have no more cause for guilt. Finally, by accepting for ourselves this freedom from guilt and this union, we offer it to everyone.

Application: Say these words to Jesus:

> *Jesus, I accept that my relationship with you is real.*
> *I accept that you are really with me, that you are really there.*
> *I will no longer withhold myself from you.*
> *I give you the gift you gave me, the gift of joining.*
> *In doing so, I am willing to join with all that is in you,*

which includes all my brothers.
I will no longer withhold myself from them either.
And thus I will have no more cause for guilt.

4.   ¹It <u>is</u> in your power to make this season holy, for it is in your power to make the time of Christ be <u>now</u>. ²It is possible to do this all at once because there is but <u>one</u> shift in perception that is necessary, for you made but <u>one</u> mistake. ³It <u>seems</u> like many, but it is all the same. ⁴For though the ego takes many forms, it is <u>always</u> the same idea. ⁵What is <u>not</u> love is always fear, and nothing else.

We can make the Christmas season holy (imagine that!), because it is in our power to enter a holy instant whenever we want. There is only one shift we need make, for there is only one shift we made away from holiness. We shifted from love to fear, and now we must shift back. Every form the ego takes is nothing but a form of fear.

5.   ¹It is not necessary to follow fear through all the circuitous routes by which it burrows underground and hides in darkness, to emerge in <u>forms</u> quite different from what it <u>is</u>. ²Yet it <u>is</u> necessary to examine each one as long as you would retain the <u>principle</u> that governs all of them. ³When you are willing to regard them, <u>not</u> as separate, but as <u>different manifestations of the same idea</u>, and <u>one you do not want</u>, they go together.

The essence of all our symptoms is fear, which is described here as a kind of evil cicada that burrows underground, gestates for years, and then emerges so different in form that it is unrecognizable as the same creature that went into the ground.

This naturally prompts the perennial question: Do we need to dig down inside ourselves to uncover the real content and cause of every single symptom we want to heal? Yes and no. Yes, if we want to get rid of a symptom yet still retain the principle that is behind all symptoms. No, if we are willing to see that they are all just manifestations of one idea. If we discard this one idea, we discard every single symptom along with it. For this one idea, which we have not yet seen, is the source of all our fear.

⁴The idea is simply this: You believe it is possible to be host to the ego or hostage to God. ⁵This is the choice you think you have, and the decision you believe that you must make. ⁶You see no other alternatives, for you can<u>not</u> accept the fact that <u>sacrifice gets nothing</u>. ⁷Sacrifice is so essential to your thought system that salvation <u>apart</u> from sacrifice means <u>nothing</u> to you. ⁸Your confusion of sacrifice and love is so profound that you cannot conceive of love <u>without</u> sacrifice. ⁹And it is <u>this</u> that you must look upon; <u>sacrifice is attack, not love</u>. ¹⁰If you would accept but this <u>one</u> idea, your fear of love would vanish. ¹¹Guilt <u>cannot</u> last when the idea of sacrifice has been removed. ¹²For if there is [Ur: *must* be] sacrifice, [Ur: as you are convinced,] someone must pay and someone must get. ¹³And the <u>only</u> question that remains is <u>how much</u> is the price, and for getting <u>what</u>.

Now we are given the one idea behind all forms of fear: We believe that the only choice we have is being host to the ego or hostage to God. Given this idea, how could we not be afraid? Being hostage to God is clearly a terrifying idea. And being host to the ego is also fearful (thought not nearly *as* fearful), for the ego, however tolerable we think it is, makes constant demands of us. In other words, no matter where we turn—to the ego or to God—someone is making demands on us. Someone is asking us to make sacrifices. This is why we are *always* afraid. This is the source of every fear we have ever had or will have.

The problem is that we have confused love and sacrifice. We think that love equals sacrificing for someone else. However, as we've seen recently, sacrificing is designed to make someone guilty, so that he will sacrifice in return. And making someone guilty is an attack. This is why we are afraid of love—it means making constant sacrifices.

If we could just uncouple love and sacrifice, everything would change. We would no longer be afraid of love, and we would no longer feel guilty. Guilt is the inevitable product of sacrifice, which always involves someone losing so that you can gain. Have you ever felt guilty when someone made a sacrifice for you? Of course you have. Guilt and sacrifice are inextricably intertwined.

6. ¹As host to the ego, you believe that you can give <u>all</u> your guilt away whenever you want [Ur: *whatever* you think], and thereby purchase peace. ²And the payment <u>does not seem to be yours</u>. ³While it is obvious that the ego <u>does</u> demand payment it <u>never</u> seems to be

demanding it <u>of you</u>. ⁴You are unwilling to recognize that the ego, which you <u>invited</u>, is treacherous <u>only</u> to those who think they are its host. ⁵The ego will <u>never</u> let you perceive this, since this recognition would [Ur: *will*] make it homeless. ⁶For when the recognition dawns clearly, you will <u>not</u> be deceived by <u>any</u> form the ego takes to protect itself <u>from</u> your sight. ⁷Each form will be recognized as but a cover for the one idea that hides behind them all; that love demands sacrifice, and is therefore <u>inseparable</u> from attack and fear. ⁸And that <u>guilt is the price of love</u>, which <u>must</u> be paid <u>by</u> fear.

When you gain because someone sacrificed for you, you feel guilty. But you figure that's OK, because you can turn around and give your guilt to someone else, either by sacrificing for him, or by just blaming him. He pays to purchase *your* peace. This strategy should be familiar to all of us. What you don't realize is that you are the one who is paying. The ego requires sacrifice *only* of its host. It "will *never* let you perceive this," for this would uncover its deepest lie—the lie that while it may victimize others, it *serves* you. If you realized once and for all, that the ego you are so devoted to, the ego you defend and beautify and listen to, is nothing but a parasite that feeds on you, you would give this unholy guest the boot, permanently.

At this point, you would see that every form it takes—all the specialness and vanity and worry and heroism and drama of every kind—is nothing but a disguise for a single idea: that love is a constant demand made on the beloved: "Sacrifice for me, my love." In this view, love is just another form of attack. The price of "love," therefore, is guilt, guilt for always demanding of your lover. You pay the penalty for this guilt in the currency of fear, fear that, because you demanded, you will therefore be demanded *of*.

> 7. ¹How fearful, then, has God become to you, and how great a sacrifice do you believe His Love demands! ²For total love would demand total sacrifice. ³And so the ego seems to demand <u>less</u> of you than God, and of the two is judged as the <u>lesser</u> of two evils, one to be feared a little, perhaps, but the other <u>to be destroyed</u>. ⁴For you see love <u>as</u> destructive, and your only question is <u>who</u> is to be destroyed, you or another? ⁵You seek to answer this question in your special relationships, in which you seem to be both destroyer and destroyed <u>in part</u>, but able to be neither completely. ⁶And this you think <u>saves you from God</u>, Whose <u>total</u> Love would <u>completely</u> destroy you.

If love demands sacrifice, then being the lover is fearful, for the constant demands you put out make you feel guilty. But being on the other end, being the *loved*, is downright frightening, for now the demands are aimed at you. From this perspective, being loved by God is mortally terrifying, for His total Love would lead to infinite demands. He would be like the ultimate Jewish mother, shrewish wife, and celebrity stalker all rolled into one—I think the appropriate name is Jehovah—and you would be the hapless object of His affections. He will never stop demanding that you read the Bible, go to church, give alms, say your prayers, stop drinking, give up sex, etc., etc., etc. Are you starting to get a sense of your underlying fear of being hostage to God?

Little do we know it, but we are all running from this fear. We catch sight of the ego and immediately grab it and say, "Quick, save me from being devoured by God!" The ego says, "Well, I have some demands, but nothing like that Guy's." And we respond, "OK, fine, anything. Just save me!" It then lays out its plan to us: "You enter into these special relationships. You'll need to satisfy some demands, but you'll get to make some demands, too. Look, love is a bitch. It's all about devouring, and you'll need to let yourself be a little devoured. But the alternative is being *totally* devoured by God, and you don't want that, do you?"

Application: Think of your relationship with your most significant other. On a scale of 1 to 10, how devoured/demanded of do you feel? On a scale of 1 to 10, how devouring/demanding do you feel? Now realize that, however unhappy of a situation this is, somewhere inside you think this is great, because it saves you from being devoured by God, which, on a scale of 1 to 10, is 100.

8. ¹You think that everyone <u>outside</u> yourself demands your sacrifice, but you do <u>not</u> see that <u>only</u> you demand sacrifice, and <u>only</u> of yourself. ²Yet the demand of sacrifice is so savage and so fearful that you <u>cannot</u> accept it <u>where it is</u>. ³[Ur: But] The <u>real</u> price of <u>not</u> accepting this has been so great that you have <u>given God away</u> rather than look at it. ⁴For if <u>God</u> would demand total sacrifice of you, it seems safer to project Him outward and <u>away</u> from you, and <u>not</u> be host to Him. ⁵To Him you ascribed the <u>ego's</u> treachery, inviting it to take His place to <u>protect</u> you <u>from</u> Him. ⁶And you do not recognize that it is <u>what you invited in</u> that

would destroy you, and <u>does</u> demand total sacrifice of you. ⁷No partial sacrifice will appease this savage guest, for it is an invader who but <u>seems</u> to offer kindness, but <u>always</u> to <u>make the sacrifice complete</u>.

What a chilling paragraph! Just think: the person in the previous application whom you see as demanding sacrifice of you—that person doesn't extract *any* sacrifice from you whatsoever. You demand it all of yourself. For within you is the ego, which demands total sacrifice of you. This demand "is so savage and so fearful that you cannot accept it where it is"—*inside* you. You have to project it outward. So you project it onto others, and think the demand is coming from them, but it's not. And you project it onto God, and think that He is the ultimate demander. You therefore throw Him out of your mind, in fear that He'll require you to be a miserable old nun who has to kneel on cold stone floors chanting prayers at 2 in the morning, all to prove your love for Him. Instead of that horrific picture, you think, "No, I'll treat myself right. Instead of asking God in as my guest, I'll ask the ego. It will have me do fun things and stick up for myself and be an important person. With it as my guide, I'll suck the marrow out of life." You don't realize, of course, that you have invited in a totally savage presence that was the real source of all the demands you saw coming from the outside.

This reminds me of the 1970's movie, *When a Stranger Calls*. In that movie, a babysitter is in a house while the parents are out for dinner and the two children are upstairs sleeping. She keeps getting these phone calls in which a man creepily whispers, "Have you checked the children?" She lowers the blinds and locks the doors, worried that this person is out there and can see in, or even get in. Finally, she gets the police to trace the call and they call back in a panic saying that the call is coming from *inside* the house. The man had killed the children and was trying to lure the babysitter upstairs, where he was waiting for her.

We are afraid of the demanding nature we see in others or in God, and so we lock the doors and won't let them in. What we don't realize is that the real demand for sacrifice, the truly savage guest, is already inside the house, waiting to kill us.

9. ¹You will <u>not</u> succeed in being <u>partial</u> hostage to the ego, for it keeps <u>no</u> bargains and would leave you <u>nothing</u>. ²Nor can you be partial <u>host</u> to it. ³You must [Ur: will have to] choose between <u>total</u> freedom

and <u>total</u> bondage, for there are no alternatives but these. [4]You have tried many compromises in the attempt to avoid recognizing the one decision you <u>must</u> make [Ur: that *must* be made]. [5]And yet it is the <u>recognition</u> of the decision, *just as it is*, that makes the decision so easy [Ur: !]. [6]Salvation is simple, being of God, and therefore <u>very</u> easy to understand. [7][Ur: But] Do not try to project it <u>from</u> you and see it <u>outside</u> yourself. [8]In <u>you</u> are both the question and the answer; the demand for sacrifice and the peace of God.

Application: Take everything you have learned from this section and funnel all of it into the following dedication. Make it personal, for you are dealing here with the central issues of your existence.

> *I cannot be partial host to the ego.*
> *I cannot invite it in a little, for it is not a polite guest.*
> *It is an invader who will never be appeased.*
> *I cannot be partial hostage to the ego.*
> *It will cut no deals with me.*
> *Its goal is total dominance.*
> *I can never be hostage to God,*
>   *for He makes no demands.*
> *He only gives.*
> *My only choice, then, is total freedom in God*
>   *or total bondage to the ego.*
> *Who have I been fooling with all the compromises I have tried?*

XI. Christmas as the End of Sacrifice
Commentary by Robert Perry

1. ¹Fear not to recognize the whole idea of sacrifice as <u>solely of your making</u>. ²And seek not safety by attempting to <u>protect</u> yourself from where it is <u>not</u> [in your brothers and in your Father]. ³Your brothers and your Father have become <u>very</u> fearful to you. ⁴And you would bargain with them for a few special relationships, in which you think you see some scraps of safety. ⁵Do not try longer to <u>keep apart</u> your thoughts and the Thought that has been <u>given</u> you. ⁶When they are brought together and perceived <u>where they are</u>, the choice <u>between</u> them is nothing more than a gentle awakening, and as simple as opening your eyes to daylight when you have no more need of sleep.

We can see this paragraph in four stages. In the first stage, we are terrified of the level of demand for sacrifice that, if unchecked, would come at us from our brothers and our Father. So, in the second stage, we try to escape that demand by withdrawing behind the walls of our own private enclave, with only a few of our closest friends. Sure, they have their demands, but we get to demand some things from them as well. There is a give and take, and this protects us from the unmitigated "take" that we see in stage one. In the third stage, we realize that the demand for sacrifice was not coming from outside at all. It came entirely from inside of us. And so, in the fourth stage, we let this thought of sacrifice come face to face with the Thought God gave to us, the Holy Spirit. There we can see the choice between them is no choice at all.

2. ¹The sign of Christmas is a star, a light in darkness. ²See it not <u>outside</u> yourself, but shining in the Heaven within, and accept it as the sign the time of Christ has come. ³He comes demanding <u>nothing</u>. ⁴No sacrifice of <u>any</u> kind, of <u>anyone,</u> is asked by Him. ⁵In His Presence <u>the</u> whole <u>idea</u> of sacrifice loses <u>all</u> meaning. ⁶For He is Host to God. ⁷And you need but invite Him [God] in Who is there <u>already,</u> by recognizing that His [God's] Host is One [the oneness of all our brothers being united in Christ], and no thought <u>alien</u> to His [God's] Oneness can abide with Him [God] there. ⁸Love <u>must</u> be total [it must be love for

all] to give Him [God] welcome, for the Presence of holiness <u>creates</u> the holiness that surrounds it. ⁹No fear can touch the Host [Christ] Who cradles God in the time of Christ, for the Host [Christ] is as holy as the Perfect Innocence [God] which He [Christ] protects, and Whose power protects <u>Him</u>.

We are used to picturing the Christmas star shining in the skies of ancient Palestine as a supernatural sign that the Messiah, the Christ, had come. Now, however, Jesus asks us to transfer this image to the sky of our own mind, to see the star shining there, as a heavenly sign that the Christ has come to us, to be born in us in the holy instant, "the time of Christ." Try, then, imagining the Christmas star in your own mind, as a sign of the coming of Christ within you. It has a powerful effect.

Rather than coming to us demanding all kinds of sacrifice, Christ comes demanding nothing. He is the overturning of the idea of sacrifice and loss, for He comes bearing everything. He comes bearing God. How do we welcome God into ourselves? We enter a state of total love, in which we unite with all our brothers. We enter the holy instant.

3.   ¹This Christmas give the Holy Spirit <u>everything</u> that would hurt you. ²<u>Let</u> yourself be healed completely that you may <u>join</u> with Him in healing, and let us celebrate our release together by releasing everyone <u>with</u> us. ³Leave nothing behind, for release is <u>total</u>, and when you have accepted it <u>with</u> me you will <u>give</u> it with me. ⁴All pain and sacrifice and littleness will disappear in <u>our</u> relationship, which is as innocent as our relationship with our Father, and as powerful. ⁵Pain [the pain of others] will be brought to us and disappear in our presence, and <u>without</u> pain there can <u>be</u> no sacrifice. ⁶And <u>without</u> sacrifice there love *must* be.

I love the subtle irony of the first line. We are so used to ads that say, "This Christmas give..." The ads, of course, are a come-on to give some "amazing" product to our family and friends. Here, Jesus begins the same sentence, but ends it with "give the Holy Spirit everything that would hurt you." The recipient is the Holy Spirit, not your uncle, and the gift is your own inner sickness, not some spiffy electric shaver. The inner sickness here is surely the special relationship thought system, focused on demand, sacrifice, guilt, and exclusion.

If we will give it all over to the Holy Spirit, then we will join Him in His job of healing the world. And we will unite with Jesus, in a relationship so innocent that it heals anyone's pain that is brought to it. Picture someone coming to you with her pain, and your union with Jesus being so deep and solid that her pain simply vanishes in your presence.

> 4. ¹You who believe that sacrifice is love must learn that sacrifice is separation from love. ²For sacrifice brings guilt as surely as love brings peace. ³Guilt is the condition of sacrifice, as peace is the condition for the awareness of your relationship with God. ⁴[Ur: For] Through guilt you exclude your Father and your brothers from yourself [you sacrifice them, lose them]. ⁵[Ur: And] Through peace you [Ur: will] invite them back, realizing that they are where your invitation bids them be. ⁶What you exclude [Ur: *excluded*] from yourself seems fearful, for you endow [Ur: *endowed*] it with fear and try [Ur: tried] to cast it out, though it is [Ur: was] part of you. ⁷Who can perceive part of himself as loathsome, and live within himself in peace? ⁸And who can try to resolve the "conflict" of Heaven and hell in him by casting Heaven out and giving it the attributes of hell, without experiencing himself as incomplete and lonely?

We *do* believe that sacrifice is love. We demonstrate this belief every day, as we give to others with the thought "It's hard to give up this [time, effort, money], but I'm doing the loving thing. I'm thereby paying off my own debt, and I'm also indebting the other person to me." The alternative to this seems to be to refrain from giving, but that is just more ego. The real alternative is true giving, which Jesus defines this way: "A gift is holy only when there is no sense at all of who will gain thereby, and not a shadow of a thought of loss" (*The Gifts of God*, p. 124).

What does he mean by saying that guilt is the condition of sacrifice? He means that when you feel guilty, you automatically sacrifice your Father and brothers; you throw them outside yourself; you lose them. Why does guilt cause you to do this? In the current context, my guess is that once you feel guilty, you feel that you *deserve* to have others demand things of you, as your punishment. So now they appear to *be* demanding. To protect yourself, then, you must put distance between you and these insatiable demanders. You must throw them outside yourself. They still want to make demands on you, but at least they are at your front gate, not inside your bedroom.

Yet your Father and brothers—the ones you have cast out—are *part* of you. So what you have really done is label part of yourself as loathsome. How can you then live with yourself in peace? Your Father and brothers are the Heaven you long for. You have therefore assigned to Heaven the attributes of hell and then cast Heaven outside yourself. How can you then not feel incomplete and lonely?

> 5.   ¹As long as you perceive the body as your reality, so long will you perceive yourself as lonely and deprived. ²And so long will you also perceive yourself as a <u>victim of sacrifice, justified</u> in sacrificing others. ³For who could thrust Heaven and its Creator aside <u>without</u> a sense of sacrifice and loss? ⁴And who could suffer sacrifice and loss without attempting to <u>restore</u> himself? ⁵Yet how could you accomplish this yourself, when the basis of your attempts is the belief in the <u>reality of the deprivation</u>? ⁶Deprivation breeds attack, <u>being</u> the belief that attack is justified. ⁷And as long as you would <u>retain</u> the deprivation, attack becomes salvation and sacrifice becomes love.

As long as we see ourselves as a tiny body rather than a limitless spirit, we will feel profoundly deprived, victimized. Yet, of course, we put ourselves in this condition; no one else did. Having fallen so far from our infinite estate, we will naturally try to restore our magnitude. But, unfortunately, we will do so within the belief that we really have been deprived, that others took our magnitude from us. Within this belief, there is only one solution: We have to take magnitude from *them*, both through direct attack and through "generous" sacrifices designed to obligate them. We set about twisting their arms, both obviously and subtly, to fill the hole in us.

> 6.   ¹So is it that, in all your seeking for love, <u>you seek for sacrifice</u> and <u>find</u> it. ²Yet you find <u>not</u> love. ³It is impossible to <u>deny</u> what love <u>is</u> and still recognize it. ⁴The meaning of love lies in what you have cast <u>outside</u> yourself, and it <u>has</u> no meaning [Ur: at all] <u>apart</u> from you. ⁵It is what you prefer to <u>keep</u> that has no meaning, while all that you would <u>keep away</u> holds all the meaning of the universe, and holds the universe together in its meaning. ⁶[Ur: For] Unless the universe were joined in you it would be <u>apart from</u> God, and to be without Him *is* to be without meaning.

We are desperately, relentlessly trying to get others to sacrifice for us, and thus prove their love. And, to some degree, they actually obey. But then we don't end up feeling truly loved. The reason is simple: *Sacrifice is not love*. Their sacrifices are not expressions of real love. These people are just paying off their guilt, and we know it.

The real meaning of love lies in our Father and brothers, whom we have cast outside ourselves. What we have kept within—the ego—has no meaning at all. We are like a father who has kicked out of the house his beloved wife and children so that he can be alone with his beautiful inflatable doll.

Real love lies in our union with the place inside us where our Father and brothers forever dwell. When we at last find this love, we won't need to take "love" from other bodies.

> 7.   ¹In the holy instant the condition of love is met, for minds are joined without the body's <u>interference,</u> and where there is communication there is peace. ²The Prince of Peace was born to re-establish the <u>condition</u> of love [which is peace] by teaching that communication remains unbroken even if the body is destroyed, <u>provided that</u> you see <u>not</u> the body as the necessary means of communication. ³And if you <u>understand</u> this lesson, you will realize that to sacrifice the <u>body</u> is to <u>sacrifice nothing</u>, and communication, which <u>must</u> be of the mind, <u>cannot</u> be sacrificed [lost]. ⁴Where, then, *is* sacrifice? ⁵The lesson I was born to teach, and still would teach to all my brothers, is that sacrifice is nowhere and love is everywhere. ⁶For communication <u>embraces everything</u>, and in the peace it re-establishes, love comes of itself.

This paragraph ties the meaning of Christmas in with the resurrection, the holy instant, communication, peace, and love. Let me try to capture the gist of it.

Jesus was born to be resurrected. He was born to show that even if his body was destroyed, his mind could still be in communication with his followers. This is the remarkable state of affairs that sparked early Christianity. Jesus had been killed, yet his followers were still having encounters with him. They were still in communication with him. Unfortunately, they interpreted this incorrectly, thinking that he had made a righteous sacrifice by sacrificing his own body and had thus been elevated to the right hand of God. What they could have understood is that by letting his body be killed he had sacrificed *nothing*. They could have seen his continuing presence as proof that nothing—not even death—can truly get in the way of the joining of minds. The union of brothers transcends the body. Bodies come and bodies go, but our relationships with each other are forever.

However little they understood it, this is what Jesus' followers experienced in those holy instants they shared with him after Easter Sunday. And this is what we can experience with him now. In this communication of minds, in which bodies cannot interfere with the sacred joining of God's holy Sons, we at last know peace. We at last know that nothing can rob us of our bond with our dear, beloved brothers. And in this peace, it finally dawns on us what love really means. Jesus was born to help this dawning occur.

> 8. ¹Let no despair darken the joy of Christmas, for the time of Christ is meaningless <u>apart</u> from joy. ²Let us join in celebrating peace by demanding no sacrifice of anyone, for so you offer me the love I offer you. ³What can be more joyous than to perceive <u>we are deprived of nothing</u>? ⁴Such is the message of the time of Christ, which I give you that <u>you</u> may give it [to others] and [thereby] return it to the Father, Who gave it to me. ⁵For in the time of Christ communication is restored, and He joins us in the celebration of His Son's creation.

We are starting to get a sense of how Jesus sees Christmas. To him, it represents entering the time of Christ, the holy instant. In this joyous instant, we join with Jesus and our brothers in the Heaven within, in the Kingdom we share with them. In this place, we are complete and nothing can rob us of our completion. In celebration of this, we release everyone from their past and from our demands. If we do this, we return to Jesus the gift he gave us, and even return the gift to God. God then joins us in celebrating the original Christmas—our birth as God's Son in Heaven.

> 9. ¹God offers thanks to the holy host [you] who would receive Him [in the holy instant], and lets Him enter and abide where He would be. ²And <u>by</u> your welcome does He welcome you into Himself, for what is contained in you who welcome Him is <u>returned</u> to Him. ³And we but celebrate <u>His</u> Wholeness as we welcome Him into ourselves. ⁴Those who receive the Father are one with Him, being host to Him

Who created them. [5]And by allowing Him to enter, the remembrance of the Father enters with Him, and with Him they remember the only relationship they ever had, and ever want to have.

This paragraph describes what we might call the further reaches of the holy instant. In the full-blown, final holy instant, we welcome God all the way into ourselves. As we do, He welcomes us into Himself; our mind is returned to Him. The memory of Him (the full, permanent awakening to Him) enters with Him, and we at last remember the only relationship we ever had, or ever want to have, our precious union with our Father.

10. [1]This is the time [Ur: week-end] in which a new year will soon be born from the time of Christ [Saturday was December 31, 1966 and Sunday was January 1, 1967]. [2]I have perfect faith in you to do all that you would accomplish. [3]Nothing will be lacking, and you will make complete and not destroy. [4]Say, then, to your brother [Ur: Say and *understand* this]:

> [5]*I give you to the Holy Spirit as part of myself.*
> [6]*I know that you will be released, unless I want to use you to imprison myself.*
> [7]*In the name of my freedom I choose* [Ur: *will*] *your release, because I recognize that we will be released together.*

[8]So will the year begin in joy and freedom. [9]There is much to do, and we have been long delayed. [10]Accept the holy instant as this year is born, and take your place, so long left unfulfilled, in the Great Awakening. [11]Make this year different by making it all the same. [12]And let all your relationships be made holy for you. [13]This is our will. [14]Amen.

As the new year of 1967 was about to be born from Christmastime 1966, Jesus was asking that a new *kind* of year be born from entering the *real* time of Christ. He was asking Helen and Bill to celebrate Christmas truly, by releasing a brother (probably each other) from all their demands. If they could do this, and do it sincerely, they would experience the time of Christ (the holy instant). Out of this, they would embark on a new kind of year. In this genuinely new year, rather than riding the rollercoaster of ever-changing purpose, they would experience the sameness that comes from having one purpose and one purpose only. This purpose would be standing next to Jesus and taking their part in the Great Awakening.

If so much could have come in their lives from just releasing one brother, it makes you wonder what might happen in *our* lives if we really did this practice and truly entered the time of Christ.

Application: Pick someone whom you have chained to your demands. First, reflect briefly on some of the demands you have laid on this person. Then choose to free him or her by sincerely repeating these words, over and over, until you feel the release. Realize that these words have the power to free both of you from prison, handing you a truly different future.

> *I give you to the Holy Spirit as part of myself.*
> *I know that you will be released,*
> > *unless **I** want to use **you** to imprison myself.*
> *In the name of **my** freedom I **will** your release,*
> > *because I recognize that we will be released **together**.*

Commentaries on Chapter 16

THE FORGIVENESS
OF ILLUSIONS

I. True Empathy
Commentary by Robert Perry

1. To empathize does not mean to join in suffering, for that is what you must *refuse* to understand. That is the ego's interpretation of empathy, and is always used to form a special relationship in which the suffering [Ur: in which *suffering*] is shared. The capacity to empathize is very useful to the Holy Spirit, provided you let Him use it in His way. His way is very different. He does not understand suffering, and would have you teach it is not understandable. When He relates through you, He does not relate through your ego to another ego. He does not join in pain, understanding that healing pain is not accomplished by delusional attempts to enter into it, and lighten it by sharing the delusion.

This section opens by saying that "To empathize does not mean to join in suffering." Yet that, of course, is exactly what it normally means. Empathy is:

> the action of understanding, being aware of, being sensitive to, and vicariously experiencing the feelings, thoughts, and experience of another of either the past or present without having the feelings, thoughts, and experience fully communicated in an objectively explicit manner; *also* : the capacity for this. (Merriam-Webster online)

Empathy means to share someone's feelings, especially (in this context) that person's feelings of pain. The idea is that you *understand* what someone is feeling, and through understanding it, you *validate* it, and through seeing the validity in it, you *feel* it with her. Finally, by feeling it with her, you lighten her suffering, for now she is not alone and she is not crazy—her feelings have been validated by someone else who is seeing and feeling the same thing she is.

Jesus, then, is taking exception with empathy itself, at least as we understand it. We can group this paragraph's criticisms into two basic ideas. First, empathy is based on *understanding* someone's suffering, and Jesus is saying that suffering is not understandable—meaning, it makes no sense. The paragraph even calls suffering "delusional." If suffering is delusional, then you release someone from suffering by helping her wake up from the delusion. Yet how can you do this if you yourself enter into the delusion and share it?

The second criticism is that empathy is really about the joining of egos. I get that from the line "relate through your ego to another ego." That's what empathy is, isn't it? Your ego is looking at another ego's suffering and saying, "I can relate." In doing that, you are validating that person's identity as an ego, and you are validating your own at the same time. And one more thing is going on. You are forming a special relationship with that ego. You are saying, "Others may not get your pain, but I get it. I am the one who understands. I'm there for you." So you are validating that person's identity as a *suffering* ego, and putting forth your identity as an *understanding* ego, and forming a bond which is the special joining of those two ego identities.

> 2. The clearest proof that empathy as the ego uses it is <u>destructive</u> lies in the fact that it is applied <u>only</u> to certain types of problems and in certain people. These it <u>selects out</u>, and <u>joins with</u>. And it <u>never</u> joins except to strengthen itself. Having identified with what it <u>thinks</u> it understands, the ego sees <u>itself</u> and would <u>increase</u> itself by sharing what is <u>like</u> itself. Make no mistake about this maneuver; the ego always <u>empathizes to weaken</u>, and to weaken is <u>always</u> to attack. You do <u>not</u> know what empathizing means. Yet of this you may be sure; if you will merely sit quietly by and let the Holy Spirit relate <u>through</u> you, you will <u>empathize with strength</u>, and will gain in strength and <u>not</u> in weakness.

This paragraph really gets to the dark underbelly of empathy. First, it notes that we don't empathize across the board, with all problems in all people. Rather, we are quite selective. The reason is not pretty. We pick those particular people because their ego is like our ego. And we pick those particular problems because their problems are like our problems. In other words, in empathizing with them, we are really seeing our own ego getting beat up by the world, and we are validating what a terrible injustice that is. With our empathy, we are really saying, "When that was done to me, how wrong they were, and how right I was!" By empathizing with them, then, we are validating our own ego. They think we are supporting them, validating them, cheering them on, but while we look at them, they don't realize that we are really staring at our own reflection in their mirror, and validating *that*.

So our ego is really just trying to strengthen itself. And as the paragraph goes on to say, it is also trying to weaken the other. How do we weaken the other with our empathy? The section doesn't really elaborate on this, but I suspect that we weaken them simply by affirming their weakness, their victimization at the hands of the world. The paragraph's later recommendation that we empathize with strength implies that right now we are empathizing with that person's weakness, with their image of being a weak, vulnerable ego under attack by the world. And what we empathize with, we reinforce. By empathizing with their weakness, then, we weaken them. Thus, we end up attacking the very person who we are trying to support.

The solution is to realize that we have no clue what empathizing means. Our job is to step back—to sit quietly by—and let the Holy Spirit relate through us. And if we do, He will empathize with that person's strength. We'll explore what that means later.

> 3. Your part is only to remember this; you do not want anything <u>you</u> value to come of a relationship. You choose neither to hurt it <u>nor to heal it</u> in your own way. You do <u>not</u> know what healing <u>is</u>. All you have learned of empathy <u>is from the past</u>. And there is <u>nothing</u> from the past that you would share, for there is nothing from the past that <u>you would keep</u>. Do <u>not</u> use empathy to <u>make the past real</u>, and so perpetuate it. Step gently aside, and let healing be done <u>for</u> you. Keep but one thought in mind and do not lose sight of it, however tempted you may be to judge any situation, and to <u>determine</u> your response *by* judging it. Focus your mind only on this:
>
> *I am not alone, and I would not intrude the past upon my Guest.*
> *I have invited Him, and He is here.*
> *I need do nothing except <u>not to interfere</u>.*

This is radical counsel. Try to forget all those things you want to come of a relationship. Don't go after them. Try to realize you don't really want them. If you try to heal the relationship in your way you'll just make the past real and thereby perpetuate it. This, in its most immediate context, refers to the fact that we learned what empathy is in the past.

But taking in a slightly broader context, it means, as we saw in the last paragraph, that what we empathize with is those things that remind us of our own past victimization. Thus, as long as we focus on empathy as conventionally understood, we cannot let go of our past.

Then we are given a priceless practice for letting the Holy Spirit relate through us (which we'll do at the end). Let's break this practice down:

I am not alone: The Holy Spirit is with me.

Intrude the past upon: to thrust my past ideas about empathy, and my past wounds, upon the Holy Spirit

My Guest: The Holy Spirit

I have invited Him: through my answering of God's Call—putting my feet on the path. The invitation need not be a recent or explicit one.

I need do nothing: The Holy Spirit will come through me and heal this person. It's not my job to heal this person.

Except not to interfere: I need only step aside, realizing I don't want what I value to come of the relationship, realizing I don't know what healing is, realizing I don't know what empathy is.

The essential dynamic here is that you have, through putting your feet on the path, invited the Holy Spirit into your life. He is your invited Guest, and He is here. Yet by trying to help this person in your way, with your ideas of how it should be done, you intrude your past on Him, which is a very rude way to treat an invited guest, especially a guest who is here to do a job for you. He's not an intruder, so why intrude on Him? Greg came up with this analogy. You invite a contractor over to do a job in your house, but then you smother him with all your ideas of how he should do his job, getting in his way, and essentially making him unable to do it. Greg said, "Those guys just hate that."

Our goal, then, is to step aside, get out of the way, and let the Holy Spirit do His job. He's the expert, why not let Him work? How does He want to relate through us to this person? What does He want to say? How does He want to empathize with this person?

I'd like to return to the earlier statement of empathizing with strength. We are prone to empathizing with the person's weakness, with their vulnerability, their fragility. The Holy Spirit, as we saw, wants to empathize with their strength. Yet, of course, they aren't feeling their strength right now. That's why they want our empathy. How can the Holy Spirit, then, empathize with their strength when they aren't feeling it? The whole nature of empathy is that you feel what *they* are feeling. For empathizing with strength to be legitimately called empathy, then, we have to assume that on some unconscious level they *are* feeling their strength. What the Holy Spirit does, therefore, is to feel with them something they aren't consciously feeling right now. And by feeling it with them, to bring it into their consciousness. Somewhere inside, they are feeling their strength, and by Him empathizing with that buried part of them, He is siding with it, and thus reinforcing it.

> 4. True empathy is of Him Who knows what it is. <u>You</u> will learn <u>His</u> interpretation of it if you let Him use <u>your</u> capacity [for empathy] for [the sake of] strength, and <u>not</u> for weakness. He will <u>not</u> desert you, but be sure that <u>you</u> desert not Him. Humility is strength in this sense only; that to recognize and <u>accept</u> the fact that you do <u>not</u> know is to recognize and accept the fact that He *does* know. You are not sure that He will do His part, because you have <u>never yet done yours completely</u>. You cannot [Ur: will *not*] know how to respond to what you do <u>not</u> understand. Be tempted not in this, and yield not to the ego's triumphant use of empathy for <u>its</u> glory.

This paragraph largely reiterates earlier points. You have a capacity for empathy, but you can use it to empathize with your brother's weakness or strength. Step aside. Realize you don't know how to use empathy, and let the Holy Spirit relate through you.

This naturally raises doubts in us about whether or not the Holy Spirit will actually come in and relate through us. This says that we only doubt that because we have never fully stepped aside and given place to Him.

> 5. The triumph of weakness is <u>not</u> what you would offer to a brother. ²And yet you recognize no triumph but this. ³This is <u>not</u> knowledge, and the form of empathy which would bring this about is so distorted that it would imprison what it would release. ⁴The unredeemed cannot redeem, yet they <u>have</u> a Redeemer. ⁵Attempt to teach Him not. ⁶<u>You</u> are the learner; <u>He</u> the Teacher. ⁷Do not confuse your role with His, for this will <u>never</u> bring peace to anyone. ⁸Offer your empathy to Him for it is *His* perception and *His* strength [Ur: His *strength*] that you would

share. ⁹And let Him offer you His strength and His perception, to be shared through you.

We need to realize just how hopeless we are when it comes to empathy. We think we are helping, but we are actually bringing about the triumph of weakness. We are imprisoning the one we would release. So again, we need to step back and let the Holy Spirit's perception and strength move through us to be shared with our brother.

> 6. The meaning of love is lost in any relationship that looks to weakness, and hopes to find love there. The power of love, which *is* its meaning, lies in the strength of God that hovers over it [the relationship] and blesses it silently by enveloping it in healing wings. Let this be, and do not try to substitute your "miracle" for this.

Conventional empathy seeks to establish relationships on the basis of joining in our victimhood. It seeks to offer a "miracle" by commiserating with another's weakness. Yet while we struggle to be the caring helper, there is a Power, a divine Guest, that hovers over the relationship and "blesses it silently by enveloping it in healing wings." Our job is merely to let this Power be.

> I have [Ur: We once] said that if a brother asks a foolish thing of you to do it. But be certain that this does not mean to do a foolish thing that would hurt either him or you, for what would hurt one will hurt the other. Foolish requests are foolish merely because they conflict [Ur: for the simple reason *that they conflict*], since they always contain some element of specialness. Only the Holy Spirit recognizes foolish needs as well as real ones. And He will teach you how to meet both without losing either.
> 7. *You* will attempt to do this only in secrecy. And you will think that by meeting the needs of one you do not jeopardize another, because you keep them separate and secret from each other. That is not the way, for it leads not to life and truth. No needs will long be left unmet if you leave them all to Him Whose function is to meet them. That is His function, and not yours. He will not meet them secretly, for He would share everything you give through Him. [Ur: And] That is why He gives it. What you give through Him is for the whole Sonship, not for part of it. Leave Him His function, for He will fulfill it if you but ask Him to enter your relationships, and bless them for you.

The above material is the famous caveat to the sentence from "The Investment in Reality": "*Recognize what does not matter*, and if your brothers ask you to do something 'outrageous,' do it *because* it does not matter" (T-12.III.4:1). This caveat really has two contexts: the earlier outrageous request discussion and the empathy discussion in this section. Given both contexts, here is what I see it as meaning:

If a brother comes to you, asking you to empathize (in the conventional sense), that is a foolish request—foolish, because he is asking you to side with him against someone else; he is asking you to give him special treatment. This is not a request you should honor—at least at face value—for it will bring hurt. Yet there is a real need underneath this foolish one, and if you follow the Holy Spirit, He can tell you how to meet the foolish one and the real one at the same time. In this case, He will have you meet the request for empathy with a *different kind* of empathy, an empathy that doesn't hurt anyone, an empathy that is for the whole Sonship, not just for part of it.

This is a feat that your empathy can't pull off. What you will try to do is meet this person's needs by siding with him against the one who "caused" his pain. Then you will try to keep what you said secret from that other person, the person you are both siding against. By keeping it secret from that person, you hope to avoid hurting him.

I think we have all been there, haven't we? You commiserate with one person, and then hope to God that the other guy—the one you commiserated *about*—doesn't find out. Something always feels wrong about that, but it seems like there is no other way to support the person in front of you. The message of this section is that, left to your own devices, there is no other way. Yet with the Holy Spirit's guidance, there is. He will empathize through you in a way that only empowers all concerned. Wouldn't that be an incredible relief?

Application: For this exercise, which will be long, please choose a situation in which you have felt called on to offer empathy as conventionally understood. It may have been a one-time request. It will be even better, though, if it is an ongoing situation, where you are asked again and again to offer empathy to the same person regarding the same situation. There must be someone in your life who has asked or repeatedly asks you to empathize, sympathize, commiserate, or understand their pain. Once you've chosen something, write the situation here and then follow the instructions below.

Are you empathizing with a problem and a person that reminds you of yourself being mistreated in the past? If so, what past injustices against you come to mind?

Did your ego feel secretly vindicated about its own past victimization by your empathizing with this person? Can you put this sense of vindication into a sentence (e.g., "When they did that same thing to me, they were wrong and I was right")?

Do you see how you were giving this person the message that they are weak and frail? Try saying silently to them, "You are weak and frail and vulnerable, at the mercy of countless attackers." How does that feel?

How does it feel to imagine that, by empathizing, your ego was trying to strengthen itself and weaken the other person?

What kind of special bond were you trying to form through your empathy? Try to put it into the following form: "Because I empathize, I show this person that I am the one who _____ and that therefore I deserve _____ from this person in the future."

By empathizing, did you subtly join in blaming the person who supposedly caused your friend's suffering? If so, did you try to therefore keep secret what you said, so that the one who "caused" her suffering wouldn't find out what you said? Who were you trying to keep the secret from?

Try to realize that you really don't know what will strengthen this person, what will help the relationship, and what will strengthen you. Say to yourself,

> *I am not alone, and I would not intrude the past upon my Guest.*
> *I have invited Him, and He is here.*
> *I need do nothing, except not to interfere.*

Say it again. Imagine this divine Guest hovering over the relationship and blessing it silently by enveloping it in healing wings. *Just let this be.* Feel the relief of not having to figure out how to help this person. Feel the relief of being able to empower all concerned. Feel the relief at being able to sit quietly by and do nothing. Trust that if you really step aside, the Holy Spirit will relate through you, and do a better job than you ever could alone.

Now try to let Him see this person through your eyes. He is looking for this person's strengths, the very strengths that could deliver them in this situation. Let Him look through you and see their strengths. Then write down whatever He sees through you.

Now try to feel Him identifying with those strengths. Join with Him in *feeling with* those strengths, feeling the strength that those strengths feel.

Now try to let Him relate through you, relating to those strengths, conveying His empathy with those strengths, and thereby drawing those strengths to the surface. What does He say through you? Please write it down.

II. The Power of Holiness
Commentary by Robert Perry

1. You may still think that holiness is impossible to understand [Ur: You still think holiness is difficult], because you cannot see how it can be extended to include <u>everyone</u>. And you have been told [Ur: *have* learned] that it <u>must</u> include everyone to *be* holy. Concern yourself not with the <u>extension</u> of holiness, for the nature of miracles you do <u>not</u> understand. Nor do you <u>do</u> them. It is their extension, far beyond the limits you perceive, that demonstrates you do <u>not</u> do them. Why should you worry how the miracle extends to all the Sonship when you do not understand the miracle itself? One <u>attribute</u> is no more difficult to understand than is the whole. If miracles *are* at all, their attributes would have to be miraculous, being <u>part</u> of them.

This paragraph sets out the problem. We have learned that real holiness extends miracles to literally everyone. Our next thought seems understandable: "But I have no clue how to extend a miracle to the entire Sonship. And if I can't understand it, how can I do it? The whole holiness enterprise sounds incredibly difficult to me."

Jesus' response, at least in this paragraph, is twofold. First, you don't do miracles, so don't worry about not understanding them. Someone else does them through you. Second, why worry about not understanding this particular attribute of miracles when you don't understand the whole *nature* of miracles?

2. There is a tendency to fragment, and then to be concerned about the truth of just a little <u>part</u> of the whole. And this is but a way of avoiding, or looking <u>away from</u> the whole, to what you think you might be better able to understand. For [Ur: And] this is but another way in which you would still try to keep understanding <u>to yourself</u>. A better and <u>far</u> more helpful way to think of miracles is this: You do <u>not</u> understand them, either in part <u>or</u> in whole. Yet they have been done through you [Ur: Yet you have *done* them]. Therefore <u>your</u> understanding <u>cannot</u> be necessary. Yet it is still impossible to accomplish what you do not understand. And so there must be Something <u>in</u> you that *does* understand.

196

The first sentences use a principle that Jesus employs several times, mostly in personal guidance to Helen. The principle is this: When you are faced with a whole that seems too big for you to understand and deal with, you will narrow your focus down to some tiny aspect of it, one that you think you can manage. Then you will suppose that by managing this one aspect, you have magically got the whole thing under control. It's a neurotic coping mechanism. This is what we are doing by troubling ourselves over how miracles can extend to the entire Sonship—thinking that if we can grasp this one aspect of miracles, we have grasped the whole thing. This is an attempt to preserve our sense that we understand, that we are in control.

We need to just give it up. We need to say to ourselves, "Look, I don't understand miracles at all, either in part *or* in whole. But that's okay, for Something in me understands them, and Its understanding is what has enabled me to actually do them."

> 3. To you the miracle <u>cannot</u> seem natural, because what you have done to hurt your mind [Ur: minds] has made it [Ur: *them*] so <u>un</u>natural that it does [Ur: they do] not remember what is natural to it [Ur: them]. And when you are told what is natural [Ur: *told* about it], you cannot <u>understand</u> it. The recognition of the part as whole, and of the whole in every part is <u>perfectly</u> natural, for it is the way <u>God</u> thinks, and what is natural to Him <u>is</u> natural to you. <u>Wholly</u> natural perception would show you instantly that order of difficulty in miracles is quite impossible, for it involves a contradiction of what miracles <u>mean</u>. And if you could understand their <u>meaning</u>, their <u>attributes</u> could hardly cause you perplexity.

It doesn't seem natural to us that a miracle could go out from one mind and reach *all* minds. Yet that is because we have put our minds in an unnatural condition. We have turned ourselves into dummies. In our minds' natural condition, they think exactly as God thinks. In this state, they innately understand that the whole Sonship is quite literally *inside* every mind. And if this is true, how could a miracle in one mind *not* affect all minds? If our minds were in their natural condition, we would immediately understand that nothing is too difficult for miracles, not even raising the dead or reaching every mind in the universe. For we would grasp what miracles really mean, and in light of that meaning, every aspect of miracles would make perfect sense.

4. You <u>have</u> done miracles, but it is <u>quite</u> apparent that you have <u>not</u> done them alone. You have succeeded whenever you have reached another mind and <u>joined</u> with it. When two minds join as one and share one idea equally, the first link in the awareness of the Sonship as one has been made. When you have made this joining as the Holy Spirit bids you, and have <u>offered</u> it to Him to use as He sees fit [Ur: as *He* knows how], His natural perception of your gift [the joining?] enables <u>Him</u> to understand it, and <u>you</u> to <u>use</u> His understanding on <u>your</u> behalf.

Here we find out that miracles are not only a collaborative venture with the Holy Spirit, but they are also a collaborative venture with the miracle receiver. The miracle succeeds when you give a healing idea to another person and that person joins with you in that idea, sharing it equally with you. Can you think of times in your life when this has happened, when you gave an idea to someone in need (even if it was just the idea of love), and that person really joined you in that idea? It is a wonderful experience. And it is the first step in the broken pieces of the Sonship being put back together again.

Yet we need the Holy Spirit to really effect this joining. He is the only one that really understands it, and so He needs to guide us into it. Without Him, it can't happen. Therefore, if it does happen, it means that He was there, helping, even if we weren't aware of it.

It is impossible to convince you of the reality of what has clearly <u>been</u> accomplished through your willingness while you believe that <u>you</u> must understand it or else <u>it</u> is not real. [Ur: You think your *lack* of understanding is a *loss* to you, and so you are unwilling to believe that what *has* happened is true. Yet can you *really* believe that all that has happened, *even though* you do *not* understand it, *has not happened*? Yet this *is* your position. You would have *perfect* faith in the Holy Spirit, and in the *effects* of His teaching, if you were not *afraid* to acknowledge what He taught you. For this acknowledgement *means* that what has happened you do *not* understand, but that you are willing to *accept* it, *because* it has happened.]

Now Jesus' real point starts becoming clear. Helen and Bill's demand that they need to understand how miracles work was getting in the way of them acknowledging all the miracles that had actually happened in their lives. Think of all that happened as the Course began to come through.

We still tell the stories decades later. Yet, in the midst of it, one suspects that Helen and Bill were not quite as floored by it all. The problem, Jesus says here, is that they had adopted the stance, "What I cannot understand cannot happen." This led directly to the insane stance, "Even if I saw it happen, if I can't understand it, then it must not have really happened." This led them to devalue the miracles that had occurred right before their eyes.

This sounds crazy, but it is a common human response. In fact, I see it as the dominant attitude of modern science toward the paranormal and mystical: "If we don't have a theory that can make sense of it, then it can't be." We also carry this attitude in our own lives. We might have some amazing experience, yet because it doesn't fit into our framework for reality, it gets mentally discarded, like a puzzle piece that doesn't fit the puzzle we are working on.

> 5. How can faith in reality be yours while you are bent on making it <u>unreal</u>? And are you <u>really</u> safer in maintaining the reality of illusions [Ur: the *un*reality of what has happened,] than you would be in joyously accepting truth [Ur: it] <u>for what it is,</u> and giving thanks for it? Honor the truth that has been given you, and be glad you do <u>not</u> understand it. Miracles are natural to [Ur: God, and to] the One Who speaks for God [Ur: Him]. For His task is to <u>translate</u> the miracle into the knowledge which it <u>represents,</u> and which <u>is</u> hidden [Ur: lost] to you. Let <u>His</u> understanding of the miracle be enough for you, and do not turn away from all the witnesses that He has given you to His reality.

Application: Try to write down one or two (or more) miraculous things that have happened to you, things that seemed to come from a higher place and could have changed your whole framework for reality, yet which instead faded too quickly from view because they seemed impossible to understand or explain. Now hear Jesus speaking to you about these experiences:

> How can faith in reality be yours, [name], while you are bent on making it *un*real?
> And are you really safer in maintaining the *un*reality of what has happened, than you would be in joyously accepting it *for what*

it is, and giving thanks for it?

Honor the truth that has been given you, [name], and be glad you do *not* understand it.

Miracles are natural to God, and to the One Who speaks for Him....

Let *His* understanding of the miracle be enough for you, [name], and do not turn away from all the witnesses that He has given you to His reality.

6. No evidence will convince you of the truth of what you do not want. Yet your relationship with Him is real * [Ur: and *has* been demonstrated]. Regard this not with fear, * but with rejoicing. The One you called upon *is* with you *. Bid Him welcome, and honor the witnesses who bring you the glad tidings He has come. It is true, just as you fear, * that to acknowledge Him is to deny all that you think you know. But what you think you know [Ur: But it] was never true. What gain is there to you * in clinging to it, and denying the evidence for truth? For * you have come too near to truth to renounce it now, and you *will* yield to its compelling attraction. You can delay this now, * but only a little while. The Host of God has called to you, and you have heard. Never again will you be wholly willing not to listen.

I hope you could think of some examples in the previous application (if you couldn't, you might want to take another crack at it), because they would make all of this make perfect sense. The Holy Spirit does act in our lives. Things do happen that are witnesses of His presence. And when these witnesses show up, we do quite often file them in the "Could that have been real?" file. Jesus is making a plea here for us to reverse that reaction. Rather than letting our current framework discard these entries of the Holy Spirit into our lives, he is asking us to let these experiences overturn our current framework. Please reread the paragraph now with this in mind, treating it as Jesus' personal plea to you and inserting your name at the asterisks.

7. This is a year of joy, in which your listening will increase and peace will grow with its increase. The power of holiness and the weakness of attack are both being brought into your awareness [Ur: have *both* been

brought into awareness]. And this has been accomplished in a mind [Ur: in minds] firmly convinced that holiness is weakness and attack is power. Should not this be a sufficient miracle to teach you that your Teacher is <u>not</u> of you? But remember also that whenever you listened to <u>His</u> interpretation the results have brought <u>you</u> joy. Would you <u>prefer</u> the results of <u>your</u> interpretation, considering honestly what they have been? God wills you better. Could you not look with greater charity on whom God loves with perfect love?

Jesus now folds the theme of the new year (which was begun at the very end of Chapter 15) into his plea that Helen and Bill really take stock of the miracles that have happened to them and through them. Hear what he is saying to them as if he is saying it to you:

"You have seen the power of holiness flow through you and produce miracles. From this, you are starting to learn that attack is actually weak, and that the real power lies in defenseless holiness. Isn't this a miracle in itself, given that you used to believe the exact opposite? Doesn't this show that Someone from beyond your thought system has become your Teacher? Isn't it also true that His interpretations, when you have listened to them, have made you far happier than your own? Face it—He is kinder to you than you are. This is the year to look at all this and make sense of it. This year, put your will behind what your experience has already proven to you."

> 8. Do not interpret <u>against</u> God's Love [Ur: for you], for you have many witnesses that speak of it so clearly that only the blind and deaf could fail to see and hear them. This year determine <u>not</u> to deny what has been given you <u>by</u> God. [Ur: He has <u>Himself</u> reminded you of Him] Awake and <u>share</u> it, for that is the only reason He has called to you. His Voice has spoken clearly, and yet you have so little faith in what you heard, because you have preferred to place still greater faith in the disaster <u>you</u> have made. Today, let us resolve <u>together</u> to accept the joyful tidings that disaster is <u>not</u> real and that reality is <u>not</u> disaster. Reality is safe and sure, and wholly kind to everyone and everything. There is no greater love than to accept this and be glad. For love asks only that <u>you be happy</u>, and will <u>give</u> you everything that makes for happiness.

Now we see the essential rub between our current framework and

201

what the miracles in our lives would tell us. It is this: Our framework is cruel to us, while the miracles (the "witnesses") testify that God loves us. Our framework amounts to faith in the disaster we have made. That, we are convinced, is the most real thing there is. The miracles, on the other hand, speak of a reality that "is safe and sure, and wholly kind to everyone and everything." How can we give our faith to that reality, no matter how convincing its witnesses are, when we know that the bottom line of our existence is the terrible mess we've made of things?

Jesus is again calling us to wake up, open our eyes. We are so lost in our hand-wringing and morbid self-pity and self-recrimination that we don't realize our Guest has arrived in a blaze of light. We invited Him and He came! He is real; He is here. And He holds out to us all of God's gifts, all of God's Love. He is dropping miracles around us like little bursts of light. Yet our eyes are closed while we whisper to ourselves long lists of all that we have done wrong and all the wrong that has been done to us. If you have ever read Helen's poem "Stranger on the Road," it captures this situation perfectly.

This year, Jesus says, is the time to pull our head out of the ashes of the past, and acknowledge our Guest.

> 9. You have never given *any* problem to the Holy Spirit He has not solved for you, nor will you ever do so. You have never tried to solve *anything* yourself and been successful. Is it not time you brought these facts *together* and made *sense* of them? This is the year for the *application* of the ideas that have been given you. For the ideas are mighty forces, to be *used* and not held idly by. They have *already* proved their power sufficiently for you to place your faith in *them*, and *not* in their denial. This year invest in truth, and let it work in peace. Have faith in Him Who [Ur: Have faith in what] has faith in *you*. Think what you have *really* seen and heard, and *recognize* it. Can you *be* alone [without the Holy Spirit] with witnesses like these?

It's almost comical when you look at how resistant Helen and Bill were in the face of all the miracles they experienced. In light of that, Jesus' plea makes such perfect sense. He is saying, "Look, this course has worked. Its ideas have proven their power to you. Calling on the Holy Spirit has really solved things. If an investment has repeatedly paid off, why keep your investment so small? Why not invest more? That is what this year is for."

It's easy to see the dark comedy in their situation. Yet *we* face the exact same situation. The amount that the Course has proven itself to us vastly exceeds our investment in it. The amount that the Holy Spirit has proven Himself to us vastly exceeds our trust in Him and reliance on Him. Are we willing to look at this and make the logical decision?

Application: Ask yourself the following questions:

On a scale of 1 to 10, what is my investment in the Course—considering where I give my time and energy, what I look to for happiness, what I look forward to each day, what kinds of things I make my plans around, and how I try to solve my problems?

If I were to invest in the Course to the degree that it has actually proven itself to me, what would my investment be then, on a scale of 1 to 10?

If my score is higher for the second question, how can I actually express that greater investment on a concrete level in my life? (You may want to ask this final question of the Holy Spirit in your mind.)

III. The Reward of Teaching
Commentary by Robert Perry

1. We have already learned that everyone teaches, and teaches all the time [Ur: This sentence appears to have been inserted by the editors, drawing from 6.In.2:2]. You may have [Ur: You have] taught well, and yet you may not have [Ur: you have not] learned how to <u>accept</u> the comfort of your teaching. If you will consider <u>what</u> you have taught, and how alien it is to what you <u>thought</u> you knew, you will be <u>compelled</u> to realize that your Teacher came from <u>beyond</u> your thought system. Therefore He could look upon it fairly, and perceive it was untrue. [Ur: And] He <u>must</u> have done so from the basis of a very different thought system, and one with <u>nothing in common with yours</u>. For certainly what He has taught, and what you have taught <u>through</u> Him, have [Ur: <i>has</i>] nothing in common with what you taught <u>before</u> He came. And the results have been to bring peace where there was pain, and suffering has disappeared to be replaced by joy.

It is important to see this as a continuation of the discussion from the previous section. The issue is this: Helen and Bill had been doing miracles. They had been giving to others, at least at times, from the Holy Spirit in them. The results were to bring peace and joy where there had been pain and suffering. This fact is perhaps most evident in the transformation of their department that they accomplished. Helen writes:

> The facts are simple. The whole climate of the department gradually changed for the better. Bill worked particularly hard on this, determined to turn hostilities into friendships by perceiving the relationships differently....Tensions lessened and antagonisms dropped away. The wrong people left, though on friendly terms, and the right ones came along almost immediately....In time the department became smooth-functioning, relaxed, and efficient. (*Absence from Felicity*, pp. 94-95)

Yet there was a problem. I have pointed out many times in these commentaries that Jesus describes a thought process we will go through, in which we will give healing ideas and then conclude that therefore

204

those ideas must be in us, which strengthens their presence inside us. What Jesus is saying here is that Helen and Bill weren't drawing that conclusion. They weren't putting two and two together.

> 2. You may have [Ur: You *have*] taught freedom, but you have <u>not</u> learned how to be free. I said earlier [Ur: Once we said], "By their fruits ye shall know them, and they shall know themselves" [9.V.9:6]. For it is certain that you judge <u>yourself</u> according to your teaching. The ego's teaching produces <u>immediate</u> results, because <u>its</u> decisions are immediately <u>accepted as your choice</u>. And this acceptance <u>means</u> that you are willing to judge yourself accordingly. Cause and effect are very clear in the ego's thought system, because all your learning has been directed toward <u>establishing</u> the relationship between them. And would you <u>not</u> have faith in what you have so diligently taught yourself to believe? Yet remember how much care you have exerted in choosing its witnesses, and in <u>avoiding</u> those which spoke for the cause of truth and <u>its</u> effects.

The cause and effect process he is talking about here is one where we look to the effects we have on others and then derive from those what kind of cause we must be. What Jesus is saying, though, is that we have a double standard in how we apply this process. When we act from our ego, we immediately think "That was my choice." Then we see the negative effect this has on others, and then immediately judge ourselves accordingly.

But the same doesn't happen when we act from the Holy Spirit. We tend to think, "That choice didn't really reflect me. It was halfhearted and a bit of a fluke." And then when we see the positive effects on others, we overlook them and think, "Yeah, but yesterday I attacked that very same person."

In other words, when it comes to letting our teaching teach us—teach us who we are—we are giving our ego teaching far more power. We are not giving our Holy Spirit teaching a fair shake.

> 3. Does not the fact that you have <u>not</u> learned what you <u>have</u> taught show you that you do <u>not</u> perceive the Sonship as one? And does it not also show you that you do not regard *yourself* as one? For it is impossible to teach successfully <u>wholly</u> without conviction, and it is equally impossible that conviction be <u>outside</u> of you. You could never

have taught freedom unless you <u>did</u> believe in it. And it <u>must</u> be that what you taught <u>came from yourself</u>. Yet this Self you clearly <u>do not know</u>, and do not recognize It <u>even though It functions</u>. What functions must be <u>there</u>. And it is <u>only</u> if you deny <u>what It has done</u> that you could possibly deny Its presence.

The fact that we are not letting our teaching teach us shows that we are split in two ways. First, we feel split off from others (from the Sonship). This is demonstrated by the simple fact that we do not see the ideas we are giving others as being ours and as applying to us. Second, we feel split off from the place in us where this teaching is coming from. To have the effects it did, our teaching must have come from real conviction. And this conviction must be within us, yet we remain disconnected from it. Obviously, we are split off from the inner source of our conviction. This conviction came from our true Self, and that means we are split off from our own Self. Yet how can we deny this Self when we see It function through us? Easy—as the last section says, we just overlook the miracles It has produced through us.

This brings to mind the image of the spiritual teacher who gets up on the stage and is full of passion and conviction, yet goes home and is moody, petty, and selfish. He must feel split off from his audience, for he expected them to embrace ideas he doesn't embrace in his day-to-day life. And he must be split off from the place in him that really does have that passionate conviction he demonstrated on stage. It's a sad image, but all too common.

4. This is a course in how to <u>know</u> yourself. You have <u>taught</u> what you are, but have <u>not</u> let what you are teach <u>you</u>. You have been <u>very</u> careful to avoid the obvious, and <u>not</u> to see the <u>real</u> cause and effect relationship that is <u>perfectly</u> apparent. Yet within you is <u>everything</u> you taught. What can it be that has <u>not</u> learned it? It must be this part [Ur: It must be this] that is <u>really</u> outside yourself, <u>not</u> by your own projection, <u>but in truth</u>. And it is this part that you have <u>taken in</u> that is <u>not</u> you. What <u>you</u> accept into your mind does not <u>really</u> change it. Illusions are but beliefs in <u>what is not there</u>. And the seeming conflict between truth and illusion can <u>only</u> be resolved by <u>separating yourself from the illusion</u> and <u>not</u> from truth.

Do you see the irony here? At times, we do teach others from some holy place in us. But then we silently say, "I'm glad that was helpful for them, but that wasn't really me." We know ourselves (or so we assume), and we know that whatever holy impulse came through us, it wasn't us; it was outside our nature. What we don't realize is that that was our real Self. And the self we know as us—that's the false self, the ego. It is what is *really* outside our nature.

So in those moments, we are showing others our real Self, but then distancing ourselves from It because it doesn't fit the false self we "know" is us. We are thus teaching others who we are, but refusing to learn it ourselves.

Application: Think of a situation in which you gave something to another from a holy place in you. Can you see how afterwards, you subtly discounted the self you were in that moment, because it wasn't your normal self? Now realize that your normal self is the false self, and *that* was your real Self.

5. Your teaching has already <u>done</u> this, for the Holy Spirit is <u>part of</u> <u>you</u>. Created by God, He left neither God nor His creation. He is both God and you, as you are God and Him together. For God's Answer to the separation added more to you than you tried to <u>take away</u>. He protected both your creations <u>and</u> you together, keeping one with you what you would <u>exclude</u>. And they will <u>take the place</u> of what <u>you</u> took in [the ego] to replace <u>them</u>. They [your creations] are <u>quite</u> real, as part of the Self you do not know. They communicate to you through the Holy Spirit, and their power and gratitude to you for <u>their</u> creation they offer gladly to your teaching of yourself, who is their home. You who are host to God are also host to <u>them</u>. For nothing real has ever left the mind of its creator. And what is <u>not</u> real was <u>never</u> there.

Amazingly, your teaching (your extension of miracles) has already separated out the true from the false in you, for this teaching came from the truth in you, from the Holy Spirit in you. To know who you are, you just need to pay attention to what you have already taught.

Most of this paragraph is rather metaphysical. It says that when we tried to leave God, our Self, and our creations, God made sure we didn't really. He created the Holy Spirit, thus adding more to our reality than we tried to take away. The Holy Spirit then guaranteed that we didn't leave our creations, who still communicate to us through the Holy Spirit. They also express their gratitude to us for creating them by adding power to our miracle working. Jesus really wants us to derive comfort from the fact that our heavenly children are still up there, funneling to us what help they can, in gratitude for our bringing them into being.

> 6. You are <u>not</u> two selves in conflict. What is <u>beyond God</u>? If you who hold Him and whom He holds <u>are</u> the universe, all else must be <u>outside</u>, where <u>nothing</u> is. <u>You</u> have taught this, and from far off in the universe, yet <u>not</u> beyond yourself, the witnesses [I believe this refers to the brothers you have healed] to your teaching have gathered to help you learn. Their gratitude has joined with yours and God's to strengthen your faith in what you taught. <u>For what you taught is true</u>. Alone, you stand <u>outside</u> your teaching and <u>apart</u> from it. But <u>with</u> them you <u>must</u> learn that you but taught <u>yourself</u>, and <u>learned</u> from the conviction you <u>shared</u> with them.

Application: Think about how many times real, true goodness has come forth from you to lift up someone else, and realize that almost every single time, you have discounted this goodness, "knowing" this wasn't the "real" you. Now imagine everyone you have ever helped gathering together around you, even people who you have never met, who've been helped by your thoughts and prayers and meditations. Each one tells you the story of what you did for them. Each one concludes by saying, "That person inside you that helped me—that is the real you. The normal you, the one you identify with—that is the illusion." See each one saying this in turn. Let their message in. Let them do what they came to do. They came to strengthen your faith in what you taught and in the Self in you that did the teaching. Let them now return your gift and be *your* teachers.

> 7. This year you will begin to learn, and make learning <u>commensurate</u> with teaching. You have <u>chosen</u> this by your own willingness to teach. Though you seemed to suffer for it, the joy of teaching will yet be yours. For the joy of teaching is <u>in the learner</u>, who offers it to the teacher in gratitude, and shares it <u>with</u> him. As you learn, your gratitude to your <u>Self</u>, Who teaches you what He <u>is</u>, will grow and help you honor Him. And you will learn His power and strength and purity, and

love Him as His Father does. His Kingdom has no limits and no end, and there is nothing in Him that is not perfect and eternal. All this is *you*, and nothing <u>outside</u> of this *is* you.

What a wonderful promise—that we ourselves could learn as much from our teaching as others do. Right now, what we have learned from our teaching (and remember, teaching is being used in the broadest sense of the word here, one which covers all forms of loving extension to others) is primarily that it drains us. It seems like such a sacrifice. As the teacher, we will never on our own realize the true joy of teaching. We need the help of our students. They are the ones who experience the benefit of our teaching. They are the ones, therefore, who understand the priceless nature of what is inside of us, the teacher.

When our learning really begins to catch up with our teaching, our self-loathing will experience a miraculous turnaround. We will become grateful to our Self. We will honor Him. We will learn of His power, purity, and perfection. Don't be misled by the "Him" here; this will be our attitude toward our Self—toward *ourselves*.

> 8. To your most holy Self all praise is due for what you are, and for what He is Who created you <u>as</u> you are. Sooner or later must everyone bridge the gap he imagines exists between his selves. Each one builds this bridge, which <u>carries him across</u> the gap as soon as he is willing to expend some little effort on behalf of bridging it. His little efforts are powerfully supplemented by the strength of Heaven, and by the united will of all [including your creations] who make Heaven what it is, being joined within it. And so the one who would cross over is literally transported there.
>
> 9. Your bridge is builded stronger than you think, and your foot is planted firmly on it. Have no fear that the attraction of those who stand on the other side and wait for you will not draw you safely across. For you <u>will</u> come where you would be, and where your Self awaits you.

Application — A visualization:

See yourself standing at the edge of a chasm.
On this side is you, identified with your false self.
On the other side is your true Self.

All of your spiritual efforts have been driven by a desire to bridge this gap.

Perhaps many of them seemed ineffectual.

But now you see what they have really accomplished.

They have built a sturdy bridge that spans this chasm, a bridge from one self to the other.

Look at this bridge, built by your efforts.

It is a strong bridge, much stronger than you realize.

Now you realize that you *can* make it to the other side.

You can make it to your true Self.

Now look at the other side of the chasm.

There you see your creations waiting for you.

And you see your brothers in their true form, also waiting for you.

And you see God, welcoming you with open Arms.

And finally, you see your own true Self, longing to reunite with you.

As you look, you realize that this is your family; this is your home.

This is where you belong.

And you experience the most powerful attraction imaginable to be on that other side.

On that side of the bridge is everything you have ever wanted.

On this side is nothing, just empty dreams.

You look down, and see your foot safely planted on the bridge.

Say to yourself, "I *will* come where I would be, and where my Self awaits me."

The attraction of the other side pulls your other foot forward.

You take step after step, with barely any effort on your part.

The attraction you feel is moving your legs for you.

After a while, your feet barely touch the bridge.

You begin to fly toward the other side.

Soon, you will be there,

   enfolded in the love and safety of your home,

   reunited with your Self,

   back where you belong.

IV. The Illusion and the Reality of Love
Commentary by Robert Perry

1. Be not afraid to look upon the special hate relationship, for freedom lies in looking at it [Ur: freedom lies here]. It would be impossible <u>not</u> to know the meaning of love, <u>except for this</u>. For the special love relationship, <u>in which the meaning of love is</u> hidden [Ur: *lost*], is undertaken <u>solely</u> to <u>offset</u> the hate [Ur: *offset* this], but <u>not</u> to <u>let it go</u>. Your salvation will rise clearly before your open eyes as you look on this. <u>You cannot limit hate</u>. The special love relationship will <u>not</u> offset it, but will merely <u>drive it underground</u> and out of sight. It is essential to bring it <u>into</u> sight, and to make <u>no</u> attempt to hide it. For it is the attempt to <u>balance</u> hate with love that makes love meaningless to you. The extent of the split [with real love] that lies in this you do <u>not</u> realize. And until you do the split will remain unrecognized, <u>and therefore unhealed</u>.

This paragraph sets out a basic dynamic that is crucial for this section. We have lots of essentially hate-based relationships. Of course, these are with people we mostly avoid. We try not to spend a ton of time with people that, in our view, don't deserve to live (though sometimes we can't help it). But if our life were only made up of relationships with people whom, for one reason or another, we wish did not exist, that would be an awful life. So we try to balance all this hate out with good, loving relationships. These relationships put up a fence around our yard, so that the hate stays safely on the outside of our lives, while inside the fence we are partying with our good friends.

This setup, however, completely fails. The reason is that we can't really limit the hate. Once it's there, it spreads out and covers everything. It simply walks right through our fences, disguised now as our "loving" relationships. We think we have found love in these relationships, but all we have found is hate wearing a smiling mask. While we believe that this is love, we have no clue what love really is. We are utterly split off from real love, as we spend our lives trying to balance naked hate with disguised hate.

As a side note, most Course students have been taught to see special relationships as coming in two types: special love and special hate. The first sentence of this paragraph, however, is the one and only reference to special hate relationships. All other references to special relationships are references to special *love* relationships.

> 2. The symbols of hate against the symbols of love play out a conflict that does not exist. For symbols stand for something <u>else</u>, and the <u>symbol</u> of love <u>is</u> without meaning if love is everything. You will go through this last undoing quite unharmed, and will at last emerge <u>as</u> <u>yourself</u>. This is the last step in the readiness for God. Be not unwilling now; you are too near, and you <u>will</u> cross the bridge in perfect safety, translated quietly from war to peace. For the <u>illusion</u> of love will <u>never</u> satisfy, but its <u>reality</u>, which awaits you on the other side, <u>will</u> give you everything.

Right now our lives are a battleground between love and hate, between our relationships with our supporters and our relationships with those who would tear us down. Which side is going to win—the forces of love or the forces of hate? If our "loving" relationships win, if they occupy center stage and have the loudest voice, then life has been a success. If, however, our detractors and competitors have the last word, then life has been an utter failure.

Yet the battle is meaningless, because it is really between mere symbols of love and symbols of hate, and these symbols don't mean anything. The symbols of love mean nothing because symbols stand outside the thing they symbolize, yet nothing stands outside of love; love is everything. The symbols of hate mean nothing for, again, love is everything, and therefore hate is not real. Its symbols, therefore, stand for nothing.

This battle between love's symbols and hate's symbols keeps us blind to what love really is. This whole thing—the symbols and the battle between them—must be undone if we are to know love's meaning. It may seem impossible to undo this; the battle has so defined our existence. We have so completely assumed that the love in our life triumphing over the hate in our life is what it's all about. Who will we be if we are not engaged in this battle? In answer, Jesus says, "You will go through this last undoing quite unharmed, and will at last emerge as yourself."

> 3. The special love relationship is an attempt to limit the destructive

effects of hate by finding a haven in the storm of guilt. It makes no attempt to rise above the storm, into the sunlight. On the contrary, it emphasizes the guilt outside the haven by attempting to build barricades against it, and keep within them. The special love relationship is not perceived as a value in itself, but as a place of safety from which hatred is split off and kept apart. The special love partner is acceptable only as long as he serves this purpose. Hatred can enter, and indeed is welcome in some aspects of the relationship, but it is still held together by the illusion of love. If the illusion goes, the relationship is broken or becomes unsatisfying on the grounds of disillusionment.

The barricades Jesus is talking about here are the same as the fence I discussed in my commentary on the first paragraph. Imagine gathering into one room all the people that you have distanced yourself from (you might want to think of or write down one or two examples for each category):

- all your ex-partners that you don't want to see again
- all your friends who stabbed you in the back, prompting you to move on
- all your former bosses and coworkers that you found unbearable
- all the people you have gladly let drop out of your life
- all the people you never let into your life because you found them objectionable

Now they are all with you in the same room. Think of all the animosity in this room, all the hate. And think of all the guilt—the guilt induced by their accusations; the guilt induced by your own hatred. That room would be filled with the storm of guilt.

Now imagine that living in that room with these people was your life. Imagine that you can't leave this room and neither can they. You just have to sit in it, day after day, simmering in this fermenting soup of hate and guilt.

What would you like to do? You'd love to open the doors to this room and push them all out. So see yourself doing that, until the last one has been escorted out of the room. Now you are alone, and they are outside.

Now invite into the room the people you want to be with and who want to be with you: the people that treat you well, the people that value you and support you, the people who are on your side, the people who think that all those people who just left are wrong about you.

Now imagine that this is your life—but of course that's not hard to imagine. This *is* your life, or at least it is to some degree. We all want to kick the former group out of our life and let the latter group in, and most of us succeed somewhat. The whole purpose of the latter group is to be a buffer, to protect us from the former group, to tell us that we aren't as bad as the former group maintains.

Unfortunately, however, the people in the room tend to eventually turn on us. They start becoming like the people we kicked out. We decide that their love was not real; it was just an illusion. So we become disillusioned, and we kick them out, too.

> 4. Love is not an illusion. It is a fact. Where disillusionment is possible, there was not love but hate. For hate *is* an illusion, and what can change was never love. It is sure that those who select certain ones as partners in any aspect of living, and use them for any purpose which they would not share with others, are trying to live with guilt rather than die of it. This is the choice they see. And love, to them, is only an escape from death. They seek it desperately, but not in the peace in which it would gladly come quietly to them. And when they find the fear of death is still upon them, the love relationship loses the illusion that it is what it is not. [Ur: For] When the barricades against it [fear] are broken, fear rushes in and hatred triumphs.

The first lines make such perfect sense. If you have become disillusioned in a love relationship, that means that what you thought was love was never love; it was hate all along.

Special relationships always bring guilt, simply because we are keeping someone to ourselves, refusing to share that person with others. We are counting on being able to live with the guilt that comes from this, rather than die of it. We are like a Nazi war criminal, who tries to escape the death that seeks him by settling down in obscurity with some loving wife in South America. He says to himself, "If she will only love me enough, I can forget my fear of them catching up with me." But when he finds himself still waking up in cold sweats, plagued by this fear, he starts to question his marriage. Finally, he realizes why he has been so afraid. She didn't love him after all. She, in fact, has secretly been informing on him to his pursuers, hoping to collect a hefty reward once he's captured.

5. There are no triumphs of love. Only hate is at all concerned with the "triumph of love." The illusion of love can triumph over the illusion of hate, but always at the price of making both illusions. As long as the illusion of hatred lasts, so long will love be an illusion to you. And then the only choice remaining possible is which illusion you prefer. There *is* no conflict in the choice between truth and illusion. Seen in these terms, no one would hesitate. But conflict enters the instant the choice seems to be one between illusions, but this choice does not matter. Where one choice is as dangerous as the other, the decision must be one of despair.

We all love the triumph of love, don't we? Two people really love each other, yet a hateful world would tear them down. But they persist, and in the end, love conquers all. That is our favorite kind of story. That is life at its best, isn't it? Not according to Jesus. He says that the "love" that would triumph is really just hate. And as long as we identify with hate, which is an illusion, love will be an illusion to us as well. Then our life becomes a sickening, hopeless choice between the illusion of hate (the illusion that hate is real) and the illusion of love (the illusion that this is something other than hate). The key is to choose not between two illusions, but between the illusion of hate and the *reality* of love. That choice is easy. Who would hesitate to choose the real thing over a fantasy?

6. Your task is not to seek for love [from special partners], but merely to seek and find all of the barriers within yourself that you have built against it. It is not necessary to seek for what is true, but it *is* necessary to seek for what is false. Every illusion is one of fear, whatever form it takes. And the attempt to escape from one illusion into another must fail. If you seek love outside yourself you can be certain that you perceive hatred within, and are afraid of it. Yet peace will never come from the illusion of love, but only from its reality.

We spend our lives seeking love from those few special people. We may realize that we are trying to escape the hatred of all the rotten people we have crossed paths with. What we certainly do *not* realize is that we are trying to escape the hatred within our own hearts. Yet all we find in our "love" relationships is just more hate, wearing a painted-on smile. This will never bring us peace. Our real task is to actually seek out the hate within (rather than run from it), look at it calmly, and decide we don't want it. When we do this, we will finally realize that true, pure, unconditional love has always lived in our hearts. It was there all along, hidden under all the hate.

> 7. Recognize this, for it is true, and truth <u>must</u> be recognized if it is to be distinguished from illusion: The special love relationship is an attempt <u>to bring love into separation</u>. And, as such, it is nothing more than an attempt to bring love into fear, and <u>make it real in fear</u>. In fundamental violation of love's one condition, the special love relationship would <u>accomplish the impossible</u>. How but in illusion <u>could</u> this be done? It is essential that we look <u>very</u> closely at exactly what it is you <u>think</u> you can do to solve the dilemma which seems very real to you, but which does not exist. You have come close to truth, and only this stands between you and the bridge that leads you into it.

We have placed ourselves in a system of separation, surrounded by strangers and enemies. How could we not be afraid? How do we solve this dilemma? The answer seems easy: Hang onto the system of separation, but right in the middle of it, carve out an island of love. This love, however, is just a variant of the theme of separation. How, then, can it be real? What can it be except a magic trick, in which love only seems to appear?

Application: Jesus asks us to look very closely at our attempt to establish a loving version of separation, an island in the middle of all the hate and fear that are part and parcel of separation. We need to ask ourselves three questions:

> Is that what I have tried to do in my life?
> Can this be real love?
> If it's not real love, will it ever really satisfy me?

> 8. Heaven waits silently, and your creations are holding out their hands to help you cross and welcome them. <u>For it is they you seek</u>. You seek but for your own <u>completion</u>, and it is they who render you complete. The special love relationship is but a shabby substitute for what makes

you whole <u>in truth,</u> <u>not</u> in illusion. Your relationship with them <u>is</u> without guilt, and <u>this</u> enables you to look on all your brothers with gratitude, because your creations were created in union <u>with</u> them. Acceptance of your creations <u>is</u> the acceptance of the oneness of creation, without which you could never <u>be</u> complete. No specialness can offer you what God has given, and what <u>you</u> are joined <u>with</u> Him in giving.

We are now back to that image of the bridge from the last section. Here we are, on this side, seeking completion from the special favor of special people, feeling guilty for keeping them to ourselves, feeling cheated when we realize what a sham this love was. And there, on the other side of the bridge wait our creations. They are what really complete us, and so they are what we are unwittingly seeking each time we pursue that special person in this world. They are not only waiting for us, they are holding out their hands to help us cross. When we remember them, we also remember the true function of our brothers—not to fill the hole in us, but to stand by our side in Heaven and join with us in the holy act of creation.

> 9. Across the bridge <u>is</u> your completion, for you will be <u>wholly</u> in God, willing for <u>nothing</u> special, but only to be wholly like to Him, completing Him by your completion. Fear not to cross to the abode of peace and perfect holiness. Only there is the completion of God and of His Son established forever. Seek not for this in the bleak world of illusion, where nothing is certain and where everything fails to satisfy. In the Name of God, be wholly willing to abandon <u>all</u> illusions. In any relationship in which you are wholly willing to accept completion, and <u>only this,</u> there is God completed, and His Son <u>with</u> Him.

We carry a deep-seated fear to cross the bridge, to leave the familiar behind, to leave form and time behind, to leave separate identity behind, and enter into something completely different. Yet only across the bridge are we complete. Only there do we fulfill our deepest desire: to be wholly like God. That completes us, and our completion completes Him. We seek this completion in this world, but it never works. It is a place "where everything fails to satisfy." Yet we can find the beginnings of completion here; we can even find it in our relationships, but not by trying to snatch it from our brother.

10. The bridge that leads to union in yourself *must* lead to knowledge, for it was built with God beside you, and will lead you straight to Him where your completion rests, wholly compatible with His. Every illusion you accept into your mind by judging it to be attainable [Ur: *by judging it attainable*] removes your own sense of completion, and thus denies the Wholeness of your Father. Every fantasy, be it of love or hate, deprives you of knowledge for fantasies are the veil behind which truth is hidden. To lift the veil that seems so dark and heavy, it is only needful to value truth beyond all fantasy, and to be entirely unwilling to settle for illusion in place of truth.

When we look at some illusion in the world and think, "If I only had that, I would be happy," we instead need to tell ourselves, "This removes my own sense of completion, and thus denies the Wholeness of my Father." When we find ourselves indulging in some fantasy, perhaps a sexual fantasy or a fantasy of revenge, we need to say, "Above all else, I want to know the truth, and fantasies are the veil that hides the truth."

11. Would you not go through fear to love? For such the journey seems to be. Love calls, but hate would have [Ur: bid] you stay. Hear not the call of hate, and see no fantasies. For your completion lies in truth, and nowhere else. See in the call of hate, and in every fantasy [of yours] that rises to delay you, but the call for help that rises ceaselessly from you to your Creator. Would He not answer you whose completion is His? He loves you, wholly without illusion, as you must love. For love *is* wholly without illusion, and therefore wholly without fear. Whom God remembers must be whole. And God has never forgotten what makes Him whole [you]. In your completion lie the memory of His Wholeness and His gratitude to you for His completion. In His link with you lie both His inability to forget and your ability to remember. In Him are joined your willingness to love and all the Love of God, Who forgot you not.

We stand here, wondering whether to stay and make it work within our current framework, or leave this framework altogether and go forward into something completely new. Love is calling us onward, but hate bids us stay—hate disguised as romance, hate dressed up as pleasurable fantasies. It is not the hate outside that is calling us; it is the hate within. We need to see this hate as our call for help, our call to God. Of course

He will answer our call. His Love for us is so great that He is literally unable to forget us.

Application: Think of some example of special love that is calling to you right now, some illusion of love that you want, some fantasy that has been cropping up in your mind.

> *This is hate disguised as love.*
> *This is my hate, calling to me, asking me to stay.*
> *Yet this hate is really my call to God, my call for help.*
> *Surely He will answer me when I am His completion,*
> *And when His Love has never ceased calling to me.*

12. Your Father can no more forget the truth in you than you can fail to remember it. The Holy Spirit is the bridge to Him, made from your willingness to <u>unite</u> with Him and created by His joy in union <u>with</u> you. The journey that <u>seemed</u> endless is <u>almost</u> complete, for what *is* endless is very near. <u>You have almost recognized it.</u> Turn with me firmly away from <u>all</u> illusions <u>now</u>, and let nothing stand in the way of truth. We will take the last useless [Ur: foolish] journey <u>away from truth</u> together, and then <u>together</u> we go straight to God, in joyous answer to His call for His completion.

This paragraph contains a very interesting comment about the Holy Spirit, that along with being created by God, He was "made from your willingness to unite with" God. This comment is also about the bridge, and seems to rule out my interpretation yesterday, that the bridge was built by our spiritual efforts. Looking back at that discussion (III.8:3-4), it appears that our efforts are what carry us *across* the bridge, not what *build* the bridge.

What does Jesus mean by saying that "we will take the last foolish journey away from truth together"? Earlier, he called his crucifixion the last foolish journey. He spoke of us having this compulsion to endlessly re-enact "the separation, the loss of power, the foolish journeys of the ego in its attempt at reparation, and finally the crucifixion of the body, or death" (4.In.3:5; Urtext version). His crucifixion was the last foolish journey apparently because in the midst of the re-enactment, he saw the futility and unreality of it. In the midst of the ego's endlessly repeating cycle, he let go of the ego.

Perhaps in this context he is asking us to re-enact the relationship dance, the one we have been repeating for who knows how long. Only this time, we take this foolish journey with Jesus. This time, we use it to undo all of our illusions of love, all of our fantasies of salvation through being loved by that special someone. This is that "last undoing" he referred to near the beginning of the section. Are we ready to carry out this dance, only this time do it with him beside us, this time use it to become truly *dis-illusioned*?

> 13. If special relationships of any kind would hinder God's completion, can they have any value to you? What would interfere with God must interfere with you. Only in time does interference in God's completion seem to be possible. The bridge that He would carry you across lifts you from time into eternity. Waken from time, and answer fearlessly the call of Him Who gave eternity to you in your creation. On this side of the bridge to timelessness you understand nothing. But as you step lightly across it, upheld *by* timelessness, you are directed straight to the Heart of God [Ur: knowledge]. At its center, and only there, you are safe forever, because you are complete forever. There is no veil the Love of God in us together cannot lift. The way to truth is open. Follow it with me.

Application: Think of some special relationship that seems to promise you salvation, and say the following to yourself:

> *The specialness in this relationship would hinder God's completion.*
> *Can I value it?*
> *It would also hinder my completion.*
> *How can I want it?*
> *Do I want to stay in ignorance or cross the bridge to knowledge?*
> *With Jesus' help, I will lift the veil of my fantasies.*
> *The way to truth is open.*
> *I will follow it with him.*

V. The Choice for Completion
Commentary by Robert Perry

This is an extremely important section. This section presents the rotten core of the special relationship. It is very dark, as well as very hard to follow. Every paragraph or two Jesus gives us a new piece of a larger picture he is assembling. It is essential, therefore, to see each new piece not by itself, but as part of the emerging puzzle. And it is even more important to not keep the puzzle's picture at arm's length, but to be willing to see it at work in our own lives.

> 1. In looking at the special relationship, it is necessary first to realize that it involves a great amount of pain. Anxiety, despair, guilt and attack all enter into it, <u>broken into</u> by periods in which they <u>seem</u> to be gone. All these must be understood for what they <u>are</u>. Whatever form they take, they are always an attack on the self <u>to make the other guilty</u>. I have spoken of this before, but there are some aspects of what is <u>really</u> being attempted that have not been touched upon.

"It is necessary first to realize that it involves a great amount of pain"—as if we didn't realize that already! What we probably don't realize, however, is that all of our *anxiety* about getting our partner to perform properly, *despair* about our partner ever performing properly, *guilt* over being so demanding ourselves, and *attack* on our partner's failure to perform is really one thing: "an attack on the self to make the other guilty." All of these negative emotions, in other words, are cases in which we voluntarily sacrifice our peace and then blame it on our partner, in order to obligate him or her to sacrifice for us in return. Jesus already covered this theme of "my sacrifice obligates you to sacrifice" in "The Needless Sacrifice" (15.VII). Yet there is more. It goes deeper, much deeper. And that is what this section is about.

> 2. Very simply, the attempt to make guilty is <u>always</u> directed against God. For the ego would have you see Him, <u>and Him alone</u>, as guilty, leaving the Sonship <u>open</u> to attack and unprotected from it. The special

221

love relationship is the ego's chief weapon for keeping you from Heaven. It does not <u>appear</u> to be a weapon, but if you consider <u>how</u> you <u>value</u> it and why, you will realize what it <u>must</u> be.

When we mope about the house, we are trying to make our partner feel guilty, to show him just how unhappy his actions have made us. But beneath that, it is *God* we are trying to make guilty. We are trying to show Him what a miserable life He has allotted us, and how desperately He needs to rectify the situation. In the ego's eyes, it is always God's fault. The ego is always trying to convince us that God has made us miserable, and that it (the ego) can give us more than He ever would. The special relationship is how it convinces us of this. It is a weapon for damning God and finding on earth the bliss that God supposedly refused us.

3. The special love relationship is the ego's most boasted gift, and one which has the most appeal to those unwilling to relinquish guilt. The "dynamics" of the ego are clearest here, for counting on the attraction of this offering, the fantasies that center around it are often quite overt [Ur: around this, are often quite open]. Here they are usually judged to be acceptable and even <u>natural</u>. No one considers it bizarre to love and hate together, and even those who believe that hate is sin merely feel guilty, but do <u>not</u> correct it. This <u>is</u> the "natural" condition of the separation, and those who learn that it is <u>not</u> natural at all seem to be the <u>unnatural</u> ones. For this world *is* the opposite of Heaven, being made to <u>be</u> its opposite, and <u>everything</u> here takes a direction <u>exactly</u> opposite of what is true. In Heaven, where the meaning of love is known, love is the same as <u>union</u>. Here, where the <u>illusion</u> of love is accepted in love's place [Ur: *in its place*], love is perceived as separation and <u>exclusion</u>.

"The special love relationship is the ego's most boasted gift"—a very chilling line. We see special love as Heaven on earth, yet it is just bait from the ego, to reel us in. What is so wrong with special love? It is not real love. Imagine walking up to a clubhouse with this sign on its door:

This is the Love Club.
It is all about love.
It is dedicated only to love.
Closed to all nonmembers.
(No one but Jan and Tom welcome.)

222

This, of course, is the sign posted on every special relationship. The unloving nature of special love is particularly evident in the fantasies we have around it, fantasies in which we get the partner while the competitors weep and gnash their teeth, in which our partner behaves as our slave, in which our partner endures humiliation or is even placed in bondage. Why don't these fantasies strike us as bizarre (okay, maybe the bondage ones do)? Because unloving love is the norm down here. It's the way things are. It's natural. What more proof do we need than this to show that this world is designed to be the exact opposite of Heaven?

> 4. It is in the special relationship, born of the hidden wish for special love from God, that the ego's hatred triumphs. For the special relationship is <u>the renunciation of the Love of God</u>, and the attempt to secure for the self the specialness that He denied. [Ur: And] It is essential to the preservation of the ego that you believe this specialness is <u>not</u> hell, but <u>Heaven</u>. For the ego would never have you see that separation could <u>only be loss</u>, being the one condition in which Heaven could not [Ur: *cannot*] be.

"The specialness He denied" is a reference to "The Fear of Redemption" (13.III.10-12), where Jesus said that the separation began when we asked for special love from God; we asked God to love us more than all our brothers. Knowing that specialness is singling out, that singling out means separation, and that separation means loneliness and loss, God refused our request, and we walked.

We need to see this paragraph in light of the first two, for it adds crucial pieces onto their picture. Here, then, is what we are unconsciously thinking while we are moping around the house: "The reason I'm unhappy is that God refused to make me His favorite. He insisted on loving me with that ever-so-holy universal Love. Well, screw that. I'll show Him how miserable that made me. When He sees my misery, He will feel so guilty that He'll *have* to grant me special favor. And He'll do that by making my husband love me. My husband's special love will be the conduit for God's special love. And then I will have no more need of His unsatisfying universal Love."

> 5. To everyone Heaven is completion [what is truly heavenly is feeling complete]. There <u>can</u> be no disagreement on this, because both the

ego <u>and</u> the Holy Spirit accept it. They are, however, in complete <u>dis</u>agreement on what completion <u>is</u>, and <u>how</u> it is accomplished. The Holy Spirit knows that [Ur: self] completion lies first in union, and then in the <u>extension</u> of union. To the ego completion lies in triumph, and in the extension of the "victory" even to the final triumph over God. In <u>this</u> it sees the ultimate <u>freedom</u> of the self, for nothing would remain to interfere with the ego [Ur: with *it*]. This <u>is</u> its idea of Heaven. And therefore [Ur: From this it follows that] union, which is a condition in which the <u>ego</u> cannot interfere, <u>must be hell</u>.

Imagine two different people. One decides that he will be complete by first joining with one person and then joining with more and more people until he is united with everyone. The other person pursues completion by first defeating one person and then going on to greater and greater victories until he finally defeats God Himself. How nasty that second picture is in comparison to the first, and how terribly lonely.

Yet we are that person when we go after special love. When we are moping about the house so that our husband will feel guilty enough to give in to us, we are first triumphing over him. And since we see him as channeling God's special love, our triumph over him is simultaneously our triumph over God. We have forced God against His Will to give us ego-love rather than God-Love. We have defeated God. This is the ego's idea of completion: total victory. We may be alone, but we are on top.

6. The special relationship is a strange and unnatural ego device for joining hell and Heaven, and making them indistinguishable. And the attempt to find the imagined "best" of <u>both</u> worlds has merely led to <u>fantasies</u> of both, and to the inability to perceive either <u>as it is</u>. The special relationship is the triumph of this confusion. It is a kind of union from which <u>union is excluded</u>, and the <u>basis</u> for the <u>attempt</u> at union <u>rests</u> on exclusion. What better example could there be of the ego's maxim, "Seek but do <u>not</u> find?"

In the special relationship, we say we are trying to join, yet everyone but our partner is excluded, and even our partner, in the end, feels shut out. Union and exclusion are total opposites—union is Heaven and exclusion is hell—but we have blended them together. We have wrapped the gift of exclusion in wrapping paper with "union" written all over it. Thinking this is Heaven, we have no idea what Heaven is. Not realizing this is hell, we have no clue what hell is.

> 7. Most curious of all is the concept of the self which the ego fosters in the special relationship. This "self" seeks the relationship to make itself complete. Yet when it finds the special relationship in which it thinks it can accomplish this it gives itself away, and tries to "trade" itself for the self of another. This is not union, for there is no increase and no extension. Each partner tries to sacrifice the self he does not want for one he thinks he would prefer. And he feels guilty for the "sin" of taking, and of giving nothing of value in return. How much value can he place upon a self that he would give away to get a "better" one?

Now Jesus adds another dimension to his unfolding picture: In our primary relationships, we are not just sacrificing a little of our time or energy, in order to get back something equally trivial in return. We are sacrificing our self, our very identity, because we want to obtain the other person's self. We are giving it all away, in order to get the biggest prize there is. We are engineering a self trade, and no one seriously thinks that a swap is a real joining.

Does this mean that we have to actually transfer one person's mind to another person's body? No, it's much simpler than that. I may remain me, but now you *own* me. You possess me. You control me. And I possess you. I control you. That is how the trade is effected. It's done all the time. It's called marriage.

> 8. The "better" self the ego seeks is always one that is more special. And whoever seems to possess a special self is "loved" for what can be taken from him. Where both partners see this special self in each other, the ego sees "a union made in Heaven." For neither one will recognize that he has asked for hell, and so he will not interfere with the ego's illusion of Heaven, which it offered him to interfere with Heaven. Yet if all illusions are of fear, and they can be of nothing else, the illusion of Heaven is nothing more than an "attractive" form of fear, in which the guilt is buried deep and rises in the form of "love."

Why would we want to make such a trade? The answer should be obvious. Our own self is so ordinary (thanks to God not granting us divine specialness) that we could never be happy being a commonplace self like this. Yet this other person's self is so amazingly special that if we only possessed it, we would be deliriously happy. If owning a really cool doll or an exotic pet makes us special, how much more special we would be if we owned a fabulous, coveted, popular person!

The trick, of course, is that we have to have something of value to offer this person. We need a self that is special enough for *her* to want to possess *it*. Otherwise, we are simply out of her league. This is why it is so hard to find the right mate. Both of us at the same time have to think that the other is more special. Both of us have to think that we are getting a real bargain in this self trade. And, unfortunately, where both of us think that, and *keep* thinking that, year after year, decade after decade, our sleep is the deepest. For we remain utterly convinced that this really is Heaven, when in fact it is only hell in Heaven's clothing. We never draw back that curtain with the angels and clouds on it to see the flames dancing behind.

Let us review what we have seen so far. We make voluntary sacrifices to make our partner feel guilty, so he will sacrifice in return. We do this by giving "gifts" (as discussed in 15.VII), by sacrificing our peace (to show him how much he's hurt us), and by giving him our very self to possess as his own. All of this is designed to control him through guilt, so that he will give us what we want, and ultimately give us his very special self for us to possess and control.

Yet the real point of this section is that these transactions with our partner are really covert transactions with God. Our sacrifices are really designed to make God feel guilty for not loving us more than others, for not making us more special. When we sacrifice our peace, we are saying to God, "Look how miserable I am because you didn't give me special love." When we give away our self to get a better one, we are saying, "Look at how worthless this self is because You didn't make it more special." And then, when our partner responds by giving us the specialness we crave, we believe that this is God giving us specialness. This represents a triumph over God, because we have forced Him to give us our kind of love (special love), rather than His kind of love (impartial, universal Love).

As an analogy, imagine a young woman who is turned down by a young man because he is giving his life to being a monk. He loves her, but not in the way she wants. He has renounced romantic love and goes off to spend years meditating in a cave, seeking to realize a love for everyone. She comes to hate him, and so many years later, she shows up at the cave as a seductress, who pretends to love him but merely wants to seduce him, in order to destroy everything he stands for.

> 9. The appeal of hell lies <u>only</u> in the terrible attraction of guilt, which the ego holds out to those who place their faith in littleness. The conviction of littleness lies in <u>every</u> special relationship, for only the deprived <u>could</u> value specialness. The <u>demand</u> for specialness, and the perception of the <u>giving</u> of specialness <u>as an act of love</u>, would <u>make love hateful</u>. [Ur: And] The <u>real</u> purpose of the special relationship, in strict accordance with the ego's goals, is to <u>destroy</u> reality and <u>substitute illusion</u>. For the ego is <u>itself</u> an illusion, and <u>only</u> illusions can <u>be</u> the witnesses to its "reality."

We only find hell dressed up as Heaven (the special relationship) appealing because we are attracted to feeling guilty and because we believe we are little. Only the little could want to be special, for specialness is just littleness blown up. If we didn't feel little, we would look at specialness and wonder how anyone could ever want it. We would instantly see that giving specialness is not an act of love, but an act of hate. Yet this is hard to believe now, isn't it? When you are telling someone that they are very special, you are insulting their magnitude. Little do you realize that what looks like love is all a game of your ego, which is trying to destroy real love, and with it reality itself, and replace it with illusory love, in order to support the illusion of its own existence.

> 10. If you perceived the special relationship as a triumph over God, <u>would you want it</u>? Let us not think of its fearful nature, nor of the guilt it <u>must</u> entail, nor of the sadness and the loneliness. For these are only <u>attributes</u> of the whole religion of separation, and of [Ur: and the] the total context in which it is thought to occur. The central theme in its litany [a series of sung or spoken liturgical prayers] to sacrifice is that <u>God must die so you can live</u>. And it is this theme that is acted out in the special relationship. Through the death of <u>your</u> self you think you can <u>attack</u> another self, and snatch it <u>from</u> the other to <u>replace</u> the self that you despise. And you [Ur: think you] despise it <u>because you do not think it offers the specialness that you demand</u>. And <u>hating</u> it [your self] <u>you</u> have made it little and unworthy, <u>because you are afraid of it</u> [of its true magnitude].

This paragraph begins the enunciation of the section's central theme.

Application: Think of a special relationship in your life. Then say to yourself,

> *This is my triumph over God.*
> *In this relationship I am chanting, "God must die so I can live."*
> *Do I want that?*

How is the special relationship a case in which we are trying to kill God so that our ego can live? This paragraph begins spelling it out, but it won't be entirely clear for a couple of paragraphs. You begin by sacrificing your worthless, non-special self to your partner. This is, in a sense, an act of killing your self, an act of suicide (why else do we get cold feet before the wedding?). By doing this, you compel your partner (through guilt) to give you her self, "to replace the self that you despise," the self that is just too ordinary to be satisfying. Now, you own her extremely special self; all the neighbors can see what a prize you have, and you feel ever so special.

> 11. How can you grant unlimited power to what [the self] you think you have <u>attacked</u> [by making it little and unworthy]? So fearful has the truth [of who you are] become to you that <u>unless</u> it is weak and little, and unworthy of value, you would not dare to look upon it. You think it safer to endow the little self <u>you</u> made [in contrast to your glorious true Self] with power you <u>wrested from</u> truth, triumphing over it and leaving <u>it</u> helpless. See how <u>exactly</u> is this ritual enacted in the special relationship. An altar is erected <u>in between</u> two separate people, on which each seeks to kill his self, and on his body raise another self to take its power from his death [Ur: *that takes his power from its death*]. Over and over and over this ritual is enacted. And it is <u>never</u> completed, nor ever will <u>be</u> completed. [Ur: For] The <u>ritual</u> of completion <u>cannot</u> complete, for [Ur: and] life arises not from death, nor Heaven from hell.

Here the special relationship is said to be a ritual, a ritual of sacrifice. The two of us erect an altar between us. On this altar, I sacrifice my self,

I kill it. And on this same altar, you sacrifice your self. I then take your self and install it in my body. I now own you.

But there is more. This new self that I possess has drawn power from my triumph over the truth in me. The fact is that the glorious truth of my being has terrified me. It is not special. It is not an inflated sense of littleness. It is far beyond all that. It is the gift of my Father's non-special Love. It is the gift of infinite magnitude. Yet this gift is precisely what has angered me. I wanted a special self, not a boundless Self.

Thus, by killing my little non-special self (in the special relationship ritual), I am also killing the non-special Self that God gave me. I see them both, in a sense, as the same: as the non-specialness that I am saddled with that can't make me happy. Thus, I am killing them both at once. In this ritual, then, I am triumphing over the truth of who I am. I have become its conqueror. As its conqueror, I take its power, and use it to light the lamps of the new very special self I have acquired from my partner.

> 12. Whenever any form of special relationship tempts you to seek for love in ritual, remember love is content, and not form of any kind. The special relationship is a ritual of form, aimed at raising [Ur: aimed at the raising of] the form to take the place of God at the expense of content. There is no meaning in the form, and there will never be. The special relationship must be recognized for what it is; a senseless ritual in which strength is extracted from the death of God, and invested in His killer as the sign that form has triumphed over content, and love has lost its meaning. Would you want this to be possible, even apart from its evident impossibility? If it were possible, you would have made yourself helpless. God is not angry. He merely could not let this happen. You cannot change His Mind. No rituals that you have set up in which the dance of death delights you can bring death to the eternal. Nor can your chosen substitute for the Wholeness of God have any influence at all upon it.

Now the full picture is present. The special relationship is a ritual. What is a ritual? It is a prescribed series of actions we perform on earth that (supposedly) bring about an actual transaction with God. In this ritual, my partner is wearing the mask of God. I sacrifice my unremarkable little self on the altar, while chanting the ritualized words, "Look what a worthless non-special self You gave me, God. It is so worthless, I am

229

going to sacrifice it, throw it away, kill it." Then my partner sacrifices her self for me, again repeating the prescribed words, "I, God, feel unbearably guilty. How could I ever think to refuse you special love? To repay you, I give you this incredibly special self, a token of My special love. With it comes My power, for you have defeated Me and my universal Love, and to the victor go the spoils."

To get a slightly better sense of this rather abstruse and complicated notion, let's go back to the jilted lover and the monk in the cave. Let's say that after the monk leaves her and goes off to his cave, she never sees him again. But every year, on the anniversary of when he went away, she finds some young man who is considering entering the monastery. She brings him to her house, lights a candle, has him repeat the vows he has been memorizing, and then proceeds to seduce him, enticing him into choosing her over his vows. Then she is done with him; he has served his purpose. Obviously, this new young man is only important for his ritual value. He is just a stand-in for the monk who turned her down long ago. By using him, she has conducted a ritual transaction with the monk who is off in his cave, unaware that any of this is going on.

Now realize that this is what we are doing in our special relationships. They have the form of love, but the form is just a ritual, a ritual designed to destroy the real content of love, and the real content of God. Which brings up two questions: First, can we really want this? Second, what makes us think that this ritual really does anything?

> 13. See in the special relationship nothing more than a meaningless attempt to raise other gods before Him, and by worshipping them to obscure <u>their</u> tininess <u>and His greatness</u>. In the name of <u>your</u> completion you do not <u>want</u> this. For every idol that you raise to place <u>before</u> Him stands before *you*, in place of what <u>you</u> are.

Application: Think of a special relationship of yours and say to yourself:

> *In my relationship with [name], I am just trying to raise up the*
> *god of specialness to replace the real God, the God of Love.*
> *In the name of my completion, I do not want this.*
> *For it stands in place of what **I** am.*

14. Salvation lies in the simple fact that illusions are not fearful because they are not true. They but seem to be fearful to the extent to which you fail to recognize them for what they are; and you will fail to do this to the extent to which you *want* them to be true. And to the same extent you are denying truth, and so are failing [Ur: and so are making *yourself* unable] to make the simple choice between truth and illusion; God and fantasy. Remember this, and you will have no difficulty in perceiving the decision as just what it is, and nothing more.

Way deep down, this ritual terrifies us. We think we are actually killing God. We think the ritual is real simply because we are deeply invested in it being real. The solution is to realize that this ritual is as real as stepping on a crack and breaking your mother's back. Choosing becomes easy when we realize that on one side is a ridiculous fantasy in which we hand someone a ring and thereby destroy all of reality, and on the other side is the eternal reality of God's never-changing Love.

15. The core of the separation illusion [Ur: delusion] lies simply in the fantasy of destruction [Ur: the fantasy *destruction*] of love's meaning. And unless love's meaning is restored to you, you cannot know yourself who share its meaning. Separation is only the decision *not* to know yourself. This [Ur: Its] whole thought system is a carefully contrived learning experience, designed to lead away from truth and into fantasy. Yet for every learning that would hurt you, God offers you correction and complete escape from all its consequences.

The core of the separation lies in the delusion that we have replaced God's universal Love with our special love. Our special relationships are a "fantasy *destruction* of love's meaning." But love's meaning is our own meaning, for we are love. And so the special relationship, and the separation itself, is simply the decision not to know ourselves. Yet God offers us a way out.

16. The decision whether or not to listen to this course and follow it is but the choice between truth and illusion. For here is truth, separated from illusion and not confused with it at all. How simple does this choice become when it is perceived as only what it is. For only fantasies make confusion in choosing possible, and they are totally unreal.

The Course holds out to us the choice between truth, seen as true, and illusion, seen as unreal fantasy. And that is how *we* must see it. It is not a choice between this sinful, God-destroying ritual and what God wants us to do. It is a choice between a silly fantasy and the eternal reality.

> 17. This year is thus the time to make the easiest decision that ever confronted you, and also the only one. You will cross the bridge into reality simply because you will recognize that God is on the other side, and nothing at all is here. It is impossible not to make the natural decision as this is realized.

This year, he told Helen and Bill, and surely he tells us now, is the time to make this choice. It's as if we have closed ourselves in a house and blacked out all of the windows, so that no sunlight can get in. Then, in the dark, we light a candle and ceremoniously blow it out, thinking that this will magically extinguish the sun. We repeat this over and over, each time hoping it will work. This year, it's time to wake up and look at the foolishness of it, to realize we will never extinguish the sun, and simply walk outdoors and bask in it.

Application: Think of a time in which you were so in love with someone that you tried to give this person all of yourself.

By giving yourself to this person, could you have been sending the message, "I sacrificed myself for you and so you are obligated to sacrifice yourself for me. You owe me your self"?

To voluntarily sacrifice your self is, in a sense, to kill your self. Why would you kill your self in order to get a better self, unless you thought your self was not good enough, not special enough?

In looking at your sacrifice of your self for this person, can you detect the feeling in you of not being whole enough, of only having to go through this process because you are not special enough?

Sacrificing your self, therefore, also sends a message to God. It says, "God, if You had favored me more, my self would already be complete. I wouldn't have to give it away to get a better one. You, therefore, are responsible for this sacrifice. You are responsible for my death."

Can you detect this feeling in you, the feeling that, if God had favored you more, made you more special, you would be so whole and complete that you wouldn't need to greedily pursue some special person out there?

If so, doesn't that make God the one to blame for you having to undertake this desperate sacrifice?

The goal here is for God to accept His guilt, and pay His debt by prompting this person to give you her precious, special self. If she does, it means that God has come under your control. Now, through this person, God has given you the specialness you sought. Can you feel the sense in yourself that not only has *she* given you specialness, but that *God* has done so too? That He has answered your prayers and, through her, bestowed on you His special favor?

God has given you special love, special favor. Reflect on what that implies. God's Love is inherently impartial, universal, given to all alike. Yet you have made Him give you *special* love. You have made Him go against His very Nature. In a sense, then, you have defeated God. You have forced Him to love you in a way that is alien to Who He is.

And hasn't Who He is felt threatening to you? For He carries a Love that loves everyone equally, a Love that overlooks your special attributes and beckons you beyond your personal boundaries? This Love does not validate you as a separate, special being. Wouldn't it be great, then, to destroy this Love?

Can you detect the remote possibility that, somewhere in your mind, that is what you believe you have done? That by forcing God to give you special love (through this person's love), you have defeated and destroyed His universal Love? Can you feel some core of your personal identity that is relieved, free of a threat that has hung over it? This same core is no longer undermined by God's formless Love; it is now validated by His special love. It has bent God to its will, changing Him from the ultimate threat into its lapdog. Can you get even the faintest sense of this?

This is the triumph of the ego over God.

Now say to yourself,

> *Do I want to destroy God?*
> *And is this even possible?*
> *My silly ritual can't really change anything.*
> *God's Love still sheds its beautiful light on everyone alike.*
> *It doesn't even know about my attempts to change it.*
> *That is the Love I want, not my empty fantasy of love.*
> *Father, let me rest in Your Love.*

Let me bask in Your eternal Smile.
My dream is ended now.
Amen.

VI. The Bridge to the Real World
Commentary by Robert Perry

1. The search for the special relationship is the sign that you equate yourself with the ego and <u>not</u> with God. For the special relationship has value <u>only</u> to the ego. To the ego [Ur: To <i>it</i>], <u>unless</u> a relationship <u>has</u> special value <u>it has no meaning</u>, for [Ur: And] it perceives <u>all</u> love as special. Yet this <u>cannot</u> be natural, for it is <u>un</u>like the relationship of God and His Son, and <u>all</u> relationships that are unlike this one <i>must</i> be unnatural. For God created love as He would have it be, and <u>gave</u> it as it <u>is</u>. Love <u>has</u> no meaning except as its Creator defined it by His Will. It is impossible to define it otherwise and <u>understand</u> it.

If you want special love—and who doesn't?—then you believe you are an ego, not a Son of God. Only the ego likes the idea of being singled out for special favor. In its perspective, if you can't do that for me, then what use are you? We have grown so accustomed to this kind of love that it seems perfectly natural. Yet it is an unnatural love—a perversion—because the only natural love is between God and His Son. Love is as God defined it. The question, then, is, are we willing to let God define what love is for <i>us</i>?

2. <u>Love is freedom</u>. To look for it by placing yourself in <u>bondage</u> is to <u>separate</u> yourself from it. For the Love of God, no longer seek for union in separation, nor for freedom in bondage! As you release, so will you <u>be</u> released. <u>Forget this not</u>, or love will be unable to find you and comfort you.

Do we believe that love is freedom? How do you feel about the idea of lifting all your demands off of everyone in your life? It's a scary thought, isn't it? Yet only by releasing your friends and family will you be released. And only by setting them free will you stop cutting yourself off from love. Only then will love be able to find you and comfort you.

3. There is a way in which the Holy Spirit asks <u>your</u> help, if you would have <u>His</u>. The holy instant is His most helpful aid [Ur: tool] in

protecting you from the attraction of guilt, the <u>real</u> lure in the special relationship. You do <u>not</u> recognize that this <u>is</u> its <u>real</u> appeal, for the ego has taught you that <u>freedom</u> lies in it. Yet the closer you look at the special relationship, the more apparent it becomes that it <u>must</u> foster guilt and therefore must <u>imprison</u>.

The special relationship is like all those fables in which some amazing gift, like having the Midas touch, promises total freedom but ends up delivering total imprisonment. The special relationship imprisons because through it we collect guilt, which is like a little devil on our shoulder, constantly telling us that jail is the only fitting place for us. Little do we know that this guilt is what actually attracts us to the relationship. We are addicted to the guilt. We are like a demented fish who thinks he wants the bait but is secretly hungering for the hook.

If we don't even know that we have this hunger for the hook, how can we possibly protect ourselves against it? We can't. We need help from the Holy Spirit. He, however, can't help us without our cooperation. His plea, therefore, (like Tom Cruise in *Jerry Maguire*) is, "Help *Me* help *you*." How do we help Him? By entering a holy instant. We will be told more about this at the end of the section.

> 4. The special relationship is totally meaningless <u>without a body</u>. If you <u>value</u> it, you must also <u>value the body</u>. And what you value you <u>will</u> keep. The special relationship is a device for limiting <u>your</u> self to a body, and for limiting your perception of others to <u>theirs</u>. The Great Rays would establish the total <u>lack</u> of value of the special relationship, <u>if they were seen</u>. For in seeing <u>them</u> the body <u>would</u> disappear, <u>because its value would be lost</u>. And so your whole <u>investment</u> in seeing it would be <u>withdrawn</u> from it.

What is romance without a body? What is any relationship without a body? What is talking? What is going out to eat? The special relationship requires a body, and therefore invests the body with value and power. All of our romance and talking and going out to eat constitutes a continual affirmation which says, "You are limited to this body."

This makes us not only see ourselves as trapped in a body; we see the other person that way, too. Yet there is a whole other way to see that person: through vision. Vision would see the Great Rays shining from her. The body would then disappear from our *mind*, even though our *eyes* would still see it. The body would be like this person's socks are now—our eyes register them but our mind doesn't pay any attention to them. It's too caught up in other things. In this case, it would be too caught up in gazing on the vast Rays of holiness radiating from this person. In light of these, the body would seem utterly valueless, and that would make the special relationship itself seem valueless.

> 5. <u>You see the world you value</u>. On this side of the bridge you see the world of separate bodies, seeking to join each other in <u>separate unions</u> and to become one <u>by losing</u>. When two <u>individuals</u> seek to become <u>one</u>, they are trying to <u>decrease</u> their magnitude. Each would <u>deny</u> his power, for the <u>separate</u> union <u>excludes the universe</u>. Far more is <u>left outside</u> than would be taken in, for God is left <u>without</u> and *nothing* taken in. If one such union were made <u>in perfect faith,</u> the universe <u>would</u> enter into it. Yet the special relationship the <u>ego</u> seeks does <u>not</u> include even <u>one</u> whole individual. The ego <u>wants</u> but part of him, and sees <u>only</u> this part and nothing else.

Now we are back to the bridge metaphor, which began three sections ago. Here, on this side of the bridge, we see a world of separate bodies, each trying to join with another body. The two are trying to become one. It sounds romantic, even spiritual, doesn't it? Yet mathematically speaking, going from two to one means that these people have just reduced themselves. They've engaged in subtraction, not addition. The problem is that their real power and magnitude lie in their identification with the entire Sonship ("the universe"), which is not invited to this party. They are taking in only one person and leaving virtually everything outside. Indeed, they *are* leaving everything outside, for they are not even taking in the one person. If they took the whole person in, the entire universe would come in along with him. But instead, they are taking just part of him in, and usually a very superficial part at that—his brains, his earning power, his impressive pecs, his handsome eyes, etc.

Application: In joining with someone and making the two one, have you ever felt like who you are got left outside, so that you became part of this joint identity that included certain superficial aspects of you, but didn't really include *you*?

6. Across the bridge it is so different! For a time the body is still seen, but <u>not</u> exclusively, as it is seen here. The little spark that holds the Great Rays within it is <u>also</u> visible, and this spark cannot be limited long to littleness. Once you have crossed the bridge, the <u>value</u> of the body is so diminished in <u>your</u> sight that you will see no need at all to <u>magnify</u> it. For you will realize that the <u>only</u> value the body has is to enable you to bring your brothers <u>to</u> the bridge <u>with</u> you, and to be <u>released together</u> there.

Across the bridge, everything looks different. On this side, it's all bodies. While we are riveted on them, we don't realize we are making a big deal out of nothing. On the other side of the bridge, we begin to see the little spark in our brothers, the spark from which the Great Rays shine. The more we look at this spark, the more we begin to see the Rays streaming from it, faint at first, but growing brighter all the time. At the same time that the spark is growing into the Great Rays in our sight, the body is diminishing. It is no longer a temple with sacred rooms and exciting secrets. It becomes purely utilitarian—like socks. Its only purpose is to bring our brothers to the other side of the bridge with us.

7. The bridge itself is nothing more than a transition in the <u>perspective</u> of reality. On this side, everything you see is grossly distorted and <u>completely</u> out of perspective. What <u>is</u> little and insignificant is magnified, and what is strong and powerful cut down to littleness. In the transition there is a period of confusion, in which a sense of actual disorientation may [Ur: seems to] occur. But fear it not, for it means only [Ur: nothing more than] that you have been willing to <u>let go</u> your hold on the distorted frame of reference that <u>seemed</u> to hold your world together. This frame of reference is <u>built</u> around the special relationship. Without <u>this</u> illusion there could <u>be</u> no meaning you would still seek here.

The bridge, of course, is not a literal bridge. It's just "a transition in perspective." Right now, you see everything in a kind of funhouse mirror, one that completely distorts *significance*. It enlarges the insignificant and shrinks the truly significant. As you cross, your perspective is slowly righted.

Try to imagine this. Right now, when you look at someone, you see a body behaving, in both the present and the past. Your image of the person inside the body is really just an amalgam of past behaviors. The holiness that resides in that person irrespective of what he or she has done is probably invisible. Now imagine making the "transition in perspective." As you do, the body and its behaviors progressively shrink in significance. The long record of past (mis)behaviors seems beside the point, irrelevant. Instead, the spark of holiness grows clearer and brighter. Then you begin to see the Great Rays, which fill your vision and become the whole basis for how you think of and relate to this person.

You can imagine that if you actually went through this process, it might be a bit disorienting, as if mountains suddenly looked the size of pebbles and each star looked like the sun. But this disorientation is a very positive sign. It means *it's happening.* You've given up on the special relationship, and this has freed you to question what bodies in general can give you.

> 8. Fear not that you will be abruptly lifted up and hurled into reality. Time is kind, and if you use it on behalf of [Ur: if you use it *for*] reality, it will keep gentle pace with you in your transition. The urgency is only in dislodging your mind from its <u>fixed</u> <u>position</u> here. This will <u>not</u> leave you homeless and <u>without</u> a frame of reference. The period of disorientation, which precedes the actual transition, is far shorter than the time it took to fix your mind so firmly on illusions. Delay will hurt you now <u>more than before,</u> <u>only</u> because you realize it *is* delay, and that escape from pain <u>is really possible</u>. Find hope and comfort, rather than despair, in this: You could not long find even the <u>illusion</u> of love in <u>any</u> special relationship here. For you are no longer <u>wholly</u> insane, and you would soon [Ur: you *would*] recognize the guilt of <u>self</u>-betrayal <u>for</u> <u>what it is.</u>

Our tendency is to stand on this side of the bridge thinking, "If bodies are going to shrink to nothing while invisible rays of holiness fill my vision, this is going to be way too disorienting. I don't think I'm ready for this." We fear that we will go through the process so quickly that we will lose our bearings entirely. This keeps us loitering endlessly on this side of the bridge, afraid to step onto it at all.

Jesus addresses this dilemma: "Just focus on getting on the bridge, and trust that, once on, you'll be watched out for. Trust that the transition will be a gentle one and the disorientation will be far briefer than you fear." What you don't realize, he says, is that it is loitering on this side that is really hurting you.

Application: Do you feel that, in some way, you are loitering on this side of the bridge, afraid to set out for fear of everything being turned upside down? Then say and mean these words:

> *Delay hurts me now more than before,*
>   *only because I realize it **is** delay,*
>   *and that escape from pain is really possible.*
> *I have come too far to find even the **illusion** of love in any special*
>   *relationship here.*
> *If I try, I will only feel guilty for betraying myself.*
> *This should not be a source of despair, but of great hope.*
> *It is time to set off across the bridge.*

9. Nothing you seek to strengthen in the special relationship is <u>really</u> part of you. And you cannot keep <u>part</u> of the thought system that taught you it <u>was</u> real, and understand the Thought that *knows* [Ur: *really* knows] what you are. You <u>have</u> allowed the Thought of your reality to enter your mind, and because <u>you</u> invited it, it <u>will</u> abide with you. Your love for it will not allow you to betray yourself, and you <u>could</u> not enter into a relationship <u>where it could not go with you</u>, for you would <u>not</u> want to be <u>apart</u> from it.

The message of this paragraph is simple: You've come too far now. There's no real going back, and there's no use in trying to compromise. Face the facts and admit that the only way to go now is *forward*.

10. Be glad you have escaped the mockery of salvation the ego offered you, and look not back with longing on the travesty it made of your relationships. Now no one need suffer, for you have come too far to yield to the illusion of the beauty and holiness of guilt. Only the wholly insane could look on death and suffering, sickness and despair, and see it thus. What guilt has wrought is ugly, fearful and very dangerous. See no illusion of truth and beauty there. And be you thankful that there *is* a place where truth and beauty wait for you. Go on to meet them gladly, and learn how much awaits you for the simple willingness to give up

nothing *because* it is nothing.

The Course often urges us to take a cue from Lot's wife and "look not back." The situation is this: By reaching the foot of the bridge, you have come a long way. Now you stand in a middle place, with the bridge in front of you, and unbridled egotism behind you. The big temptation now is to *look back.* You look back at those special relationships and think, "Ah, the good old days! Why am I even *thinking* about crossing this bridge?" What you need to realize is that the good old days only look good from a distance, and only because you are afraid of what lies ahead. If you were to actually dive back into the manic pursuit of specialness, you would feel really ill really fast. What looked so beautiful before was just guilt wearing a red dress. Now that you've begun to see that, it's time to move forward. It's time to be thankful that real beauty and real truth await you—on the other side of the bridge.

> 11. The new perspective you will gain from crossing over will be the understanding of <u>where Heaven *is*</u>. From this side [Ur: From *here*], it seems to be outside and <u>across</u> the bridge. Yet as you cross to <u>join</u> it, <u>it</u> will <u>join with you</u> and <u>become one</u> with you. And you will think, in glad astonishment, that for all this <u>you gave up *nothing*</u>! The joy of Heaven, which <u>has</u> no limit, is <u>increased</u> with each light that returns to take its rightful place within it. Wait no longer, for the Love of God and *you*. And may the holy instant speed you on the way, as it will surely do if you but <u>let</u> it come to you.

On this side of the bridge, Heaven seems so far away, on the other side of lots and lots of toil and sacrifice. Yet that thought is part of the distorted perspective of this side of the bridge. As you reach the other side, you will suddenly think, "My God, Heaven is one with me. It has *always* been one with me. And to think, to gain all its infinite joys, *I gave up nothing!*" If only we could see this now, for surely it is the fear of all that we will have to give up that keeps us from crossing the bridge.

> 12. The Holy Spirit asks only this little help of you: Whenever your thoughts wander to a special relationship which still <u>attracts</u> you, enter with Him into a holy instant, and there <u>let Him release you</u>. He needs only your willingness to <u>share</u> His perspective to give it to you

completely. And your willingness need not be complete <u>because His is</u> <u>perfect</u>. It is His task to atone for your <u>un</u>willingness by His perfect faith, and it is <u>His</u> faith you share with Him there. Out of <u>your</u> recognition of your <u>un</u>willingness for your release, His <u>perfect</u> willingness is <u>given</u> you. Call upon Him, for Heaven is at His call. And <u>let</u> Him call on Heaven <u>for</u> you.

Here comes the practice in which we apply all that we have learned in this section. It is not a particularly welcome practice. I remember leading a group through this in a workshop I was conducting, and I felt like the room turned to stone. What makes it challenging is that it asks us to let go, not of anger or fear, but of the thrill of *attraction*.

Application: Is there a relationship in your life that is particularly attracting you right now? Maybe it's someone new in your life, someone you have hopes about. Try to find some glint of attraction somewhere in your life, and say these lines. When you reach the end, just open your mind to the Holy Spirit, occasionally repeating the final line.

> *The specialness in this relationship is the ugliness of guilt dressed*
> *up as beautiful.*
> *I have already learned that.*
> *Therefore, I will not look back.*
> *Holy Spirit, I don't want the past anymore.*
> *I want to be released from my attraction to the past.*
> *I want to enter a holy instant with You.*
> *I know my willingness isn't perfect.*
> *But that's all right, because Your perfect willingness will make*
> *up for it.*
> *Let me enter a holy instant with You.*

VII. The End of Illusions
Commentary by Robert Perry

1. It is impossible to let the past go <u>without</u> relinquishing the special relationship. For the special relationship is an attempt to <u>re-enact</u> the past <u>and change it</u>. Imagined slights, remembered pain, past disappointments, perceived injustices and deprivations all enter into the special relationship, which becomes a way in which you seek to restore your wounded <u>self</u>-esteem. What basis would you have for choosing a special partner <u>without</u> the past? <u>Every</u> such choice is made because of something "evil" in the past <u>to which you cling</u>, and for which must <u>someone else</u> atone.

This is one of the great "shadow figure" paragraphs, even though the term isn't mentioned. In the special relationship, we choose someone strictly for his suitability to play a role in our vengeance theater. This vengeance theater puts on a restaging of our past. This is the past in which we didn't get the love we wanted, and instead got slights, pain, disappointments, injustices, and deprivations (at least in our perception). The new partner is there to play the role of past partners, only this time to do it right, to reverse all the indignities the past ones dished out. Through this, we restore our wounded self-esteem (what a phrase!). Yet this occurs via the new person atoning for the sins of the old ones. He, then, has to pay for sins he didn't commit, and only because *you* are clinging to them. Is this remotely fair?

2. The special relationship <u>takes vengeance on the past</u>. By seeking to remove suffering <u>in the past</u>, it <u>overlooks</u> the present in its preoccupation with the past and its <u>total commitment</u> to it. <u>No special relationship is experienced in the present</u>. Shades of the past envelop it, and make it what it is. It <u>has</u> no meaning in the present, and if it means nothing <u>now</u>, it cannot have any <u>real</u> meaning at all. How can you change the past <u>except</u> in fantasy? And who can give you what you think <u>the past</u> deprived you of? The past is nothing. Do not seek to lay the blame for deprivation on it, for the past <u>is</u> gone. You cannot <u>really</u> *not* let go what has <u>already</u> gone. It <u>must</u> be, therefore, that <u>you</u> are maintaining the

illusion that it has <u>not</u> gone because you think it serves some purpose that you <u>want fulfilled</u>. And it must also be that this purpose <u>could not be fulfilled in the present</u>, but <u>only</u> in the past.

Let's face it—the previous paragraph was right. Our special relationships are there to make up for our past, in which we didn't get the love we wanted. By getting the new guy to do it right, to give us what we want, we gain a kind of symbolic vengeance on those who, for some bizarre reason, refused to do so. As the new partner showers us with love, we silently address the ghosts in the attic: "See? See what you were supposed to do, and how wrong you were for not doing it?" This is why I called it vengeance theater.

In the special relationship, then, we live in the past. We live in the fantasy that we are actually changing the past. We are showing "them." We are entering a grudge match in which past losses are erased from the scoreboard because this time we win.

Jesus here is trying to make us disturbed by the notion that we are living in the past, living a fantasy existence. The paragraph ends by suggesting that we are doing this on purpose. We know the past is gone; we know we can't change it. But it suits our purposes to act like it *hasn't* and we *can*. How sick is that?

> 3. Do not underestimate the intensity of the ego's drive for vengeance on the past. It is <u>completely</u> savage and <u>completely</u> insane. For the ego remembers everything <u>you</u> have done that has offended it, and seeks retribution of <u>you</u>. The fantasies it brings to its chosen relationships in which to act out its hate are fantasies of <u>your</u> destruction. For the ego holds the past <u>against you</u>, and in your <u>escape</u> from the past it sees <u>itself</u> deprived of the vengeance it believes you so justly merit. Yet without your <u>alliance</u> in your own destruction, the ego could not hold you to the past. ⁷In the special relationship <u>you are allowing your destruction to be</u>. That this is insane is obvious. But what is <u>less</u> obvious is that the <u>present</u> is useless to you while you pursue the ego's goal as its ally.

The temptation is to read this section and think, "No, I've put the past behind me. I'm not trying to prove anything to them. I'm not trying to get from new people what they wouldn't give me." That's called denial. Only when we are willing to acknowledge our deep drive to settle the score with the past can we look at the next layer down. That next layer is that the ego wants to gain vengeance on *us*, for all the times we forgave instead of resented, for all the times we questioned the value of worldly things and events, for all the times we questioned the reality of the ego itself. It hasn't forgotten a single one of these times, and it merely waits until it can punish us in full for all these transgressions. How does it get its vengeance on us? By impelling us to get vengeance on our own past. There is that old saying, "He who seeks revenge better dig two graves." The ego knows this full well. It tells us to dig a grave for the other guy as a way of getting us to dig that second grave.

> 4. The past is gone; seek not to preserve it in the special relationship that binds you to it, and would teach you <u>salvation</u> is past and so you must <u>return</u> to the past to <u>find</u> salvation. There is <u>no</u> fantasy that does not contain the dream of retribution for the past. Would you <u>act out</u> the dream, or let it go?

While we fantasize about how to show them, about how we'll prove all of them wrong, we become trapped in the past. We keep returning to it, again and again, thinking that this is where salvation lies. Is this the kind of shadow existence we really want to lead? To escape the past, we have to give up the special relationship.

> 5. In the special relationship it does not <u>seem</u> to be an acting out of vengeance that you seek. And even when the hatred and the savagery break briefly through [Ur: into awareness], the illusion of love is not profoundly shaken. Yet the one thing the ego <u>never</u> allows to reach awareness is that the special relationship is the acting out of <u>vengeance on yourself</u>. Yet what else <u>could</u> it be? In seeking the special relationship, you look not for glory <u>in yourself</u>. You have <u>denied</u> that it is there, and the relationship becomes your <u>substitute</u> for it. And vengeance becomes <u>your</u> substitute for Atonement, and the <u>escape</u> from vengeance becomes your <u>loss</u>.

There are really three levels of vengeance here, each one more unconscious than the last. The first level is vengeance on the past idiots, the ones who didn't love us like they should have. That is clearly apparent at times. It's not all that hidden. The second level is vengeance on the current partner. This vengeance is basic to the special relationship, simply because the partner is playing the role of the past idiots. This vengeance on our partner, I believe, is "the hatred and the savagery" that break briefly through into awareness. Yet even when this happens—and we all know it does—it does not really shake the illusion of love. It is only when it happens too often that that illusion slowly crumbles.

The third level is the most unconscious. It is what the ego never allows to reach awareness. The third level is vengeance on ourselves. Who suspects that this third level is even there? Who of us thinks, "When I was taking vengeance on my wife (second level) for being just like my mother (first level), I was really taking vengeance on myself (third level)"? Yet there is evidence that that level is indeed there. After all, in the special relationship we are seeking what is ultimately a very demeaning view of ourselves, a view in which we are needy, greedy takers. Why would we seek a self-perception that is basically an attack on ourselves?

> 6. Against the ego's insane notion of salvation the Holy Spirit gently lays the holy instant. We said before that the Holy Spirit must teach through comparisons, and uses opposites to point to truth. The holy instant is the <u>opposite</u> of the ego's fixed belief in salvation through vengeance for the past. In the holy instant it is understood [Ur: *accepted*] that the past is gone, and <u>with</u> its passing the drive for vengeance <u>has been</u> uprooted and has disappeared. The stillness and the peace of *now* enfold you in perfect gentleness. Everything is gone <u>except the truth</u>.

The alternative to our pitiful habit of living in the past is the holy instant. The ego thinks, "Thank God I can prove how wrong they were! I'm really going to enjoy this." But in the holy instant we think, "Thank God the past is gone. In the stillness of now, I feel enfolded in perfect gentleness. I really *am* enjoying this." We stop living in fantasies and find, to our surprise, that the truth is perfectly satisfying.

> 7. For a time you may attempt to bring illusions <u>into</u> the holy instant, to hinder your full awareness of the <u>complete difference</u>, in <u>all</u> respects, between your <u>experience</u> of truth and illusion. Yet you will not attempt this long. In the holy instant the power of the Holy Spirit <u>will</u> prevail, <u>because you joined Him</u>. The illusions you bring with you will weaken

the <u>experience</u> of Him for a while, and will prevent you from <u>keeping</u> the experience in your mind. Yet the holy instant <u>is</u> eternal, and your illusions of time will <u>not</u> prevent the timeless from being what it is, nor you from <u>experiencing</u> it as it is.

This paragraph shows that we can experience diluted holy instants. They come in varying strengths, not because they actually vary, but because we bring into them some of our past illusions. In a meditation, for instance, we have a beautiful experience of the eternal present and we think, "What an amazing spiritual person I am. This will show all those people who thought I was nothing." This weakens the experience and makes it fade from memory faster. But Jesus promises here that we won't keep doing that (thank God). The holy instant will eventually draw us all the way in.

8. What God has given you is truly given, <u>and will be truly received</u>. For God's gifts <u>have</u> no reality <u>apart</u> from your receiving them. <u>Your</u> receiving completes <u>His</u> giving. You will receive *because* it is <u>His</u> Will to give. He gave the holy instant to be given you, and it is impossible that you receive it not *because* He gave it. When He willed that His Son be free, His Son *was* free. In the holy instant is His reminder that His Son will <u>always</u> be <u>exactly</u> as he was created. And <u>everything</u> the Holy Spirit teaches is to remind you that you <u>have</u> received what God has given you.

Application: Do you feel a sense of hopelessness about receiving the holy instant? If so, dwell on these words:

God's gifts have no reality apart from my receiving them.
*I **will** receive **because** it is His Will to give.*
He gave the holy instant to me to be received.
*It is impossible that I receive it not, **because** He gave it.*
In the holy instant, I will experience the freedom that God gave me.
And I will know that I will always be exactly as God created me.

9. There is nothing you <u>can</u> hold against reality. All that must be forgiven are the <u>illusions</u> you have held against your brothers. Their reality <u>has</u> no past, and <u>only</u> illusions can <u>be</u> forgiven. God holds nothing against <u>anyone</u>, for He is <u>incapable</u> of illusions of <u>any</u> kind. Release your brothers from the slavery of <u>their</u> illusions by forgiving them for the illusions <u>you</u> perceive in them. Thus will you learn that <u>you</u> have been forgiven, for it is <u>you</u> who offered them illusions. In the holy instant this is done for you <u>in time,</u> to bring you the true condition of Heaven.

The special relationship is there to make up for all those things we hold against people from our past. They took everything they could, but our special partner is going to give it all back, and more. Isn't that what we hope for? What we don't realize is that we can't hold anything against what is real. We only resent our brothers for *illusions*, and by this resentment we reinforce their slavery to their illusions.

There are two approaches we can take. One is to try to extract from them what they withheld. The other is to forgive them, realizing that they didn't deprive us; we did. We forgive them, then, for the *illusions* we have seen in them. This is how we learn that *we* have been forgiven, for the guilt we carry around comes from chaining them to illusions. This forgiveness is what happens in the holy instant. There, we let the past go, and let everyone off the hook.

10. Remember that you <u>always</u> choose between truth and illusion; between the <u>real</u> Atonement that would heal and the ego's "atonement" that would destroy. The power of God and all His Love, without limit, will support you as you seek only your place in the plan of Atonement arising from His Love. Be an ally of God and <u>not</u> the ego in seeking how Atonement can come to you. His help suffices, for His Messenger understands how to restore the Kingdom <u>to</u> you, and to place <u>all</u> your investment in salvation in your relationship with Him.

We have two choices before us: to go for the ego's "atonement" (in which someone else atones for those past sins against us) or for the real Atonement (in which we enter the holy instant, and let our illusions of past sins be replaced with truth). We can be God's ally and seek our place in His plan. Or we can be the ego's ally, in which we ally with it in our own destruction (as the third paragraph said). It may seem harder to choose God, as the ego's voice is so insistent, so loud and strident. Yet we have help: "The power of God and all His Love, without limit, will support you as you seek only your place in the plan of Atonement arising from His Love."

> 11. Seek and *find* His message in the holy instant, where <u>all</u> illusions are forgiven. From there the miracle extends to bless everyone and to resolve <u>all</u> problems, be they perceived as great or small, possible or impossible. There is <u>nothing</u> that will not give place to Him and to His majesty. To join in close relationship with Him is to accept relationships <u>as real</u>, and through <u>their</u> reality to give over <u>all</u> illusions for the reality of your relationship with God. Praise be to your relationship with Him and to no other. The truth lies there <u>and nowhere else</u>. You choose this or <u>nothing</u>.

In the holy instant, we discover that our illusions have been forgiven, because the past is gone. From this blessed time, the miracle will go out from us, healing all problems, big or small. This is because the power of God is present in the holy instant, ready to flow out from us. For there in this instant is God, waiting to join with us in close relationship. In this eternally satisfying relationship with Him, we discover the reality in all our relationships, and we give over all of our illusions, for they get in the way of the one relationship that our whole being yearns for.

> 12. *Forgive us our illusions, Father, and help us to accept our true relationship with You, in which there are no illusions, and where none can ever enter. Our holiness is Yours. What can there be in us that needs forgiveness when Yours is perfect? The sleep of forgetfulness is only the unwillingness to remember Your forgiveness and Your Love. Let us not wander into temptation, for the temptation of the Son of God is not Your Will. And let us receive only what You have given, and accept but this into the minds which You created and which You love. Amen.*

Application: This beautiful prayer, which is clearly a Course version of the Lord's Prayer, is meant to be prayed, so let us do just that. I recommend fixing a line in your mind and then closing your eyes and saying that line to God, believing that He will really hear. Work your way through the prayer in this way, realizing that it concludes with a request to experience the holy instant, to receive what God has given.

> *Forgive us our illusions, Father,* [forgive us the illusions of sin
>   we have seen in our brothers]
> *and help us to accept our true relationship with You,*
>   *in which there are no illusions, and where none can ever enter.*
> *Our holiness is Yours.* [Our game of vengeance has not turned us
>   into sinners.]
> *What can there be in us that needs forgiveness when Yours is*
>   *perfect?*
> *The sleep of forgetfulness is only the unwillingness to remember*
>   *Your forgiveness and Your Love.*
> *Let us not wander into temptation, for the temptation of the Son*
>   *of God is not Your Will.*
> *And let us receive only what You have given,* [the holy instant]
>   *and accept but this into the minds which You created and which*
>   *You love.*
> *Amen.*

Final application: Think about a current special partner, and then ask yourself the following questions:

1. What people from your past is this person there to make up for? Who are the ones that first come to mind?
2. What did they do wrong that this person is supposed to do right? What were the past people *supposed* to give that you hope (or hoped) that this person *will* give you?
3. Can you see how, if this person gives those things to you, this will prove how wrong the past people were?
4. Can you see that this is an act of vengeance on them?
5. Can you also see how you have hired this person to atone for (pay for) *their* sins?
6. Is that fair?
7. How has this person, in your perception, mainly failed you? Is it for some form of *repeating* of the past that he or she was supposed to make up for?
8. Are there moments when you overtly take vengeance on this

person for repeating the past, for doing it wrong just like the
past people did?

9. How do those moments make you feel about yourself?
10. Can you see that by using this person to give you what the past
refused, you are really living in the past, living in a fantasy of
trying to change the past? How does that idea feel?
11. Do you feel that this quest for what the past denied you
reinforces the idea that glory is not in you, or that it reinforces
a demeaning self-perception in which you need to claw "love"
greedily from others?
12. Could it be that these negative results—feeling guilty,
living in a fantasy of the past, reinforcing a demeaning self-
perception—were the ego's plan from the start?
13. Could it be that the ego is using your quest for vengeance on
others to take vengeance on *you*? How does that possibility
make you feel?

Realize that the holy instant is the solution to this entire approach to
life, and invite it with these words:

> *I choose this instant as the one to offer to my Father.*
> *Let me fully enter this present moment.*
> *Let me discover that the past is over.*
> *Let me set everyone free from the past illusions I have held*
> *against them.*
> *Let me realize that the innocence God gave me is forever intact.*
> *Father, this holy instant would I give to You.*
> *Let me experience the beauty of my relationship with You.*

Commentaries on Chapter 17

FORGIVENESS AND THE HOLY RELATIONSHIP

I. Bringing Fantasy to Truth
Commentary by Robert Perry

1. The betrayal of the Son of God lies <u>only</u> in illusions, and <u>all</u> his "sins" are but his own imagining. His <u>reality</u> is forever sinless. He need not be forgiven but <u>awakened</u>. In his dreams he <u>has</u> betrayed himself, his brothers and his God. Yet what is done in dreams has not been <u>really</u> done. It is impossible to convince the <u>dreamer</u> that this is so, for dreams are what they are *because* of their illusion of reality. Only in waking is the full release from them, for only then does it become <u>perfectly</u> apparent that they had <u>no</u> effect upon reality at all, <u>and did not change it</u>. <u>Fantasies change reality</u>. That is their purpose. They <u>cannot</u> do so <u>in</u> reality, but they *can* do so in the mind that would <u>have reality be different</u>.

In our dreams we have betrayed ourselves (by giving in to the lure of special relationships), our brothers (by using them to feed our specialness), and God (by using our special relationships to supposedly kill Him). Yet for all the guilt we carry over what we've done, we haven't really done any of it. When you kill someone in a dream, are they really dead? Has anything really happened? Is there any actual reason to feel guilty?

Yet you can't fully know this until you wake up from the dream, for the whole point of dreams is to change reality. That is why we have them, because we want to reshape reality to suit our tastes. Hence, we show ourselves convincing scenarios in which reality has magically changed to conform to our wishes. This combination of internal desire and external "proof" makes dreams convincing as long as we are in them.

2. It is, then, only your <u>wish</u> to change reality that is fearful, because <u>by</u> your wish you think you have <u>accomplished</u> what you wish. This strange position, in a sense, <u>acknowledges</u> your power. Yet by <u>distorting</u> it and devoting it to "evil," it also <u>makes it unreal</u>. You cannot be faithful to two masters who ask conflicting things of you. What you use in fantasy you <u>deny</u> to truth. Yet what you <u>give</u> to truth to use <u>for</u> you is <u>safe</u> from fantasy.

We think it is the dream that scares us, but what is really frightening is our own wish to change reality, to twist it to suit our likes. We are frightened by our own autocratic wishes. Our mind is so powerful that as soon as we wish to change reality, a "reality" rises before our eyes in which the wish has been accomplished.

Imagine that you had a fleeting wish for someone you know to die, and then instantly you saw that person fall dead in front of you from a bullet. Wouldn't you become absolutely terrified of your wishes? Thankfully, when you wish to change reality, your mind only produces fantasies, dreams, which merely trick you into thinking that your wish has been accomplished. Yet you could use this same power in a healthy way, to acknowledge reality as it is. These are the only two ways to use the power of your mind, and you can't be faithful to both at once.

> 3. When you maintain that there <u>must</u> be an order of difficulty in miracles, all you mean is that there are some things you would <u>withhold</u> from truth. You believe truth cannot deal with them <u>only</u> because <u>you</u> would keep them <u>from</u> truth. Very simply, your lack of faith in the power that heals <u>all</u> pain arises from <u>your</u> wish to retain some <u>aspects</u> of reality <u>for fantasy</u>. If you but realized what this <u>must</u> do to your appreciation of the whole! What you <u>reserve for yourself</u>, you <u>take away</u> from Him Who would release you. Unless you <u>give it back</u>, it is inevitable that <u>your</u> perspective on reality be warped and uncorrected.

When we read a line like we read yesterday, about the miracle healing all problems, great or small (16.VII.11:2), our skepticism immediately unsheathes its claws. We automatically assume that the miracle is like an engine: the bigger the problem, the harder time this engine will have moving it. This seems backed up by experience, in that miracles only very rarely heal the really big things. But Jesus says here that this has a whole other explanation. Some problems seem harder to heal not because of their objective mass, but because our grip on them is tighter. To put it bluntly, we are attached to our fantasies about them. This grip of ours takes them out of the Holy Spirit's hands, making Him unable to heal them.

Application: Is there some big problem in your life that you would like healed, but that seems too big to heal? Realize that the difficulty in healing it comes not from its objective size, but from the strength of your attachment to the situation acting out your fantasies. What fantasies are you clinging to in this situation?

4. As long as you would have it so, so long will the <u>illusion</u> of an order of difficulty in miracles <u>remain</u> with you. For <u>you</u> have established this order in <u>reality</u> by giving some of it to one teacher, and some to another. And so you learn to deal with <u>part</u> of the truth in one way, and in <u>another</u> way the <u>other</u> part. To <u>fragment</u> truth is to <u>destroy</u> it by rendering it meaningless. <u>Orders</u> of reality is a perspective without understanding; a frame of reference <u>for</u> reality to which it cannot <u>really</u> be compared at all.

The order of difficulty, then, is not established by how big versus how small the problem is. It is established by how much we give the problem over to the Holy Spirit versus how much we give it to our ego. The more we want it to conform to our fantasies, the more we hold it away from the Holy Spirit, and the harder it is going to be to heal.

Doling things out to two different teachers seems to fragment reality itself into different pieces, some of which are small and easy to heal and others of which are huge, inoperable masses. Yet can reality really be like this, in which some things are less real and some are more real? Shouldn't everything within reality be *equally* real?

5. Think you that you can bring truth to fantasy, and learn what truth <u>means</u> from the perspective of illusions? Truth *has* no meaning in illusion. The frame of reference <u>for</u> its meaning <u>must be itself</u>. When you try to bring <u>truth</u> to illusions, you are trying to make illusions real [Ur: *make them real*], and <u>keep</u> them by <u>justifying</u> your belief in them. But to give illusions to truth is to enable truth to teach that the <u>illusions</u> are unreal, and thus enable you to <u>escape</u> from them. Reserve not one idea aside from truth, or you <u>establish</u> orders of reality that <u>must</u> imprison you. ⁷There <u>is</u> no order in reality, because <u>everything</u> there is true.

What does it mean to bring truth to fantasy (or illusions)? It means to bring truth before the judgment seat of fantasy, and let fantasy, from its perspective, dictate what truth is. This brings to mind a story told by Carl Jung, in which a man was for years obsessed from a distance with a woman. Finally, one day he pursued her down an alley, and there, cornered and desperate, she exposed to him a breast eaten away by cancer. Up until that moment, he let his fantasies completely dictate what she was. But finally, he was shocked into letting truth (in the sense here of conventional, factual truth) dispel his fantasies, showing him that she was not the object his fantasies had invented. This is a great symbol for the process we all need to go through. Everything we are attached to is some version of this woman for us, and we need to let the truth, rather than our fantasies, dictate what that thing is.

Application: What is your version of the man's obsession? Look at it in your mind and realize that what you see is a fantasy that you have conjured up. You are not seeing reality. Then say,

> *Holy Spirit, I give this fantasy over to You, to be undone for me.*
> *Only the truth will satisfy me; I want only that.*
> *What is the truth that You want me to see here?*

Then listen for His answer.

6. Be willing, then, to give <u>all</u> you have held <u>outside</u> the truth to Him Who <u>knows</u> the truth, and in Whom all is <u>brought</u> to truth. Salvation from separation would be <u>complete,</u> or will not be at all. Be not concerned with anything except <u>your willingness to have this be accomplished.</u> <u>He</u> will accomplish it; not you. But forget not this: When you become disturbed and lose <u>your</u> peace of mind because <u>another</u> is attempting to solve his problems through fantasy, you are refusing to <u>forgive yourself</u> for just this same attempt. And you are holding <u>both</u> of you <u>away</u> from truth and from salvation. As you <u>forgive</u> him, you <u>restore</u> to truth what was denied by <u>both of you.</u> And you <u>will</u> see forgiveness where <u>you</u> have given it.

We should have one concern and one concern only: to be willing to have all that we have held outside truth be given to Him Who knows the truth. Very seldom will the truth confront us in an alley. We need to voluntarily give our fantasies over to it, to be undone. The undoing is the

Holy Spirit's job, but He can't do that job until we let Him.

As we try to give up our fantasies, we will notice that everyone around is trying to solve their problems through fantasy. We will see them going after some solution that will "solve everything," a solution that they *have* to have, yet which is obviously a pseudo-solution and a substitute for solving the real problem. We usually see this better than they do, and we are often tempted to get upset and judge them. Yet when we do that, we are simultaneously condemning ourselves for *our* fantasy solutions, of which there are many.

Application: Is there someone in your life you are judging for chasing a fantasy solution, a solution that won't work and that conveniently avoids solving the real problem? Once you identify an example, then ask yourself, "What is *my* version of this fantasy solution?" Now repeat,

> *By judging you, [name], for your fantasy solution,*
> *I simultaneously judge myself for my own version of it.*
> *I am thus holding both of us away from truth and from salvation.*
> *As I forgive you, however, I forgive myself.*
> *As I forgive **you**, I forgive **myself**.*
> *And I restore the truth to both of us.*

II. The Forgiven World
Commentary by Robert Perry

1. Can you imagine how beautiful those you forgive will look to you? In <u>no</u> fantasy have you ever seen anything so lovely. Nothing you see here, sleeping or waking, comes near to such loveliness. And nothing will you value like unto this, nor hold so dear. Nothing that you remember that made your heart [Ur: seem to] sing with joy has ever brought you even a little part of the happiness this sight will bring you. <u>For you will see the Son of God</u>. You will behold the beauty the Holy Spirit loves to look upon, and which He thanks the Father for. He was created to see this <u>for</u> you, until <u>you</u> learned to see it for yourself. And all His teaching leads to seeing it and giving thanks with Him.

Application: It is best to do this one on paper. Fill in the blanks in writing, and then go through the whole thing, reading it slowly and personally. Take your time.

Can you imagine how beautiful _____ and _____ (people in your life) will look to you when you have forgiven them?

In no fantasy, not even in your favorite fantasy about _____ (a favorite fantasy), have you ever seen anything so lovely.

Nothing you see here, including _____ (something beautiful you've seen with your waking eyes) and _____ (something beautiful you've seen in a dream), comes near to such loveliness.

And nothing, even _____ (something you deeply value in this world), will you value like unto this, nor hold so dear.

Nothing that you remember that made your heart sing with joy, Including _____ (an event that made your heart sing with joy), has ever brought you even a little part of the happiness this sight will bring you.

For you will see the Son of God in _____ and _____ (the same individuals you used at the beginning).

You will behold the beauty the Holy Spirit loves to look upon, and which He thanks the Father for.

This loveliness is not a fantasy.

It is the real world....

2. This loveliness is <u>not</u> a fantasy. It is the real world, bright and clean and new, with everything sparkling under the open sun. Nothing is hidden here, for everything has <u>been</u> forgiven and there <u>are</u> no fantasies to hide the truth. The bridge between that world and this is <u>so</u> little and <u>so</u> easy to cross, that you could not believe it is the meeting place of worlds so different. Yet this little bridge is the strongest thing that touches on this world at all. This little step, so small it has escaped your notice, is a stride through time into eternity, beyond all ugliness into beauty that will enchant you, and will never cease to cause you wonderment at its perfection.

What does it mean to see the real world? It means to see the ecstatic vision of the Son of God in everyone, and to thereby experience a happiness that no happiness in this world can come near. In the real world, no gems are hidden under heavy rocks of fantasy; everything is out in the open, sparkling under the warm sun.

The image of the bridge comes in again here. In picturing the bridge before, we probably imagined one of those long suspension bridges, with crumbling slats and gaps to watch out for. But Jesus clearly has in mind something more like a very sturdy wooden bridge over a two-foot-wide stream. The bridge is incredibly short and unbelievably easy to cross, if one simply wants to. Are we willing to see the bridge in these terms?

3. This step, the smallest ever taken [Ur: by anything], is still the greatest accomplishment of all in God's plan of Atonement. All else is learned, but <u>this</u> is <u>given,</u> complete and wholly perfect. No one but Him Who <u>planned</u> salvation could complete it thus. The real world, in its loveliness, <u>you</u> learn to reach. Fantasies are all undone, and no one and nothing remain still bound by them, and by <u>your own</u> forgiveness you are <u>free to see.</u> Yet [Ur: And] <u>what</u> you see is only what <u>you made,</u> with the blessing of your forgiveness on it. And with this final blessing of God's Son <u>upon himself,</u> the <u>real</u> perception, born of the new perspective he has learned, has served its purpose.

Strangely, in this paragraph, the small step across the bridge from this world into the real world now becomes the step from the real world into Heaven. This switch has always puzzled me. Anyway, both processes are actually in this paragraph. We gain the real world through the work of undoing our fantasies. Rather than chaining people to our fantasies, we forgive people for not acting them out. Yet even in the real world we see something slightly short of true reality. We see the same old illusions, only forgiven. This blanket forgiveness represents a final blessing on ourselves, and at that point this new kind of perception has served its purpose.

> 4. The stars will disappear in light, and the sun that opened up the world to beauty will vanish. Perception will be meaningless when it has been perfected, for everything that has been used for learning will have no function. Nothing will ever change; no shifts nor shadings, no differences, no variations that made perception possible will still occur. The perception of the real world will be so short that you will barely have time to thank God for it. For God will take the last step swiftly, when you have reached the real world and have been made ready for Him.

The opening sentence is a great twist on the usual image of the end of the world: "Immediately after those horrible days end, the sun will be darkened, the moon will not give light, the stars will fall from the sky, and the powers of heaven will be shaken" (Matthew 24:29, NIV). Here, instead of the sun and stars disappearing in darkness, they disappear in *light*. This is how the Course describes what happens in the final step. We have reached perfect perception and just a split second later God lifts us into knowledge. There, "nothing will ever change." Just try to imagine that. There will be no shifts. There will be no shadings from light to dark. You will not have a bright light surrounded by darkness (which is why the stars had to go). One thing will not be different from another. Nothing will vary from time to time or place to place. All of the changes and differences that made perception possible will be gone forever. There will just be pure, endless light.

> 5. The real world is attained simply by the <u>complete</u> forgiveness of the old, the world you see <u>without</u> forgiveness. The Great Transformer of

perception will undertake <u>with</u> you the careful searching of the mind that <u>made</u> this world, and uncover <u>to you</u> the <u>seeming</u> reasons for your making it. In the light of the <u>real</u> reason that He brings, as you follow Him, He will <u>show</u> you that there is <u>no</u> reason here at all. Each spot <u>His</u> reason touches grows alive with beauty, and what <u>seemed</u> ugly in the darkness of your <u>lack</u> of reason is suddenly released to loveliness. Not even what the Son of God made in insanity could be without a hidden spark of beauty that gentleness could release.

6. All this beauty will rise to bless your sight as you look upon the world with forgiving eyes. For forgiveness literally <u>transforms</u> vision, and lets you see the real world reaching quietly and gently across chaos, removing <u>all</u> illusions that had twisted your perception and fixed it on the past. The smallest leaf becomes a thing of wonder, and a blade of grass a sign of God's perfection.

Here is a powerful account of the Last Judgment (though not mentioned by name), the process by which our perception undergoes its final purification, in preparation for the last step. At the point at which our perfection is *almost* perfect, the Holy Spirit will open ancient vaults in our mind, vaults that have been closed for billions of years, and there we will discover our "seeming reasons" for making this world, for making all the stars and planets and grass and trees. In light of His *real* reason, we will discover that our *seeming* reasons were actually an *absence* of reason. We made the world out of irrational hate.

Yet as we sift through these seeming reasons, we will discover that even in the midst of this hate there was a tiny spark of love that went into the making of the world. And now we will see everything we made *only* in light of this tiny spark of love. We will see it as one sees a child's sculpture—clumsy, made for petty reasons, but containing one small feature that speaks of his dear love for his mother. What do you think his mother will see in this sculpture? She'll see only that spark of love, of course. And that's how we'll see everything in this world. We'll see each thing as having that spark behind it, overlooking the hate and insanity that shaped the bulk of it. This explains that line, "The smallest leaf becomes a thing of wonder, and a blade of grass a sign of God's perfection."

This actually fits the Course's second definition of seeing the real world. The first is seeing the Son of God in everyone. The second is seeing only the loving thoughts that went into the making of this world.

7. From the forgiven world the Son of God is lifted easily into his home. And there he knows that he has <u>always</u> rested there in peace. Even salvation will become a dream, and vanish from his mind. For salvation <u>is</u> the end of dreams, and with the closing of the dream will have no meaning. Who, awake in Heaven, <u>could</u> dream that there could ever be <u>need</u> of salvation?

When you see only the forgiven world, forgiven for all the hate you injected into its very DNA, then God will lift you home. There, you will not only forget the ego; you will even forget *salvation*. The whole drama of problem *and* solution will vanish from your mind. All you will know is that you have been here forever. And you will be right.

8. How much do you <u>want</u> salvation? It will <u>give</u> you the real world, trembling with readiness to <u>be</u> given you. The eagerness of the Holy Spirit to give you this is so intense He would not wait, although He waits in patience. <u>Meet</u> His patience with your <u>impatience</u> at delay in meeting Him. Go out in gladness to meet with your Redeemer, and walk with Him in trust out of this world, and into the real world of beauty and forgiveness.

How much do we want salvation? It will give us a world whose loveliness and joy vastly exceed anything we've ever experienced in this world. What are we waiting for? This real world is not holding itself apart from us. It actually *trembles* with readiness to be given us, and the Holy Spirit is intensely eager to give it. Let us not grow impatient with Him for mysteriously withholding it from us, as we so often do. He has been knocking eagerly at the door for untold eons, with this very gift in hand, wrapped and ready for us. Rather, we must become actually impatient with our own delay in answering the door. We must get out of bed and rush out in gladness to meet Him, "and walk with Him in trust out of this world, and into the real world of beauty and forgiveness."

Application: Are you impatient with the slow pace of your spiritual progress? Then say,

How can I be impatient with the Holy Spirit?
He is intensely eager to give to me,

and the gift itself trembles with readiness to be given me.
*I choose instead to be impatient with my **own** delay.*

Then ask yourself, "How am I delaying in meeting the Holy Spirit to accept His gift of the real world?"

III. Shadows of the Past
Commentary by Robert Perry

1. To forgive is merely to remember only the loving thoughts you gave in the past, and those that were given you. All the rest must be forgotten. Forgiveness is a selective remembering, based not on your selection. For the shadow figures you would make immortal are "enemies" of reality. Be willing to forgive the Son of God for what he did not do. The shadow figures are the witnesses you bring with you to demonstrate he did what he did not. Because you bring [Ur: brought] them, you will hear them. And you who keep [Ur: *kept*] them by your own selection do not understand how they came into your mind, and what their purpose is. They represent the evil that you think was done to you. You bring them with you only that you may return evil for evil, hoping that their witness will enable you to think guiltily of another and not harm yourself. They speak so clearly for the separation that no one not obsessed with keeping separation could hear them. They offer you the "reasons" why you should enter into unholy alliances to support the ego's goals, and make your relationships the witness to its power.

This is perhaps the most important section on the shadow figures—our images of people from our past who didn't give us what we wanted.

To forgive means remembering only the love from the past, the love you gave and that was given you. This doesn't mean that love was most of what happened (it probably wasn't). It means that only the love was real. The rest is past; it is over. And it was never truly real in the first place. What people did to hurt us was never really done. Imagine really seeing people from this vantage point: "The love you gave to me was eternally real. The rest of what you did was never really done."

This requires a highly selective remembering, a remembering only of the love. Unfortunately, we already engage in selective remembering, a remembering of the attack. That's what the shadow figures are all about. They are our lopsided memories of the people who wronged us. We carry them around like a parade of witnesses, who one by one offer testimony in support of our case against the world. The testimony makes constant reference to facts, but the facts are distorted, cherry-picked, and artfully woven together to create a case that is utterly convincing even though completely false, the essence of which is, "I was done wrong by."

This case then becomes the justification for everything we do. It gives us permission to attack others and remain completely innocent. It gives us reasons to enter into unholy alliances with other people to boost our ego. With this parade of witnesses, dutifully recounting their long story of injustice, we can justify literally anything.

> 2. It is these shadow figures that would <u>make the ego holy</u> in your sight, and teach you what you do to keep <u>it</u> safe is really <u>love</u>. The shadow figures <u>always</u> speak for vengeance, and <u>all</u> relationships into which they enter are totally insane. <u>Without exception</u>, these relationships have <u>as their purpose</u> the <u>exclusion</u> of the truth about the other, <u>and of yourself</u>. This is why you see <u>in both</u> what is not there, and <u>make</u> of both the slaves of vengeance. And why whatever reminds you of your past grievances attracts you, and seems to go by the name of love, no matter how distorted the associations by which you arrive at the connection may be [Ur: And why whatever reminds you of your *past* grievances, no matter how distorted the associations by which you *arrive* at the remembrance may be, *attracts* you, and seems to you to go by the name of love]. And finally, why all such relationships become attempts [Ur: the attempt] at union <u>through the body</u>, for <u>only</u> bodies <u>can</u> be seen as means for vengeance. That bodies are central to all unholy relationships is evident. Your <u>own</u> experience has taught you this. But what you may not [Ur: do *not*] realize are <u>all</u> the reasons that go to <u>make</u> the relationship unholy. For <u>unholiness</u> seeks to <u>reinforce</u> itself, as holiness does, by gathering <u>to</u> itself what it perceives as <u>like</u> itself.

These paragraphs describe the shadow figures as speaking. We can imagine them (as I said above) as a series of witnesses that take the stand. Mom (actually, our distorted memory of Mom) gets up on the stand and says, "I never loved Sally as much as her sister, simply because her sister so outperformed her in school." Distorted Memory of Dad takes the stand and says, "I just never spent much time with Sally. I really wanted a son." Distorted Memory of First Husband gets up and says, "Sally put on weight and, after a while, my secretary looked so much more attractive."

The tape of their testimony runs in our head on a continuous loop. Having listened to this loop countless times, we—the judge, jury, and prosecuting attorney—have come to some firm conclusions. First, given the injustices done to our ego in the past, whatever we do to protect it now is absolutely necessary. Second, our sole purpose in life is to get these people back, which we do by having someone in the present happily give us all the love that they withheld. Third, the person to do this in the present must remind us of the shadow figures (even if the way they remind us is extremely convoluted and indirect), or else this person's love is not so relevant. If someone just like Mom gives us the love Mom wouldn't, that shows just how appallingly wrong Mom was. Fourth, payment must be made by our current partner's body. By joining with our partner's body we (think we) gain vengeance on the bodies of the shadow figures. This is why bodies are so crucial in the special relationship.

> 3. In the unholy relationship, it is <u>not</u> the body of the other with which union is attempted, but the bodies of those <u>who are not there</u>. For even the <u>body</u> of the other, <u>already</u> a severely limited perception of him, is <u>not</u> the central focus as it is, or in entirety. What can be used for fantasies of vengeance, and what can be most readily associated with those on whom vengeance is <u>really</u> sought, is centered on and <u>separated off</u> as being the only parts <u>of value</u>. Every step taken in the making, the maintaining and the breaking off of the unholy relationship is a move toward further fragmentation and unreality. The shadow figures enter more and more, and the one in whom they <u>seem</u> to be <u>decreases</u> in importance.

This is one of the more uncomfortable points about shadow figures. Sex with the current partner is, on an emotional level, sex with the shadow figures. It is "ghost sex." By having sex with the current partner, we are (again, on an emotional level) forcibly extracting from the shadow figure's body the love he or she wouldn't give us, and thus gaining vengeance on the shadow figure at the same time. You may think you were closing your eyes and fantasizing that your lover was really Brad Pitt, but little did you realize that, given that the main shadow figures are parents…well, I'll let you complete that sentence. (You definitely don't want to think about this while in the act.)

It gets worse. You have not only reduced your partner to a body, you have really reduced him or her to particular body parts that you especially focus on. You may assume that these parts are defined by being attractive or sexually significant. But they are really defined by being "most readily associated with those on whom vengeance is really sought." They, in other words, are the parts that most remind you of the shadow figures.

In other words, the current partner is just a projection screen for the shadow figures, and the more time goes on, the more you are living and interacting with the ghosts in the attic.

> 4. Time is indeed unkind to the unholy relationship. For time *is* cruel in the ego's hands, as it is kind when used for gentleness. The attraction of the unholy relationship begins to fade and to be questioned almost at once. Once it is formed, doubt <u>must</u> enter in, because its purpose <u>is</u> impossible. [Ur: The only such relationships which *retain* the fantasies which center on them, are the ones which have been *dreamed* of, but have *not* been made at all. Where *no* reality has entered, there is *nothing* to intrude upon the *dream* of happiness. But consider what this means; the more *reality* that enters into the unholy relationship, the *less satisfying* it becomes. And the more the *fantasies* can encompass, the greater the satisfaction seems to be.] The "ideal" of the unholy relationship thus becomes one in which the <u>reality</u> of the other does not <u>enter at all</u> to "spoil" the dream. And the <u>less</u> the other <u>really</u> brings to the relationship, the "better" it becomes. Thus, the attempt at union becomes a way of <u>excluding</u> even the one with whom the union was sought. For it was <u>formed</u> to <u>get him out of it</u>, and join with fantasies in uninterrupted "bliss."

This paragraph is a sad explanation of why relationships erode over time. When we start out, we have that rush of excitement about all that this person is and all that he could be for us. Little do we realize that this excitement comes from projecting onto him our shadow figures. We are really thinking, "Wow! Here is Dad again, and this time he is going to love me *so* much!"

The problem is that this only works when we don't yet know the person. Once we do get to know him more, his behavior starts to instill little doubts. Remember those first doubts you had about that special someone? These doubts inevitably snowball. We gradually switch from "This is the new reformed Dad" to "Oh no, this is the old Dad all over again!" We slowly realize, in light of accumulating evidence, that the dream won't come true.

What is ideal, then, is a relationship in which the other brings very little to the relationship, and therefore leaves the projection screen nice and blank so that our fantasies can go up on the screen without any competing images from their side. We want a mail-order bride that is demure, subservient and speaks no English. Even there, however, there will be some disappointment of the fantasy. The only relationships where the fantasies can remain completely undimmed over time (as the extra Urtext material says) are those relationships that are nothing *but* fantasies, relationships that never actually happen. Have you ever noticed how those can stay pristine and perfect for years and years?

5. How can the Holy Spirit bring <u>His</u> interpretation of the body as a means of communication into relationships whose <u>only</u> purpose is <u>separation</u> from reality? What forgiveness *is* enables Him to do so. If all <u>but</u> loving thoughts have been forgotten, what remains <u>is</u> eternal. And the <u>transformed</u> past is made <u>like the present</u>. No longer does the past <u>conflict</u> with *now*. <u>This</u> continuity <u>extends</u> the present by increasing its reality <u>and its value</u> in your perception of it. In these loving thoughts is the spark of beauty hidden in the ugliness of the unholy relationship where <u>hatred</u> is remembered; yet [though hidden, the spark is] there to <u>come alive</u> as the relationship is given to Him Who <u>gives</u> it life and beauty. That is why Atonement centers <u>on the past</u>, which is the <u>source</u> of separation, and where it must be undone. For separation must be corrected <u>where it was made</u>.

Application: Think of someone with whom you have a long and checkered history, and silently speak these lines to them.

*The only thing real about our past was the love you gave me and
    I gave you.*
All the rest was never real in the first place.
The real past, then, is like the real present.
Both are beautiful and clean and free of guilt.
*The love we gave each other is the spark of beauty in our
    relationship.*
*And this spark will come alive as I give the relationship to the
    Holy Spirit.*
Let all the separation from our past be undone.

6. The <u>ego</u> seeks to "resolve" <u>its</u> problems, <u>not</u> at their source, but where they were <u>not</u> made. And thus it seeks to guarantee there <u>will</u> be no solution. The Holy Spirit wants [Ur: wills] only to make <u>His</u> resolutions complete and perfect, and so He seeks and <u>finds</u> the source of problems <u>where it is,</u> and there <u>undoes</u> it. And with each step in <u>His</u> undoing is the <u>separation</u> more and more undone, and <u>union</u> brought closer. <u>He</u> is not at all confused by <u>any</u> "reasons" for separation. <u>All</u> He perceives in separation is that it <u>must be undone.</u> Let Him uncover the hidden spark of beauty in your relationships, and <u>show</u> it to you. Its loveliness will so attract you that you will be unwilling ever to lose the sight of it again. And you will <u>let</u> this spark transform the relationship so you can see it more and more. For you will <u>want</u> it more and more, and become increasingly unwilling to <u>let</u> it be hidden from you. And you will learn to seek for and <u>establish</u> the conditions in which this beauty <u>can</u> be seen.

The ego never tries to solve the real problem. Once you let it define what the problem is, then, you are doomed to pursue fantasy solutions. The ego tells you to listen to the testimony of the shadow figures and *they* will tell you the problem. In this view, the problem is that in your past nobody loved you, not really, not enough.

The Holy Spirit takes an opposite tack. He says that the problem is in how you *look on* the past. Do you see it as a heavy drama in which nobody loved you? If so, the past becomes a continual justification for separation. After all, how could you unite with others given the way they've treated you? Instead, He teaches you to see in the past only the spark of beauty, the love that you gave and that was given you. If you just let Him show you this hidden spark, you will find it so incredibly lovely that you will never want it hidden again. You will learn how to make sure that it is always out in the open, where everyone can see it and love it.

7. All this you will do gladly, if you but let Him hold the spark before you, to light your way and make it <u>clear</u> to you. God's Son is one. Whom God has <u>joined</u> as one, the ego <u>cannot</u> put asunder. The spark of holiness <u>must</u> be safe, however hidden it may be, in <u>every</u> relationship. For the Creator of the one relationship has <u>left</u> no part of it without <u>Himself.</u> <u>This</u> is the only part of the relationship the Holy Spirit sees, because He knows that <u>only</u> this is true. <u>You</u> have made the relationship unreal, and <u>therefore</u> unholy, by seeing it <u>where</u> it is not and as it <u>is</u> not.

Give the past to Him Who can change your mind about it for you. But first, be sure you fully realize what you have made the past to represent, and why.

Every relationship was created by God as holy. Every relationship is a sacred part of the One Relationship between Father and Son, and thus every one contains God. Therefore, outside of time, we already have a full-blown, total relationship with each and every Son of God, a relationship of pure, undivided love. The love that we give and receive in this world—the spark of beauty—is a manifestation of the love at the primordial foundation of the relationship.

Because of that foundation, the spark of beauty *must* be there in every single relationship. There is no use saying, "Look, there was just no spark of beauty in my relationship with my father." Your memory may be so selective that it's invisible to you, but it's still there. And when the Holy Spirit looks on that relationship, that is *all He sees*. Therefore, give the past to Him. Let Him show you the spark, and it will light your way home.

Application: Think of a relationship in which the love seems obscured, hidden. Now ask the Holy Spirit,

> *Holy Spirit, what is the spark of beauty, the spark of love, in this relationship?*
> *Show it to me.*

Then listen quietly, until you get a sense of His answer. If your confidence in getting an answer starts to wane, or your mind beings to wander, repeat your question again, and keep listening.

8. The past becomes the [Ur: In brief, the past is *now* your] justification for entering into a continuing, unholy alliance with the ego against the present. For the present *is* forgiveness. Therefore, the relationships the unholy alliance dictates are not perceived nor felt as *now*. Yet the frame of reference to which the present is referred for meaning is an *illusion* of the past, in which those elements that fit the purpose of the unholy alliance are retained, and all the rest let go. And what is thus let go is

all the truth the past could ever <u>offer</u> to the present as witnesses for <u>its</u> reality. [Ur: While] what is <u>kept</u> but witnesses to the reality of dreams.

Why have you made the past into what it is for you? To justify teaming up with your ego in a war against the present. Why is the present seen as such a threat? Because it *is* forgiveness. In the present, the past is gone, and thus everyone is off the hook. That's forgiveness.

How do you and your ego defeat the present? You experience your relationships not in the present, but as a mere footnote on the page of the past. More plainly put, you interpret them from a past frame of reference. This can seem quite reasonable. After all, past experience should tell us *something* useful about the present and future. And it could, if we saw the past truly. As it is, though, we see the present in light of a fake past, a fictional story that we wrote, "inspired" by selected past events. We have been the ultimate spin doctor, spinning all the facts so as to make our ego the hero and make others the villains. And we simply ignore all evidence to the contrary. Yet this discarded evidence—the love, the spark of beauty—"is all the truth the past could ever offer."

> 9. It is still up to you to choose [Ur: to be willing] to join with truth or with illusion. But remember that to choose <u>one</u> is to <u>let the other go</u>. Which one you choose <u>you</u> will endow with beauty and reality, because the choice <u>depends</u> on which you value more. The spark of beauty or the veil of ugliness, the real world or the world of guilt and fear, truth or illusion, freedom or slavery—it is all the same. For you can <u>never</u> choose <u>except</u> between God and the ego. Thought systems are but true or false, and all their <u>attributes</u> come simply from what they <u>are</u>. Only the Thoughts of God <u>are</u> true. And all that follows <u>from</u> them <u>comes from</u> what they are, and is as true as is the holy Source from Which they came.

It all comes down to our choice. Every choice the Course has been talking about is just another permutation of the one choice between God and the ego. We don't like the lack of wiggle room implied here. We want the freedom to choose both, or choose a different one at different times. We approach God and the ego as if they were editorialists writing a series of opinions. "In this case, I agree with what God has to say, but over here, the ego sounds more right to me." What we don't realize is that everything they say is all of a piece and flows directly from their foundation. God's Thoughts are all true because they come from God. The ego's thoughts are all false because they come from the father of lies. The choice becomes easy if we will just acknowledge this one thing.

> 10. My holy brother [Ur: brothers], I would enter into all your relationships, and step between you and your fantasies. Let my relationship to you be real to you, and let me bring reality to your perception of your brothers. They were not created to enable you to hurt yourself through them. They were created to create with you. This is the truth that I would interpose between you and your goal of madness. Be not separate from me, and let not the holy purpose of Atonement be lost to you in dreams of vengeance. Relationships in which such dreams are cherished have excluded me. Let me enter in the Name of God and bring you peace, that you may offer peace to me.

Application — a visualization:

Picture in front of you a special relationship partner, and ask yourself the following questions.

How do you want this person to be?

What do you want this person to give you?

If he (you can substitute "she" if you want) is and does everything you want, what will that prove to the people of the past?

Now realize that what you are seeing in front of you isn't the actual person at all.

It is just an amalgam of various shadow figures and fantasies about how they will behave now.

What you are looking at is a picture of your fantasies of vengeance.

You are trying to join with ghosts.

Now hear Jesus speak to you:

"My holy brother, I would enter into this relationship, and step between you and your fantasies."

See him do just that: See him step in between you and the fantasy image you see in front of you.

Notice how, as he does, the desire for the fantasy immediately grows cold.

Recognize that Jesus is real, far more real than the fantasy you were
seeing.

He says,

"Let my relationship to you be real to you, and let me show you your
real brother, behind the veil of your fantasies."

While the fantasy image remains behind Jesus, a shining figure joins
Jesus by his side.

This is your brother as he really is; picture him however you like.

Jesus says, "He was not created to enable you to hurt yourself through
him.

He was created to *create* with you."

Now both Jesus and your brother walk over and join hands with you.

You feel a renewed commitment to a real joining with this real person,
not with your fantasies.

In closing, Jesus says,

"Do not exclude me from your relationships.

Let me enter in the Name of God and bring you peace, that *you* may
offer peace to me."

IV. The Two Pictures
Commentary by Robert Perry

1. God established <u>His</u> relationship with you <u>to make you happy,</u> and nothing <u>you</u> do that does <u>not</u> share His purpose <u>can</u> be real. The purpose <u>God</u> ascribed to anything <u>is</u> its only function. Because of <u>His</u> reason for creating <u>His</u> relationship with you, the function of relationships became forever "to make happy." *And nothing else.* To fulfill this function you relate to your creations as God to His. For nothing God created is <u>apart</u> from happiness, and nothing God created but would <u>extend</u> happiness as its Creator did. Whatever does not fulfill this function [Ur: Whatever fulfills this function *not,*] <u>cannot be real</u>.

To think that God established His relationship with me to make me happy feels wonderful. It also feels great to think that in doing so, He cast the die for all relationships. All of them are supposed to follow the template laid down by that original relationship. All of them exist in order to make happy. Note the contrast with our current relationships. There is a difference between "I am establishing this relationship with you to make you happy" and "I am just using you to take vengeance on my mother by making you atone for her sins." To the extent we establish relationships for the latter reason, they are not real relationships, for only what fulfills the function of making happy can be real.

2. In this world it is impossible to create [creating does *not* happen in this world, only in Heaven]. Yet it *is* possible to make happy. I [Ur: We] have said repeatedly [see 15.V.5] that the Holy Spirit would not <u>deprive</u> you of your special relationships, but would <u>transform</u> them. And all that is meant by that is that He will <u>restore</u> to them the function <u>given</u> them by God. The function <u>you</u> have given them is clearly <u>not</u> to make happy. But the holy relationship <u>shares</u> God's purpose, rather than aiming to make a <u>substitute</u> for it. Every special relationship <u>you</u> have made <u>is</u> a substitute for God's Will, and glorifies yours instead of His <u>because of the illusion</u> [Ur: *delusion*] <u>that they are different</u>.

It is in our relationship with our creations that we most resemble

God's relationship with us, but our creations are in Heaven, not on earth. Yet our relationships on earth *can* share the function of these heavenly relationships, the function of making happy. Therefore, rather than dumping relationships altogether, we need to let the Holy Spirit transform their function. They need to express God's Will of making happy, rather than our will of taking vengeance.

This is an important point, because it is very easy to think that we should just jettison the whole relationship enterprise. Jesus, however, says no; we should transform it.

> 3. You have made <u>very real</u> relationships even in this world. Yet you do not recognize them because you have raised their <u>substitutes</u> to such predominance that, when truth calls to you, as it does constantly, <u>you answer with a substitute</u>. Every special relationship you have made has, as its fundamental purpose, the aim of occupying your mind so completely that <u>you will not hear</u> the call of truth.

So, we *have* made real relationships (a synonym for holy relationships) in this world. The problem is, we don't expect them to really deliver happiness. When we feel that call of truth rise up in our mind, when we feel that yearning for the infinite, we automatically assume that the answer is a special relationship. We think, "If I could only get that ring on Jerry's finger, that yearning would be satisfied." We assume this so quickly and thoughtlessly, because we aren't *really* listening to that call. Its real nature has been drowned out in all the excitement over this relationship. And that's the whole idea. Have you ever noticed how effective a new special relationship is in drowning out everything else, especially God?

> 4. In a sense, the special relationship was the <u>ego's</u> answer to the creation of the Holy Spirit, Who was God's Answer to the separation. For although the ego did not understand <u>what</u> had been created, it <u>was</u> aware of threat. The whole defense system the ego evolved to <u>protect</u> the separation from the Holy Spirit was in response to the gift with which God blessed it, and <u>by</u> His blessing enabled it to be <u>healed</u>. This blessing holds <u>within itself</u> the truth about everything. And the truth is that the Holy Spirit <u>is</u> in close relationship with you, because in Him is your relationship with God restored to you. The relationship with Him

has never been broken, because the Holy Spirit has not been separate from anyone <u>since</u> the separation. And through Him have all your holy relationships been carefully preserved, to serve God's purpose <u>for</u> you.

The special relationship is the answer to the Answer; the ego's answer to God's Answer, the Holy Spirit. It's as if there is a cosmic arms race going on. The ego sensed, through its intelligence network, that God had created the ultimate separation-busting weapon (so to speak). So the ego had to respond with its own new weapon, something that had power to drown out the sweet call of the Holy Spirit in our mind.

It is appropriate that the ego used relationships to entice us away from the Holy Spirit, for relationship is His keynote. He is in close relationship with us. In Him, our relationship with God is preserved intact and unbroken. And in Him, all our holy relationships with each other have also been preserved. This makes the Holy Spirit a powerful draw for us, simply because our desire for relationship runs so deep. So the ego thought, "The only way I can draw these guys away from that Holy Spirit is by offering them the same thing: relationship. I need to offer a relationship with so many bells and whistles and necklaces and undergarments that they will never notice I have sold them a counterfeit relationship."

> 5. The ego is always alert [Ur: *is* hyperalert] to threat, and the part of your mind into which the ego was accepted is <u>very</u> anxious to preserve its reason, <u>as it sees it</u>. It does <u>not</u> realize that it is totally insane. And <u>you</u> must realize <u>just what this means</u> if <u>you</u> would be restored to sanity. The insane <u>protect</u> their thought systems, <u>but they do so</u> [Ur: *do it*] <u>insanely</u>. And <u>all</u> their defenses are <u>as insane as what they are supposed to protect</u>. The separation has <u>nothing</u> in it, no <u>part</u>, <u>no</u> "reason," and <u>no</u> attribute that is <u>not</u> insane. And its "protection" <u>is</u> part of it, as insane as the whole. The special relationship, which is its chief defense, <u>must</u> therefore be insane.

This paragraph begins a discussion (well, it actually began in paragraph 3) that is hard to follow. Its key line, "Defenses do what they would defend," is one we think we already understand. Yet we completely misunderstand it. So please try to open your mind and follow very carefully what I will say. Understanding it properly is the key to the whole section.

The situation is this: The ego is under threat from the Holy Spirit, which means the Holy Spirit could potentially lure us away from the ego. That's the threat. So the ego has to protect itself. It has to defend itself. This means offering us enticements that lure us back to the ego, away from the Holy Spirit. The problem, however, is that the ego is totally insane. Everything in it is insane. And so its enticements are also insane. The special relationship is its chief enticement (remember, the ego defends itself with enticements), so it too must be insane.

As an analogy, imagine that you are with a totally crazy person (who represents the ego). He is absolutely mad, which results in his being an abusive partner. Now imagine that a potential partner comes along who has a heart of gold, is goodness personified, and wants nothing more than to be with you (he, of course, represents the Holy Spirit). Your current partner is going to be incredibly threatened, right? So he now has to lure you back with gifts, with enticements. He will do his best to make these look ultra-desirable. But remember, he is insane. So his enticement will ultimately be insane as well. They look attractive, but underneath that layer of paint they are pure madness, just like he is.

> 6. You have but little difficulty now in realizing that the thought system the special relationship protects is but a system of delusions. You recognize, at least in general terms, that the ego is insane. Yet the special relationship still seems to you somehow to be "different." Yet we have looked at it far closer than we have at many other aspects of the ego's thought system that you have been more willing to let go. While this one remains, you will not let the others go. For this one is not different. Retain this one, and you have retained the whole.

Continuing my analogy, let's imagine that when your crazy partner offers you his enticements, they work. You get sucked back in. Wouldn't one of your friends say, "Don't you know him by now? He's crazy. These gifts he's holding out are bound to be crazy, too, however good they look now."

That's what Jesus is saying here: "You've learned that the ego is delusional. Yet somehow you think that the special relationship is different, that it's somehow sane. Yet the special relationship is the ego's chief enticement. Why would you expect it to be any different from the rest of the ego? You cannot keep it and let the other aspects of the ego go. They stay or go together."

7. It is essential to realize that <u>all</u> defenses *do* what they would <u>defend</u>. The underlying basis for their effectiveness is that they <u>offer</u> what they defend. What they defend is placed <u>in</u> them for safe-keeping, and as <u>they</u> operate <u>they bring it to you</u>. Every defense operates <u>by giving gifts</u>, and the gift is <u>always</u> a miniature of the thought system the defense protects, set in a golden frame. The frame is very elaborate, all set with jewels, and deeply carved and polished. Its purpose is to be of value *in itself*, and to divert <u>your</u> attention from what it encloses. But the frame <u>without</u> the picture you <u>cannot</u> have. Defenses operate <u>to make you think you can</u>.

Now we are in a position to understand that universally misunderstood first line. We all assume that it means "defenses do the very thing they try to defend us against." But wait—the word "against" is not in there. That's no small detail. For there are two parties in any defense, what is being *defended* and what is being *defended against*. And in this sentence, defenses "do" what they would defend, *not* what they would defend *against*.

Remember, the ego is defending itself from your leaving it (by answering the Holy Spirit's call). It does so by offering you gifts, enticements. You look at its gift and think, "Oh, I guess that ol' ego isn't so bad." Yet remember, this gift, which defends the ego from being abandoned, will do to you the same thing that the *ego* does to you. That is the meaning of "defenses *do* what they would defend."

Let's go back to my analogy of the crazy partner. Let's say that, because he's abusive, you leave him. But then he offers you this wonderful gift, a picture in a stunning frame, and you think, "Maybe he's not so bad." What you don't realize is that, since he is abusive, the gift will be subtly designed to deliver more abuse.

You, however, are so caught up in staring at the frame that you don't notice that the picture—which is a little blurry and hard to make out—is a picture of his face glaring at you in hate. On the picture is painted a tiny, fuzzy caption that says, "I hate you, you worthless scum."

The gift, then, is brilliantly designed. For you accept it because of the frame, but in doing so, what you are actually accepting is the "gift" of abuse. That, after all, is what this guy always gives you.

In sum, then, the gift is an enticement. By enticing you to stay, it's a defense against your leaving. But, ironically, this enticing defense ends up doing to you what your abusive partner *always* does to you. *Defenses do what they would defend.* They defend the ego and hence do to you what the ego always does to you. Do you get that line now?

> 8. The special relationship has the most imposing and deceptive frame of all the defenses the ego uses. Its thought system is offered here, surrounded by a frame so heavy and so elaborate that the picture is almost obliterated by its imposing structure. Into the frame are woven all sorts of fanciful and fragmented illusions of love, set with dreams of sacrifice and self-aggrandizement, and interlaced with gilded threads of self-destruction. The glitter of blood shines like rubies, and the tears are faceted like diamonds and gleam in the dim light in which the offering is made.

The ego, of course, is this abusive lover of ours. It is profoundly threatened by the possibility of the Holy Spirit luring us away from it. So it brings out its biggest kiss-and-make-up gift: the special relationship. This gift has the most incredibly ostentatious and eye-popping frame. It's massive. It's set with all kinds of jewels and gilded threads. Your breath is taken away. You can't believe what an amazing gift the ego has given you. Of course, the ego makes sure the lights are low when it gives the gift, so you don't realize that the diamonds are really tears and the rubies are drops of blood.

What is this frame in literal terms? It is everything that this gift—the special relationship—promises to give you. The frame might as well have neon lights on it saying, "Here you will find love and joining. Your delicious dreams of someone sacrificing for you will be fulfilled. Your fantasies of self-aggrandizement will come true. All that you have ever dreamed of is here. At last it is all yours."

> 9. Look at the *picture*. Do not let the frame distract you. This gift is given you for your damnation, and if you take it you will believe that you *are* [Ur: are] damned. You cannot have the frame without the picture. What you value is the frame, for there you see no conflict. Yet the frame is only the wrapping for the gift of conflict. The frame is not the gift. Be not deceived by the most superficial aspects of this thought system, for these aspects enclose the whole, complete in every [Ur: with *every*] aspect. Death lies in this glittering gift. Let not your gaze dwell on the hypnotic gleaming of the frame. Look at the picture, and realize that death is offered you.

The frame is the promise of the special relationship; the picture is what you actually get. The frame is the advertising; the picture is the actual product. The frame is the bait; the picture is the hook.

Application: Let's now apply this to a particular special relationship, ideally one that has been enticing you of late.

First imagine that your ego has noticed you being dissatisfied with it.
It's been watching you get involved with the Holy Spirit.
It's getting worried.
So one day it shows up with a huge gift, all wrapped up.
The ego presents this gift to you with great ceremony and says, "I love you. Come back to me."
You unwrap it and discover that it's an enormous framed picture.
Well, actually, it's a surprisingly small picture set within a gigantic frame.
This gift represents your special relationship with [fill in the name].
The lights are turned down low, so you can't see things very clearly.
But you can't stop looking at the gorgeous frame.
On this frame are written or pictured all the things this relationship promises you.
See those promises somehow depicted on the frame.
What do you see on it? Great sex? Unbridled affection? Total encouragement and affirmation?
Notice how these promises excite you.
Here is everything you ever wanted.
Without thinking, you reach out to touch one of the rubies on the frame,
and you find that it is liquid.
You realize it is a drop of blood.
Horrified, you start to question what this gift really is.
So finally, you focus your eyes on the picture, squinting in the dim light.
The picture is very hard to make out, both because the light is dim and because the picture itself is dark and out of focus.
While trying to make it out, it occurs to you that while the frame advertised the relationship's *promise*, the picture shows you what

the relationship actually *delivers*.

What, you wonder, does this relationship really deliver?

Finally, you make out what the picture is.

It's a picture of you, but rather than smiling, you're dead.

It's a picture of your corpse.

You put the whole thing down and, without saying a word to the ego, you walk out.

To recap what we've seen so far: When the Holy Spirit was created, the ego felt profoundly threatened, for the Holy Spirit had the potential to win us away from the ego. To counteract the pull of the Holy Spirit, the ego offered us the special relationship, a prize so enticing, so alluring, that it seemed capable of drowning out the "threat" of the Holy Spirit for good.

As we progress on this path, we may have a relatively easy time seeing the ego's system in general as a batch of lies and a field of misery. But when it comes to the special relationship, it seems different. It seems like something to keep. The problem is that the special relationship is not different from the rest of the ego. It is not a shining star of hope and happiness amidst the pain and delusions of the ego. It is just the ego's usual pain and misery dished up in an attractive form.

The way the ego defends itself from being abandoned is to offer us enticements, but these enticements are just delivery devices for the ego's customary attack on us. The special relationship is the biggest enticement of them all. Jesus portrays it as a tiny picture surrounded by a massive, hypnotic frame. The frame contains all the promise of the special relationship, all the happiness the ego tells us the relationship will deliver. Yet of course, it is the picture that is the actual gift. The picture is what the relationship really delivers. We are so busy excitedly gazing on the frame that we don't even notice that the picture is a picture of death.

> 10. That is why the holy instant is so important in the defense of truth. The truth itself <u>needs</u> no defense, but <u>you do</u> need defense against your <u>acceptance</u> of the gift of death. When you who <u>are</u> truth accept an idea so <u>dangerous</u> to truth, <u>you threaten truth with destruction</u>. And <u>your</u> defense must now be undertaken, <u>to keep truth whole</u>. The power of

Heaven, the Love of God, the tears of Christ, and the joy of His eternal Spirit are marshalled to defend you from your own attack. For you attack <u>Them</u>, being <u>part</u> of Them, and They must <u>save</u> you, for They love Themselves.

The ego's defense—the special relationship—is so alluring to us that the Holy Spirit needs to respond with a counterdefense. This is the holy instant, a gift so much more attractive than the special relationship that it has the power to win us away from our deadly mating rituals. Unlike the ego, the Holy Spirit is not winning us back as a defense of Himself. Rather than defending Himself, He is defending *us*. For we are part of truth, and if we were to dedicate ourselves to illusions forever, we would actually shatter the unity of Heaven.

> 11. The holy instant is a miniature of Heaven, sent you *from* Heaven. It is a picture, too, set in a frame. Yet if you accept <u>this</u> gift you will <u>not</u> see the frame at all, because the gift can only <u>be</u> accepted through your willingness to focus <u>all</u> your attention <u>on the picture</u>. The holy instant is a miniature of eternity. It is a picture of timelessness, set in a frame of time. If you focus on the picture, you will realize that it was only the frame that made you <u>think</u> it *was* [Ur: was] a picture. <u>Without</u> the frame, the picture <u>is seen as what it represents</u>. For as the whole thought system of the ego lies in <u>its</u> gifts, so the whole of Heaven lies in this instant, borrowed from eternity and set in time for <u>you</u>.

Notice how opposite the holy instant is from the special relationship. The holy instant is a picture that you can only have if you focus all your attention on the picture, ignoring the frame. And the way it is framed facilitates this—the frame is light, modest, spare; it doesn't detract attention from the picture. Furthermore, the picture is presented to you in full light, not dim light. And finally, the picture is not really a picture at all. It's more like a window onto true reality.

So what is the frame of the holy instant? Jesus says the holy instant is "set in a frame of time." I would say that the frame is the time and circumstances in which you experienced the holy instant. "It was 3:15 on Wednesday, April 25, 2004. I was sitting on my porch reading the Course, when all of a sudden my mind felt transported to somewhere else." The physical details leading up to "when all of a sudden"—that's the frame. You have the holy instant by ignoring the frame; the setting is ultimately inconsequential.

> 12. Two gifts are offered you. Each is complete, and cannot be partially accepted. Each is a picture of all that you can have, <u>seen very differently</u>. You can<u>not</u> compare their value by comparing a picture to a frame. It <u>must</u> be the <u>pictures only</u> that you compare, or the comparison is wholly without meaning. Remember that it is the picture that is the gift. And <u>only</u> on this basis are you <u>really</u> free to choose. <u>Look at the pictures</u>. <u>Both</u> of them. One is a tiny picture, hard to see at all beneath the heavy shadows of its enormous and disproportionate enclosure. The other is lightly framed and hung in light, lovely to look upon for what it <u>is</u>.

We have to compare the two pictures. We probably want to compare the two frames. The frame of the special relationship (great sex on the kitchen floor) is so exciting, while the frame of the holy instant (reading the Course on the porch) is *bo-o-oring*.

Or perhaps we want to compare the *frame* of the special relationship with the *picture* of the holy instant. For those two are actually not so very different. Many of the things we see in the frame of the special relationship—all the joy and completion promised in the special relationship—are the very things we actually *experience* in the holy instant. But that's not a fair comparison. Again, we have to compare the pictures, which is the last thing we want to do.

> 13. You who have tried so hard, and are <u>still</u> trying, to fit the better picture into the wrong frame and so combine what cannot <u>be</u> combined, accept this and be glad: These pictures are each framed perfectly for what they represent. One is <u>framed</u> to be out of focus and <u>not</u> seen. The other is framed for perfect clarity. The picture of darkness and of death grows less convincing as you search it out amid its wrappings. As each senseless stone that <u>seems</u> to shine from the frame in darkness is <u>exposed to light,</u> it becomes dull and lifeless, and ceases to distract you from the picture. And finally you look upon the <u>picture itself</u>, seeing at last that, unprotected by the <u>frame,</u> it <u>has</u> no meaning.

That first line says it all: We want the *experience* of the holy instant inside the *frame* of the ego. We want the peace, completion, and love we experienced that day when we read the Course on the porch, both during and *after* the great sex on the kitchen floor. This really does happen;

unfortunately, it only happens in novels. What we need to accept is that there is a reason the pictures are framed as they are. The picture of the special relationship is framed to distract you from the picture, for you could only want it when you're not looking at the picture. However, when you finally turn a bright light on and look carefully at the picture, you realize it's just a picture. It's not a horrifying photograph of your death. It's a quaint fiction, nothing more.

14. The other picture is lightly framed, for time cannot contain eternity. There is no distraction here. The picture of Heaven and eternity grows more convincing as you look at it. And now, by real comparison, a transformation of both pictures can at last occur. And each is given its rightful place when both are seen in relation to each other. The dark picture, brought to light, is not perceived as fearful, but the fact that it is just a picture is brought home at last. And what you see there you will recognize as what it is; a picture of what you thought was real, and nothing more. For beyond [Ur: *behind*] this picture you will see nothing.

15. The picture of light, in clear-cut and unmistakable contrast, is transformed into what lies beyond the picture. As you look on this, you realize that it is not a picture, but a reality. This is no figured representation of a thought system, but the Thought itself. What it represents is there. The frame fades gently and God rises to your remembrance, offering you the whole of creation in exchange for your little picture [the picture of the special relationship], wholly without value and entirely deprived of meaning.

When you look at the special relationship's picture calmly, in full light, you see that it's just a picture. Nothing to be afraid of, and definitely nothing to crave. But when you look at the picture of the holy instant, the opposite happens. The more you focus on the picture, the more the convincing and desirable it grows. As your become increasingly absorbed in the picture, the frame fades from view. And without the frame ("I was reading the Course on the porch"), you realize "This is no picture. It is a window, a window onto reality."

16. As God ascends into His rightful place and you to yours, you will experience again the meaning of relationship and know it to be true. Let us ascend in peace together to the Father, by giving Him ascendance

in our minds. We will gain <u>everything</u> by giving Him the power and the glory, and keeping <u>no</u> illusions of where they are. They <u>are</u> in us, through <u>His</u> ascendance. What He has given is <u>His</u>. It shines in every part of Him, as in the whole. The whole reality of your relationship with Him lies in <u>our</u> relationship to one another. The holy instant shines alike on <u>all</u> relationships, for in it they *are* one. For here is only healing, <u>already</u> complete and perfect. For here is God, and where <u>He</u> is only the perfect and complete <u>can</u> be.

As the frame fades away and we become fully absorbed in the reality of the holy instant, we will remember God, and we will at last know what relationship really means. As long as we were eagerly clutching that massive, gaudy frame, we had no clue. As long as we thought relationships were about glorifying our ego, they could only disempower us. But now we realize that if we give God the ascendance in our mind, we will find the power and the glory in us.

Application: "Two Pictures" exercise

To do this exercise, you'll need to get a sheet of paper out and draw a simple diagram. Turn the paper to a "landscape" position, so that the long side goes *left to right*.

Now draw a vertical line down the very middle of the page.

Now, in the left-hand side of the page, draw a big rectangle that almost fills the page. This is the frame of the special relationship.

In the very middle of this rectangle, draw a small rectangle (about two inches high). If you want, you can draw a little skull in the middle of this small rectangle.

On the right hand side of the page, simply draw a big oval. This is the picture frame of the holy instant. The space inside the oval is of course the picture. Leave that blank.

Okay, you're done. Now for the exercise.

The picture on the left represents the special relationship. Its massive frame depicts all of what you hope to get from such relationships. The picture of death in the middle represents what such relationships *really* offer you.

Now think of a particularly important special relationship, either one from your past or one that has been going on a long time. Think first about all that you hoped for from that relationship, all the things you fantasized about getting. Write those down in the *frame* area. Now broaden your search and think about the things you hoped to get from other special relationships, and write those down in the same area.

Now think about the forms of death that you experienced in that relationship, especially after the "honeymoon" was over. For instance, you might have experienced a great deal of guilt, or frustration, or rage, or physical illness. Whatever forms of death come to mind, write those down inside the *picture* area (not in the frame area).

Think further about forms of death you have experienced in other special relationships, again, especially after the honeymoon period. If any other forms of death appear to you in this context, write those down.

The picture on the right represents the holy instant. A holy instant is defined as any instant in which you momentarily leave the past and your normal mental framework and experience something beyond their boundaries. It may be an elevated moment during meditation, or a heightened experience while out in nature. It may be a profound spiritual experience. It may be a joining with another human being that seemed to be about truth or reality, about something that transcended your separate interests.

Thinking of the holy instants you've experienced—what you might call your greatest spiritual moments—write down the words that apply to those moments on the right-hand picture, the oval one. If you want to write down some of the details of the setting(s) in which these occurred (such as, "reading the Course on the porch"), you can write these along the edge of the frame, outside the oval. This part is optional.

Once, you're done, take about sixty seconds, and simply look at both pictures. Ignore the frame on the left. Just look at the pictures. Look back and forth rapidly in order to compare them with each other.

Finally, write down a sentence that captures your thoughts, feelings, and observations during this comparison process.

V. The Healed Relationship
Commentary by Robert Perry

This is an extremely important section. It is the beginning of the holy relationships discussions, which extend into Chapter 23, and thus last more than twice as long as the special relationship discussions. These discussions are central to the Text. Indeed, the longest and arguably the most important section in the Text, "The Obstacles to Peace," is really about the holy relationship.

The holy relationship, however, is almost completely misunderstood by Course students. Most students assume (because most teachers teach) that the holy relationship exists in the mind of one person, rather than between two people. In this view, the relationship is holy to me when I am in a holy state of mind about it. It has to be said that this viewpoint is utterly alien to the Course. It sounds nice, but it's not founded on any actual discussions of the holy relationship by the Course. It is founded on mere assumption and opinion—on air, in other words. In the Course itself, this is not a vague, wishy-washy, or subtle issue. The Course itself is always perfectly clear about the holy relationship being a joining between two people in a holy goal. The harm in believing that "it only takes one" is that you will completely misunderstand this central topic in the Course, along with the sections in which it is discussed.

To really appreciate the holy relationship discussions in the Text, you need to see them as addressing Helen and Bill's relationship in particular. As you may know, they had worked together for seven difficult years before Bill gave his speech to Helen, saying "there must be another way." When she said, "You're perfectly right, and I'll join in this new approach with you," they had a holy instant and joined in a common purpose. Their purpose was to demonstrate the "better way" Bill had proposed, a way that focused on cooperation, harmony, and emphasizing the positive, rather than competition, attack, and focusing on the mistakes. Joining in this purpose is what made their relationship holy, which really means a relationship whose goal is holy and which is therefore on the journey to that goal.

All of this is crucial background for understanding this section.

> 1. The holy relationship is the <u>expression</u> of the holy instant in living in this world. Like <u>everything</u> about salvation, the holy instant is a <u>practical</u> device, <u>witnessed</u> to by its results. The holy instant <u>never</u> fails. The <u>experience</u> of it is <u>always</u> felt. Yet without <u>expression it is not remembered</u>. The holy relationship is a constant reminder of the experience in which the relationship became what it is. And as the <u>un</u>holy relationship is a continuing hymn of hate in praise of <u>its</u> maker, so is the holy relationship a happy song of praise to the <u>Redeemer</u> of relationships.

Once we have a holy instant, we generally have difficult keeping the memory of it in front of us, where it can do real good in our lives. This paragraph says that the way to keep it in mind is through its expression, the holy relationship. The holy relationship is the expression of the holy instant in which it was born. And the expression is what makes you remember the source of that expression (the holy instant).

To put this more concretely, let's say that you had a beautiful, idyllic wedding ceremony, which felt like a moment of Heaven on earth. That, in this case, was "the experience in which the relationship became what it is." Now let's say that it's six months later and there are two possible scenarios. In one, you've spent much of that six months in the afterglow of that heavenly wedding day. In the other, you've spent much of that six months in bitter arguments. In which scenario are you more likely to clearly and frequently remember that idyllic wedding ceremony?

> 2. The holy relationship, a <u>major</u> step toward the perception of the real world, is <u>learned</u>. It is the old, unholy relationship, transformed and seen anew. The holy relationship is a phenomenal teaching accomplishment. In all its aspects, as it begins, develops and becomes accomplished, it represents the <u>reversal</u> of the unholy relationship. Be comforted in this; the <u>only</u> difficult phase is the beginning. For here, the <u>goal</u> of the relationship is abruptly shifted to the <u>exact opposite</u> of what it was. This is the <u>first</u> result of <u>offering</u> the relationship to the Holy Spirit, to use for <u>His</u> purposes.

Notice that the holy relationship "begins, develops, and becomes accomplished." It is a *process*, which goes something like this: In the midst of the pain and difficulty of a special relationship, two people invite the Holy Spirit into the relationship, by joining in a common goal. He then begins to guide them toward that new goal. Now the relationship is holy, not because the two are constantly forgiving and at one, but because that is the goal that shines at the heart of their relationship. The rest of the relationship will be the story of it *developing* toward this goal, and finally *accomplishing* this goal.

But the hard part, as he says, is the beginning. Why this is the hard part will be made abundantly clear as we proceed.

> 3. This invitation is <u>accepted immediately</u>, and the Holy Spirit wastes no time in introducing the practical results of asking Him to enter. <u>At once His</u> goal <u>replaces</u> yours. This is accomplished very rapidly, but it makes the relationship seem disturbed, disjunctive and even quite distressing. The reason is quite clear. For the relationship <u>as it</u> *is* is out of line with its own goal, and clearly unsuited to the purpose that has been <u>accepted</u> for it. In its <u>un</u>holy condition, *your* goal was all that <u>seemed</u> to give it meaning. Now it seems to make <u>no</u> sense. Many relationships have been broken off at this point, and the pursuit of the old goal re-established in <u>another</u> relationship. For once the unholy relationship has <u>accepted</u> the goal of holiness, it can never again be what it was.

This paragraph talks as if you invite the Holy Spirit in *and then* He changes the goal. In practice, I think these two events are much more intertwined. Let's look at Helen and Bill's case. They joined in a new goal, the goal of learning how to really get along with people. This invited the Holy Spirit into their relationship, Who then saw their goal in His terms, as the goal of holiness. After all, who but a holy person could really *only* cooperate, be harmonious, and emphasize the positive, never competing, never attacking? The Holy Spirit then set *that* as the goal of the relationship.

With the Holy Spirit holding this new goal at the heart of the relationship, the goal becomes like a powerful magnet, drawing the relationship to itself. But this new goal makes the relationship "seem disturbed, disjunctive and even quite distressing." Why? Because we evaluate things entirely in relation to their goal. If you want your car, for instance, to get you places, get good mileage, be comfortable, and look good, what happens if it is unsuited to these goals, if it constantly breaks down, guzzles gas, has no temperature control, and is a complete eyesore? Being so unsuited to its goals, it has no meaning and no value to you.

That's the position the new holy relationship is in. It appears to be totally unsuited to the goal of holiness. You think, "The two of us are *never* going to make it to the goal of holiness. We are about the most unholy twosome there could be!"

This makes it very tempting just to end the relationship, because now it can't go back. It's like a platonic friendship where the two have had sex; they can't reel it back to just the friendship. The (ego's) solution? Dump the relationship and its new goal, and find a relationship where you can pursue the old goal.

> 4. The temptation of the ego becomes extremely intense with this shift in goals. For the relationship has <u>not</u> as yet been changed sufficiently to make its former goal completely <u>without</u> attraction, and its structure is "threatened" by the recognition of its inappropriateness for meeting its new purpose. The conflict between the goal and the structure of the relationship is <u>so</u> apparent that they <u>cannot</u> coexist. Yet now <u>the goal will not be changed</u>. Set firmly in the unholy relationship, there <u>is</u> no course except to <u>change the relationship</u> to fit the goal. Until this <u>happy</u> solution is seen and accepted as the <u>only way out</u> of the [Ur: this] conflict, the <u>relationship</u> may seem [Ur: seems] to be severely strained.

Now the two are in a real bind. The relationship as it is (its "structure") is totally unsuited to its goal. Unless these two things are in accord, the relationship becomes utterly pointless, like the car in my earlier analogy. Now the two apparently have two options in front of them. First option: They can change the goal to fit the relationship. In other words, they can go back to the old goal of specialness, which the relationship already *does* fit. Going back to the old goal seems very attractive, but it's not possible. As Jesus said earlier, the new goal can't be undone.

Second option: They can change the relationship to fit the goal. They can bring the relationship into conformity with the new goal of holiness. This seems infinitely harder, but it's the only way out. Their task now is to realize that this *is* the only way out, because the goal is not budging. I once heard this analogy: Let's say you are standing twenty feet from your goal, and let's say you take a huge rubber band and stretch it to put one end around your waist and other end around your goal. How do you resolve the tension created in that rubber band? One option is to stand your ground and have the goal pulled closer to where you already are. The other option is to consider the goal immovable, in which case the only way to resolve the tension is to allow the rubber band to pull *you* closer to where the *goal* is.

That latter option is what these two people have to do.

> 5. It would <u>not</u> be kinder to shift the goal more slowly, for the <u>contrast</u> would be obscured, and the ego given time to reinterpret each slow step according to its liking. Only a radical shift in purpose <u>could</u> induce a <u>complete</u> change of mind about what the whole relationship <u>is for</u>. As this change develops and is finally accomplished, it grows increasingly beneficent and joyous. But at the beginning, the situation is experienced as very precarious. A relationship, undertaken by two individuals for their unholy purposes, suddenly has <u>holiness</u> for its goal. As these two <u>contemplate</u> their relationship from the point of view of this new purpose, they are inevitably appalled. Their perception of the relationship may even become quite disorganized. And yet, the <u>former</u> organization of their perception no longer serves the purpose <u>they</u> have agreed to meet [Ur: set].

Imagine that you are pretty happy with your car. It gets you places, it gets decent mileage, and it looks pretty nice. Now imagine that the Holy Spirit shows up and says, "The purpose of this car is now…to *fly*." If you believed that, what would that do to your perception of your car? Couldn't you imagine your perception of the car becoming "quite disorganized"? Couldn't you imagine looking at your nonflying car and being "appalled" at how ridiculously unsuited it is to its goal? Might you not say to the Holy Spirit, "Can we just shift this goal more gradually?" Maybe you'd suggest that the goal for now is for it merely go faster. After that, there could be a new goal of it learning to hop, and so on.

This is what's happening to the two holy relationship partners. They had a normal relationship, and then the Holy Spirit came along and said it had to become actually holy, like two living saints being in constant communion with each other. In this light, the relationship as it is now seems to make no sense to them. They are appalled at how unsuited it seems to its goal. They wish the goal could be changed more slowly and gradually. But Jesus says no. They are never going to get there unless they can change their whole concept of what the relationship is for. Even if the relationship won't fly for a long time, it will *never* fly unless they see that as the goal and refuse to settle for anything less.

> 6. <u>This is the time for</u> *faith*. You <u>let</u> this goal be set for you. That <u>was</u> an act of faith. Do not <u>abandon</u> faith, now that the <u>rewards</u> of faith are being introduced. If you believed the Holy Spirit was <u>there</u> to <u>accept</u> the relationship, why would you now not <u>still</u> believe that He is there [Ur: there,] to <u>purify</u> what He has taken under His guidance? Have faith in your brother [Ur: *each other*] in what but <u>seems</u> to be a trying time. <u>The goal</u> *is* <u>set</u>. And your relationship has <u>sanity</u> as its purpose. For now you find yourself in an <u>insane</u> relationship, <u>recognized</u> as such <u>in the light of its goal</u>.

"This is the time for *faith*"—faith in what? Faith that the goal can be reached. This means faith that the two of you can actually reach the goal, faith that the other person can reach it with you, and faith that the Holy Spirit is there to guide it along the way. This faith is absolutely crucial, for without it, you just give up. Who pours their energies into a goal they feel no hope of reaching? Yet this faith is actually nothing new, for it took faith to allow the goal to be set in the first place. No goal is set without some faith that it can be reached. All Jesus is saying is to take the faith that was there in the *setting* of the goal and hang onto it while *pursuing* the goal.

> 7. Now the ego counsels thus; substitute for this <u>another</u> relationship to which your <u>former</u> goal was <u>quite</u> appropriate. You can <u>escape</u> from your distress only by getting rid of your brother [Ur: *only by getting rid of each other*]. You need not part entirely if you choose not to do so. But you <u>must</u> exclude <u>major areas</u> of fantasy from your brother, <u>to save your sanity</u>. *Hear not this now!* [Ur: Hear not this now!] Have faith in Him Who <u>answered</u> you. He heard. Has He not been very explicit in His answer? You are <u>not</u> now wholly insane. Can you <u>deny</u> that He <u>has</u> given you a <u>most</u> explicit statement [the Course]? Now He asks for faith a little longer, even in bewilderment. For this will go, and you will see the <u>justification</u> for your faith emerge, to bring you shining conviction. Abandon Him not now, nor your brother [Ur: *nor each other*]. This relationship <u>has been</u> reborn as holy.

Let's expand the ego's counsel a bit: "I think you've gotten a bit too absorbed in this 'holy relationship' of yours. What about *your* needs? This relationship is doomed; face the facts. Why not put your focus on a more promising relationship, one that promises more real happiness and pleasure, rather than just pie-in-the-sky idealism? You don't need to cut off contact with this 'holy relationship' person. Just take all your fantasies of the perfect relationship and funnel them into another relationship, where those dreams can really come true. You can still do this 'holy' thing on the side; just be a bit more practical. Let's look at the big picture, please."

What the ego counsels, in other words, is to opt for a disguised version of giving up. The Holy Spirit's response? *"Hear not this now!"* Come on, the Holy Spirit is here. Sanity has peeked its head out. The holy relationship has arrived. The light has come. Why stick it away in a dresser drawer and go back to fumbling in the dark?

Commentary by Greg Mackie

A review of paragraphs 1-7: In a holy instant, two people (originally Helen and Bill) mutually join in a common goal, which invites the Holy Spirit into their special relationship. He enters and changes its goal to holiness, making it a holy relationship. Now they enter a period of distress, because the structure of the relationship—built originally to serve the ego's goals—is out of accord with its new goal of holiness. The distress is so intense that the two are tempted to give up, dump each other, and find another special relationship. Instead, they must have faith: faith that they can actually reach the goal, that each person will do his or her part, and that the Holy Spirit will guide them. This faith will carry them through this trying time to the joy the new goal will bring.

> 8. Accept with gladness what you do not understand, and <u>let</u> it be explained to you as you perceive its purpose work in it to <u>make</u> it holy. You will find many opportunities to blame your brother [Ur: *blame each other*] for the "failure" of your relationship, for it will seem at times to have <u>no</u> purpose. A sense of aimlessness will come to haunt you, and to remind you of all the ways you once <u>sought</u> for satisfaction and thought you found it. Forget not now the misery you <u>really</u> found, and do not breathe life into your failing ego [Ur: egos]. For your relationship has <u>not</u> been disrupted. <u>It has been saved.</u>

When the two partners joined in a common goal, their relationship was "reborn as holy" (T-17.V.7:14). But at this point, it sure doesn't *look* holy. In fact, now that the goal and the structure no longer fit together, it looks worse than ever. The temptation here is twofold: to look back and reminisce about how wonderful it used to be, and to blame the partner for messing it up. "Things were great until *you* gummed up the works." I can imagine Helen blaming Bill for his getting them into this whole "better way" thing, and Bill blaming Helen for taking down this crazy course.

When this happens, the two need to look back on their past relationship without the rose-colored glasses and see how miserable it *really* was. If Helen and Bill's situation was so wonderful before, why did Bill plead for a better way in the first place? Looking at the relationship honestly opens both partners' minds to the truth: Their relationship has not been disrupted from the Heaven it was; it has been saved from the *hell* it was. They may not get this in the midst of their distress, but they need to have faith that the One who changed the goal will lead them from hell to the real Heaven they are now dedicated to reaching.

> 9. You are very new in the ways of salvation, and think you have <u>lost</u> your way. *Your* way *is* lost, but think not this is <u>loss</u>. In your newness, remember that you and your brother have started again, *together*. And take his [Ur: each other's] hand, to walk together along a road far more familiar than you now believe. Is it not certain that you will remember a goal unchanged throughout eternity? For you have chosen but the goal of God, from which your true intent was <u>never</u> absent.

The two holy relationship newbies lament the loss of their old familiar road. They've conveniently forgotten that it was full of thorns and shards of broken glass, and led them into bad neighborhoods full of violence and despair. Now they've been given something everyone yearns for: a fresh start. Now they can take each other's hand and walk together down a brand new road. When they do, they will make a joyous discovery: This road is not as unfamiliar as they thought. It is the road to God, and deep down their goal has *always* been God. They're on the outskirts of the hometown they forgot so long ago, and as they see the road that leads home, something within them says, "I remember this! Everything I always loved is just around the bend."

10. Throughout the Sonship is the song of freedom heard, in joyous echo of your choice. You have joined with many in the holy instant, and they have joined with you. Think not your choice will leave you comfortless, for God Himself has blessed your holy relationship [Ur: special relationship]. Join in His blessing, and withhold not yours upon it. For all it needs now is your blessing, that you may see that in it rests salvation. Condemn salvation not, for it has come to you. And welcome it together, for it has come to join you and your brother together in a relationship in which all the Sonship is together blessed.

They do not travel this new road alone. When they joined in the holy instant that gave birth to their holy relationship, the entire Sonship joined with them in joyous thanks. God has blessed this holy relationship, and this relationship in turn blesses everyone. As long as the distress and disorientation lasts, it will be difficult for the partners to see that *they too* have been blessed by what has happened. But if together they welcome and bless what has happened instead of succumbing to the temptation to bolt, they will realize that their joining in the goal of holiness has brought salvation to everyone, *including* themselves.

11. You undertook, together, to invite the Holy Spirit into your relationship. He could not have entered otherwise. Although you may [Urtext omits "may"] have made many mistakes since then, you have also made enormous efforts to help Him do His work. And He has not been lacking in appreciation for all you have done for Him. Nor does He see the mistakes at all. Have you been similarly grateful to your brother [Ur: each other]? Have you consistently appreciated the good efforts, and overlooked mistakes? Or has your appreciation flickered and grown dim in what seemed to be the light of the mistakes? Perhaps [Urtext omits "Perhaps"] you are now entering upon a campaign to blame him [Ur: *each other*] for the discomfort of the situation in which you find yourself [Ur: yourselves]. And by this lack of thanks and gratitude you make yourself [Ur: *yourselves*] unable to express the holy instant, and thus [Ur: you] lose sight of it.

Though this material applies to any holy relationship, I find it helpful to think of Helen and Bill. In that holy instant when they joined in search of a better way, the Holy Spirit entered and blessed their new goal. As they worked toward that goal they made plenty of mistakes.

(One personal message from Jesus describes a "chain of miscreation" on their part, a long list of mistakes the two of them had made in the course of a single day.) But the Holy Spirit (and Jesus) overlooked those and instead expressed appreciation for all the positive efforts they made. Unfortunately, they weren't always so charitable to each other. They *did* blame each other for their discomfort—there was no "perhaps" about it. They tended to focus on each other's mistakes and thus lost sight of the goal they agreed to in that original holy instant. Sound familiar?

Application: Think of a relationship in which you and another have joined in a common goal. Have you focused on the other's mistakes? Have you been on a campaign to blame him or her for the discomfort in the relationship? Or have you consistently appreciated the good efforts and overlooked mistakes?

> 12. The experience of an instant, however compelling it may be, is easily forgotten if you allow time to close over it. It must be kept shining and gracious in your awareness of time, but not concealed within it. The instant remains. But where are you? To give thanks to your brother [Ur: each other] is to appreciate the holy instant, and thus enable its results to be accepted and shared. To attack your brother [Ur: each other] is not to lose the instant, but to make it powerless in its effects.

Many spiritual teachers say that when you have a powerful spiritual experience, it is critical to maintain your day-to-day spiritual practice afterwards so you can make that experience a permanent part of you. Otherwise, it will probably fade and be forgotten as you slip back into your old ego patterns. This paragraph describes a similar phenomenon: the holy instant which sparks a holy relationship will fade and be forgotten if the two partners don't work to maintain it. It will still be there, but it will have no power to truly transform their daily lives. How do they maintain it? By resisting the temptation to attack each other for their mistakes, by constantly appreciating each other's positive efforts toward the goal.

> 13. You *have* received the holy instant, but you may [Urtext omits "may"] have established a condition in which you cannot use it. As a

result, you do not realize that it is <u>with you still</u>. And by <u>cutting yourself off</u> from its <u>expression</u>, you have denied yourself its benefit. You <u>reinforce</u> this every time you attack your brother [Ur: *you attack each other*], for the attack <u>must</u> blind you to <u>yourself</u>. And it <u>is</u> impossible to <u>deny</u> yourself, and to [Urtext omits "to"] recognize what has been given and <u>received</u> by you.

Again, there was no "may" in Helen and Bill's case. They had received the holy instant when they joined to find a better way, but their constant attacks on each other established a condition in which it couldn't be used—they lost sight of the goal by getting lost in their old "stuff," and thus couldn't fulfill it. We can all relate to this. How often have you joined with others in some high-minded goal, only to see the whole thing disintegrate into backbiting and office politics and pissing contests? When we are embroiled in a battle of egos, it can be easy to forget the goal that brought us together in the first place.

14. You and your brother stand together in the holy presence of truth itself. Here is the goal, together <u>with</u> you. Think you not the goal <u>itself</u> will gladly arrange the <u>means</u> for its accomplishment? It is just this same <u>discrepancy</u> between the purpose that has <u>been</u> accepted and the means as they stand now which <u>seems</u> to make you suffer, but which makes Heaven glad. If Heaven were <u>outside</u> you, you could <u>not</u> share in its gladness. Yet because it is <u>within</u>, the gladness, too, <u>is</u> yours. You <u>are</u> joined in purpose, but remain still separate and divided on the means. Yet the <u>goal</u> is fixed, firm and unalterable, and the means will surely fall in place <u>because</u> the goal is sure. And <u>you</u> will share the gladness of the Sonship that it is so.

Here again is the dilemma this whole section has been talking about. How can this relationship (the "means"), so flawed that the two partners are "inevitably appalled" when they look at it (as the fifth paragraph said), accomplish the exalted goal of holiness? It can because "the goal itself will gladly arrange the means for its accomplishment." The goal is not just an endpoint; it is a power within the relationship, directing its course. Heaven knows that the goal is so certain and unchanging that the relationship cannot help but fall into line eventually. And because Heaven is within, the partners can access that certainty *right now*.

Application: Bring to mind a relationship in which you have joined with another in a holy goal. Think of the doubts you have about this relationship reaching its goal, and apply the following words:

> *[Name] and I stand together in the holy presence of truth itself.*
> *Here is the goal, together with us.*
> *Think we not the goal itself will gladly arrange the means for its*
>   *accomplishment?*
> *Heaven is glad, because it knows that the goal is fixed, firm and*
>   *unalterable,*
>   *and the means—our relationship—will surely fall in place*
>   *because the goal is sure.*
> *Because Heaven is within us, we can share its gladness,*
>   *a gladness shared by all the Sonship.*

15. As you begin to recognize and <u>accept</u> the gifts you have so freely given to your brother [Ur: *each other*], you will also accept the <u>effects</u> of the holy instant and use them to correct <u>all</u> your mistakes and free you from <u>their</u> results. And learning this, you will have <u>also</u> learned how to release <u>all</u> the Sonship, and offer it in gladness and thanksgiving to Him Who gave you <u>your</u> release, and Who would <u>extend</u> it through you.

When the two partners entered the holy instant and joined in the goal of holiness, the Holy Spirit released them. Deep in the heart of the relationship, the goal of holiness is already accomplished. Now, to keep this holy instant "shining and gracious in [their] awareness of time" (as the twelfth paragraph said), they must accept and recognize the gifts they have given to each other. They must have faith in each other, overlook mistakes, and appreciate the good efforts. If they do this, they will experience the *effects* of the holy instant—its transforming effects on their relationship—which will correct all their mistakes and set them free. This will teach them how to extend freedom to everyone, giving the Sonship gladly over to the Voice that gave them their freedom.

VI. Setting the Goal
Commentary by Greg Mackie

1. The practical application of the Holy Spirit's purpose is extremely simple, but it <u>is</u> unequivocal. ²In fact, in <u>order</u> to be simple it *must* be unequivocal. ³The simple is merely what is <u>easily understood,</u> and for this it is apparent that <u>it must be clear</u>. ⁴The setting of the Holy Spirit's goal is <u>general</u>. ⁵Now He will work <u>with</u> you <u>to make it specific,</u> for application *is* specific. ⁶There are certain <u>very</u> specific guidelines He provides for <u>any</u> situation, but remember that you do not yet realize their universal application. ⁷Therefore, it is essential at this point to use them in each situation separately, until you can more safely look <u>beyond</u> each situation, in an understanding far broader than you now possess.

While much of the material in this section can be applied more broadly, it is talking specifically about the holy relationship—originally, Helen and Bill's holy relationship. In the holy relationship, two people have joined in a common goal and thus accepted "the Holy Spirit's purpose": the goal of holiness or "truth" (as this section will say later). This is a general, abstract goal; now, the Holy Spirit must teach the partners how to make the goal specific in order to practically apply it to their lives, "for application *is* specific." To do this, He will now give simple guidelines for goal-setting in a specific situation. These guidelines apply to all situations, but only through applying them to each specific situation as it comes up will their universal application be recognized.

2. In any situation in which <u>you</u> are uncertain, the <u>first</u> thing to consider, very simply, is "What do I want to come of this? ²What is it *for*?" ³The clarification of the goal belongs at the <u>beginning</u>, for it is this which will determine the outcome. ⁴In the ego's procedure this is reversed. ⁵The <u>situation</u> becomes the determiner of the outcome, <u>which can be anything</u>. ⁶The reason for this disorganized approach is evident. ⁷The ego does not know what it <u>wants</u> to come of the situation. ⁸It <u>is</u> aware of what it does <u>not</u> want, but only that. ⁹It has no <u>positive</u> goal at all.

Here's the primary guideline: In each situation, ask at the very beginning, "What is it *for*?" The goal set at the beginning—here, the goal of truth—will determine the outcome.

The ego, however, can't set a goal at the beginning, because it *has* no positive goal. Now, elsewhere the Course says that the ego has some very definite deep-level goals—guilt, for instance. Here, though, I think Jesus is talking more about the surface manifestation of our ego. Most of us just drift through life without a clear, unequivocal sense of what we want. We do have goals, but they are usually weak, conflicting, and ever-changing, so we "have no unified outcome in mind" (W-pI.24.6:2). We often have a clear idea of what we *don't* want to happen—"anything but *that*"—but most of the time we're pretty confused about what exactly we're shooting for. The outcome truly "can be anything."

> 3. Without a clear-cut, positive goal, set at the outset, the situation just seems to happen, and makes no sense until it has <u>already happened</u>. ²Then you look <u>back</u> at it, and try to piece together what it <u>must</u> have meant. ³<u>And you will be wrong</u>. ⁴Not only is your judgment <u>in the past</u>, but you have no idea what should happen [Ur: *should* have happened]. ⁵No goal was set with which to bring the means <u>in line</u>. ⁶And now the only judgment <u>left</u> to make is whether or not the ego <u>likes</u> it; is it acceptable, or does it call for vengeance? ⁷The absence of a criterion for outcome, <u>set in advance</u>, makes understanding doubtful and evaluation impossible.

This paragraph describes so well how our lives generally work. Something happens and then we say, "What the heck was that all about?" With hindsight, we try to piece things together and put together a theory about what it all meant.

But with this approach, "you will be wrong." Why? Because we had no preset goal by which to evaluate what happened. When we have a goal, the situation becomes a means to the goal, and we evaluate it by the standard of how well it meets the goal. For instance, if I set a goal of running a race in a certain time, I will evaluate that race by looking at my stopwatch as I finish. But without a goal, we have no standard for evaluation; my race becomes little more than running around in circles. Without a clear goal, our only way of evaluating situations is to determine whether our ego likes what happened. "I loved it when she said that nice thing about me. I hated it when he fired me—he's gonna get his!" Is this really a good way to evaluate what happens in our lives?

4. The value of deciding in advance what you <u>want</u> to happen is simply that you will perceive the situation as a means to *make* it happen. ²You will therefore make every effort to <u>overlook</u> what interferes with the accomplishment of your objective, and concentrate on everything that helps you meet it. ³It is quite noticeable that <u>this</u> approach has brought you closer to the Holy Spirit's <u>sorting out</u> of truth and falsity. ⁴The true [Ur: "true"] becomes what can be used to <u>meet</u> the goal. ⁵The false [Ur: "false"] becomes the useless <u>from this point of view</u>. 6The situation now <u>has</u> meaning, but only because the goal has <u>made</u> it meaningful.

This is the alternative to the scenario in the last paragraph. If we are in a holy relationship, the goal of truth has already been set for our relationship by the Holy Spirit. Now our job becomes to set that goal in advance for every situation we enter. The situation then becomes a means to make the goal happen—this is what it is all about. We overlook what interferes with the goal and focus on what makes it happen (a great example from the last section: overlooking our holy relationship partner's mistakes and focusing on his or her good efforts). This is what gives the situation meaning: instead of evaluating it on the basis of our ego's fickle preferences, we evaluate it on the basis of how well it serves the goal of truth.

5. The goal of truth has further practical advantages. ²If the situation is used for truth and sanity, its outcome <u>must</u> be peace. ³And this is quite <u>apart</u> from what the outcome *is*. ⁴If peace is the <u>condition</u> of truth and sanity, and <u>cannot</u> be <u>without</u> them, where peace is they <u>must</u> be. ⁵Truth comes of itself. ⁶If you experience <u>peace</u>, it is because the truth <u>has</u> come to you and you <u>will</u> see the outcome truly, for deception cannot prevail against you. ⁷You will <u>recognize</u> the outcome *because* you are at peace. ⁸Here again you see the <u>opposite</u> of the ego's way of looking, for the <u>ego</u> believes the situation <u>brings</u> the experience. ⁹The Holy Spirit knows that the situation <u>is</u> as the goal determines it, and is experienced <u>according</u> to the goal.

Here we see one of the major "practical advantages" of the goal of truth: If the goal is truth, the outcome for us will be *peace*, whatever the external outcome looks like. Peace, in fact, is the evidence that we have dedicated the situation to the goal of truth. The ego thinks that the situation determines the experience: If I like what happens, I am at peace; if I don't like it, I'm upset. But the Holy Spirit knows that the *goal* determines the experience: If I dedicate the situation to truth from the start, I will experience peace no matter what.

> 6. The goal of truth <u>requires faith</u>. ²Faith is implicit in the acceptance of the Holy Spirit's purpose, <u>and this faith is all-inclusive</u>. ³Where the goal of truth is set, there faith <u>must</u> be. ⁴The Holy Spirit sees the situation <u>as a whole</u>. ⁵The goal establishes the fact that <u>everyone</u> involved in it <u>will</u> play his part in its accomplishment. ⁶<u>This is inevitable.</u> ⁷No one will fail in anything. ⁸This <u>seems</u> to ask for faith <u>beyond</u> you, and beyond what you can <u>give</u>. ⁹Yet this is so <u>only</u> from the viewpoint of the ego, for the ego believes in "solving" conflict [Ur: conflicts] through <u>fragmentation</u>, and does <u>not</u> perceive the situation as a whole. ¹⁰Therefore, it seeks to split off <u>segments</u> of the situation and deal with them <u>separately</u>, for it has faith in separation and <u>not</u> in wholeness.

Now we return to a theme from the previous section: the need for *faith*. Here, we must recognize that our acceptance of the Holy Spirit's goal of truth in our holy relationship was an act of faith on our part, and this faith will carry us through. This faith is all-inclusive, so applying it to this situation means having faith that because of the goal, everyone involved in the situation will play his or her part in accomplishing the goal. "No one will fail in anything": what wonderful news! The Holy Spirit sees this because He sees the situation as a whole; if we see the situation with His eyes, we will have the same all-encompassing faith He does.

> 7. Confronted with any <u>aspect</u> of the situation that <u>seems</u> to be difficult, the ego will attempt to <u>take this aspect elsewhere</u>, and resolve it there. ²And it will <u>seem</u> to be successful, except that this attempt <u>conflicts with unity</u>, and <u>must</u> obscure the goal of truth. ³And peace will not be experienced <u>except</u> in fantasy. ⁴Truth has <u>not</u> come because faith has been <u>denied</u>, being <u>withheld</u> from where it rightfully belonged. ⁵Thus do you <u>lose</u> the understanding of the situation the goal of truth would bring. ⁶For fantasy solutions bring but the <u>illusion</u> of experience, and the illusion of peace is <u>not</u> the condition in which truth can enter.

Unlike the Holy Spirit, the ego does not see situations as a whole. It sees them from the perspective of separation, so when it sees a problem in a situation, it will try to "take this aspect elsewhere, and resolve it there."

What is Jesus talking about here? Recall the previous section's discussion of the temptation to abandon our holy relationship when the going gets tough—either literally leaving our partner or mentally bailing out by excluding "major areas of fantasy" (T-17.V.7:4) from her. The ego's "taking this aspect elsewhere" seems to be a form of that. We have a problem within our holy relationship, and we try to find some sort of solution outside the relationship. Perhaps we complain about the problem to someone else, hoping to find an external ally. Perhaps we look for another relationship in which to fulfill the need that's not getting met in the problem area.

These external "solutions" are really fantasy solutions that block the real solution: remembering our shared goal of truth, and having faith in that goal and in each other. Our fantasy solutions may seem to bring peace, but it is only an *illusion* of peace. What we must do is remember the goal of truth at the heart of our holy relationship and restore our faith to where it rightfully belongs. As we were told earlier, "If the situation is used for truth and sanity, its outcome *must* be peace"—*real* peace.

Application: Let's apply this section's counsel to a specific situation. (You can apply what it says about setting goals even if you are not in a holy relationship.) Think of a situation you are facing in your life and ask the Holy Spirit: "What do I want to come of this? What is it *for?*" You may want to write down what you receive.

Whatever you've written down, if that goal has truly come from the Holy Spirit, then its inner content is *truth.* Affirm your commitment to this goal by saying: *"Holy Spirit, I dedicate this situation to the goal of truth."*

Now that you have made this dedication, repeat the following:

> *Having dedicated this situation to the goal of truth,*
> *I will perceive the situation as a means to make this goal happen.*
> *I will make every effort to overlook what interferes with meeting*
>   *this goal,*

and concentrate on everything that helps me meet it.

The goal itself will gladly arrange the means for its accomplishment.

It will give me faith in everyone to play his or her part in its accomplishment.

This is inevitable. No one will fail in anything.

By clarifying the goal at the beginning, I have guaranteed the outcome.

If the situation is used for the goal of truth and sanity, its outcome must be peace.

This is true regardless of what the external outcome looks like.

I will recognize the true outcome because I am at peace.

My experience of peace will show me that the truth has come to me,

and thus I have accomplished the goal of truth.

VII. The Call for Faith
Commentary by Greg Mackie

This section looks awfully cryptic unless we place it in its larger context: the discussion of the holy relationship. This section is a continuation of the discussion in the last two paragraphs of the previous section. We have a problem situation in our holy relationship, and the ego counsels us to take the problem outside of our relationship and try to solve it elsewhere. This is an act of faithlessness against the goal of our relationship and our partner, which robs us of the peace that only faith—which must ultimately be extended to *everyone* and *every* situation—can bring.

> 1. The substitutes for <u>aspects</u> of the situation are the witnesses to your <u>lack</u> of faith. They demonstrate that you did <u>not</u> believe the situation <u>and the problem</u> were in the same place. The problem *was* the [Ur: this] lack of faith, and it is <u>this</u> you demonstrate when you <u>remove</u> it [the problem] from its source and place it elsewhere. As a result, <u>you do not see the problem</u>. Had you not lacked faith that it <u>could</u> be solved, the <u>problem</u> would be gone. And the situation would have been <u>meaningful</u> to you, because the <u>interference</u> in the way of understanding would have been removed. To remove the problem <u>elsewhere</u> is to <u>keep</u> it, for you remove yourself <u>from</u> it and <u>make</u> it unsolvable.

In the last section, I mentioned some of the ways in which we might take problems outside of our holy relationship to solve them elsewhere: speaking against the partner to another person or finding another relationship to meet our needs in our problem area (having an affair is a classic example). I'm sure you can think of many other ways. But whatever method we choose to check out of our relationship, it is evidence of our lack of faith. This lack of faith is our way of holding onto the problem: it blinds us to the real problem which, ironically, *is* our lack of faith. If we had faith that the solution could be found within our relationship, the situation would have been meaningful to us—we would have seen it in light of the goal of our relationship—and the problem would have been solved.

Note: The idea of finding the solution within the relationship doesn't mean we can't get relationship help from "outside" sources like counseling, asking a trusted friend for guidance, etc. These things, when guided by the Holy Spirit, can be helpful means of finding the solution within the relationship, expressions of faith in the relationship.

> 2. There is <u>no</u> problem in <u>any</u> situation that faith will not solve. There is no <u>shift</u> in any <u>aspect</u> of the problem but will make <u>solution impossible</u>. For if you shift <u>part</u> of the problem elsewhere the meaning of the problem <u>must</u> be lost, and the <u>solution</u> to the problem is <u>inherent</u> in its meaning. Is it not possible that <u>all</u> your problems <u>have been</u> solved, but you have removed <u>yourself</u> from the solution? Yet faith <u>must</u> be where something has <u>been</u> done, and where you <u>see</u> it done.

These are the two options available to us: If we remove even part of the problem from the situation we will not see the situation's meaning, and since the solution is part of its meaning, this makes solution impossible. Our removing the problem from the situation, in essence, removes *ourselves* from the solution. But if we keep the problem and the situation together, we will see the situation's meaning and our faith will be sufficient to solve it. In fact, we will see that it is *already* solved, and how can we *not* have faith if what we're hoping for is already accomplished?

> 3. A situation is a relationship, being the joining of thoughts. If problems are perceived, it is because the thoughts are judged to be <u>in conflict</u>. But if the goal is <u>truth</u>, this is impossible. Some idea of bodies <u>must</u> have entered, for minds cannot [Ur: can *not*] attack. The thought of bodies <u>is</u> the sign of faithlessness, for bodies <u>cannot</u> solve anything. It is their <u>intrusion</u> on the relationship, an error in <u>your</u> thoughts <u>about</u> the situation, which then becomes the <u>justification</u> for your lack of faith. You <u>will</u> make this error, but be not at all concerned with that. The error does not matter. [Ur: But do not *use* the error to what *seems* to be to your advantage, for this *does* matter.] Faithlessness brought to faith will never interfere with truth. But faithlessness used *against* truth will <u>always</u> destroy faith. If you lack faith, ask that it be restored <u>where it was lost</u>, and seek not to have it <u>made up to you</u> elsewhere, as if you had been unjustly <u>deprived</u> of it.

All situations represent the joining of thoughts between people. When we perceive a problem within our holy relationship, it is because there seems to be *discord* between our thoughts. There can never be any real discord between our true minds, however, and we recognize this when we remember the goal of truth at the core of our relationship.

The only way apparent discord can enter is if we focus on each other's *bodies*. Isn't every problem we have in a relationship some form of dissatisfaction with our partner's body, especially its behavior? "Take out the trash. Say 'I love you' more often. Lose weight. Stop nagging." This focus on bodies is both evidence of our faithlessness and seeming justification *for* our faithlessness: How can I have faith that the two of us will reach this lofty goal when you're constantly dropping the ball?

The solution to this problem? *Do not use your faithlessness.* We will inevitably make the error of faithlessness, but this is nothing to be concerned about as long as we don't try to use our faithlessness to our ego's advantage. We need to resist the temptation to use our faithlessness by seeking a solution to our problem outside our relationship, seeking to have the apparent lack in our relationship made up to us elsewhere. Instead, we should bring our faithlessness to faith, the faith inherent in our acceptance of the goal of truth. We need to ask the Holy Spirit to restore the faith we have temporarily lost sight of.

> 4. Only what *you* have not given <u>can</u> be lacking in <u>any</u> situation. But remember this; the goal of holiness was set for <u>your</u> relationship, <u>and not by you</u>. <u>You</u> did not set it because holiness cannot be seen [Ur: can *not be seen*] except through faith, and your relationship was not holy <u>because</u> your faith in your brother [Ur: one another] was so limited and little. Your faith must grow to meet the goal that has been set. The goal's <u>reality</u> will call this forth, for you will see that peace and faith will not come separately. What situation can you be in <u>without faith</u>, and remain faithful to your brother [Ur: each other]?

The real reason for our relationship problem is not our partner's body misbehaving, but our own faithlessness. In fact, withholding our faith is the real problem in *any* situation. When we are tempted to be faithless to our partner and to the goal of our relationship, we need to remember that the Holy Spirit gave us the goal of holiness, and the reality of this goal will call forth from us the faith we need to grow to meet the goal. If He was able to give us enough faith in each other to turn our special relationship into a holy relationship, will He not also be able to increase our faith to the point where we can make it to the goal?

> 5. <u>Every</u> situation in which you find yourself is but a means to meet the purpose set for <u>your</u> relationship. See it as something <u>else</u> and you <u>are</u> faithless. <u>Use not your faithlessness</u>. Let it enter and look upon it calmly, but <u>do not use it</u>. Faithlessness is the servant of illusion, and wholly faithful to its master. <u>Use</u> it, and it will carry you straight to illusions. Be tempted not by what it offers you. It interferes, not with the goal, but with the <u>value</u> of the goal <u>to you</u>. Accept not the illusion of peace it offers, but look upon its offering and recognize it *is* illusion.

When we have accepted the Holy Spirit's goal and entered a holy relationship, literally every situation we enter becomes a means to accomplish our goal—even situations that don't directly involve our partner. We are to see everything in our life—from the guy who cuts us off in traffic to our abandonment issues with our father to the war in the Middle East—from the perspective of this lofty goal. Anything else is an act of faithlessness, but again, this is not a problem as long as we don't *use* our faithlessness. Using it will bind us to illusions and blind us to our real goal. But if we simply look at it dispassionately and see that it offers only an illusion of peace, our faith our partner and in our goal will be restored.

Application: Bring to mind a relationship in which you and another person have joined in a holy goal. Is there a situation within this relationship in which something your partner has done has tempted you to lose faith in him and in the relationship's ability to reach the goal? If so, dispel your faithlessness with the following words:

> *I will not use my faithlessness here.*
> *I will not let myself be tempted by the "peace" it seems to offer me,*
> *because it will cause me to lose sight of the value of the goal of our relationship.*
> *Instead, I will let my faithlessness enter and look upon it calmly.*
> *When I do, I will see that the "peace" it offers me is only an illusion,*

and I will remember that only the goal of holiness will bring me real peace.

6. The goal of illusion is as closely tied to faithlessness as faith to [the goal of] truth. If you lack faith in anyone to fulfill, and perfectly, his part in any situation dedicated in advance to truth, your dedication is divided. And so you have been faithless to your brother [Ur: to each other], and used your faithlessness against him [Ur: against each other]. No relationship is holy unless its holiness goes with it everywhere. As holiness and faith go hand in hand, so must its faith go everywhere with it. The goal's reality will call forth and accomplish every miracle needed for its fulfillment. Nothing too small or too enormous, [Ur: nothing too insignificant or too imposing,] too weak or too compelling, but will be gently turned to its use and purpose. The universe will serve it gladly, as it serves the universe. But do not interfere.

Once we have dedicated every situation in our life in advance to our holy relationship's goal of truth, our faith must follow. If we lack faith in *anyone* to perfectly do his or her part in accomplishing that goal, our dedication is actually divided between truth and faithlessness. This divided dedication is an abandonment of our goal and is thus using our faithlessness against our partner—the one thing we must not do. What we must do is realize that for our relationship to be truly holy, our faith must extend not only to our partner, but to everyone everywhere. This universal faith may seem daunting to us, but fortunately the power of the goal itself will bring forth every miracle we need to accomplish it. All we need to do is get our faithlessness out of the way.

7. The power set in you in whom the Holy Spirit's goal has been established is so far beyond your little conception of the infinite that you have no idea how great the strength that goes with you. And you can use *this* in perfect safety. Yet for all its might, so great it reaches past the stars and to the universe that lies beyond them, your little faithlessness can make <u>it</u> useless, if you would use the faithlessness instead.

Such immense power is unleashed in us through the simple act of joining with another person in a common goal. Really take this in: A holy relationship has within it power that "is so far beyond your little conception of the infinite that you have no idea how great the strength that goes with you." Yet all of this power can be dammed up by using just a "little faithlessness" against our partner. This is something to remember the next time we're tempted to attack our holy relationship partner for some petty offense.

> 8. Yet think on this, and learn the cause of faithlessness: You think you hold against your brother [Ur: the other] what he has done to you. But what you really blame him for is what *you* did to *him* [Ur: *what you did to him*]. It is not his past but yours you hold against him. And you lack faith in him because of what you were. Yet you are as innocent of what you were as he is. What never was [your past "sins" against your partner] is causeless, and is not there to interfere with truth. There is no cause for faithlessness, but there *is* [Ur: a] Cause for faith. That Cause has entered any situation that shares Its purpose. The light of truth shines from the center of the situation, and touches everyone to whom the situation's purpose calls. It calls to everyone. There is no situation that does not involve your whole relationship, in every aspect and complete in every part. You can leave nothing of yourself outside it [the situation] and keep the situation holy. For it shares the purpose of your whole relationship, and derives its meaning from it.

Here we see the real reason for our faithlessness against our partner: It isn't all the rotten things she's done to us, but all the rotten things *we've* done to *her*. We secretly feel guilty for all of the ways *we've* dropped the ball in the relationship, and we've projected that guilt onto our partner in a vain attempt to escape it. Yet we don't really need to escape it, because none of our past "sins" had any real effect on the innocence of who we are.

There is, then, no real cause for faithlessness. We have every reason for faith, because the Cause Who entered our relationship and blessed it with His holy purpose now blesses every situation we enter. Every situation is now a means to meet the goal of our relationship, and as we bring our goal of truth wholeheartedly to it, the light of truth shines forth from every situation and leaves no one untouched.

Application: Bring to mind the same relationship you used in the previous application. Now, "Think on this and learn the cause of faithlessness":

I think I hold against [name] what he has done to me [think of
  some examples].
But what I really blame him for is what I did to him [think of some
  examples].
It is not his past but mine I hold against him.
I lack faith in him because of what I was.
Yet I am as innocent of what I was as he is.
Both my past and his never existed in truth.
Therefore, I have perfect cause for faith in both [name] and
  myself.
The Cause for faith has blessed our relationship and every
  situation we enter.

9. Enter each situation with the faith you give your brother [Ur: the
faith that you would give each other], or you <u>are</u> faithless to your own
relationship. <u>Your</u> faith will call the others to <u>share</u> your purpose, as
the [Ur: this] same purpose called forth the faith in you. And you will
see the means you once employed to lead you to illusions transformed
to means for truth. Truth calls for faith, and faith makes room <u>for
truth</u>. When the Holy Spirit <u>changed</u> the purpose of your relationship
by exchanging yours for His, the goal He placed there <u>was</u> extended
to every situation in which you enter, or will <u>ever</u> enter. And <u>every</u>
situation was thus <u>made free</u> of the past, which <u>would</u> have made it
purpose<u>less</u>.

As we've seen, when the Holy Spirit gave our relationship the goal
of truth, every situation from then on was transformed into a means to
that goal. Therefore, we are not only called to have faith in our partner,
but to extend that same faith to every situation and everyone involved in
it. If we do this, something amazing will happen: others will respond to
our faith by *joining* us in the goal of truth. When this happens, "you will
see the means you once employed to lead you to illusions transformed to
means for truth." Every situation, scrubbed clean of the past that hid its
light, will now lead us *to* the light.

10. You call for faith because of Him Who walks with you in every
situation. You are no longer wholly insane, <u>nor no longer alone</u>. For

313

loneliness in God <u>must</u> be a dream. You whose relationship <u>shares</u> the Holy Spirit's goal are <u>set apart</u> from loneliness because the truth has come. Its call for faith is strong. Use not your faithlessness against it, for it calls you to salvation and to peace.

The first line here reminds me of Lesson 156 in the Workbook: "I walk with God in perfect holiness." When we joined with our partner in the Holy Spirit's goal, we joined with the Holy Spirit and God as well. How could we possibly be lonely with companions like these? Yet to fully join with our mighty companions, we must access the faith that the goal of truth calls forth in us. We do this by following this section's repeated counsel: "Use not your faithlessness against it." Only by steadfastly refusing to let our faithlessness get in the way of truth can we find the salvation and peace that the goal of truth offers us.

VIII. The Conditions of Peace
Commentary by Greg Mackie

This is another section that emphasizes not using our faithlessness. Defined broadly in a down-to-earth way, "using your faithlessness" means being cynical, engaging in a situation from a viewpoint that says, "I don't believe in a higher, self-transcending goal or in anyone involved here. I'm here to extract what my ego needs from all these untrustworthy idiots." Peace lies in setting aside this faithlessness, thus opening our minds to faith in the goal of truth and in everyone in every situation to play his or her part in accomplishing that goal.

> 1. The holy instant is nothing more than a special case, or an extreme example, of what <u>every</u> situation is <u>meant</u> to be. The meaning that the Holy Spirit's purpose has <u>given</u> it [the holy instant] is also given to <u>every</u> situation. It calls forth just the same <u>suspension</u> of faithlessness, withheld and left <u>unused,</u> that faith might answer to the call of truth. The holy instant is the shining example, the clear and unequivocal demonstration of the meaning of <u>every</u> relationship and <u>every</u> situation, <u>seen as a whole.</u> Faith has <u>accepted</u> every <u>aspect</u> of the situation, and faithlessness has not forced <u>any</u> exclusion on it. It is a situation of perfect peace, simply because <u>you</u> have <u>let it be what it is.</u>

Remember, all of this material is about the holy relationship and originally addressed Helen and Bill's holy relationship. In a holy instant, the two of them joined in the common goal of finding a better way of relating with each other and with their work colleagues. That holy instant, unbeknownst to them at the time, was a dedication to the Holy Spirit's goal of truth that changed their lives forever, leading to a string of events they never could have anticipated, most importantly the scribing of *A Course in Miracles*.

That instant, however, was not meant to be just a one-time phenomenon: It was an "extreme example" of what *every* situation is meant to be. Every situation is meant to be a holy instant in which faithlessness is set aside and faith is placed in the goal of truth. This is what gives meaning to every relationship and every situation. This enables us to see every situation as a whole through faith instead of fragmented by faithlessness. And as we learned in the "Setting the Goal" section, "If the situation is used for truth and sanity, its outcome must be peace" (T-17.VI.5:2).

> 2. This simple courtesy is all the Holy Spirit asks of you. Let truth be what it is. Do not <u>intrude</u> upon it, do not <u>attack</u> it, do <u>not</u> interrupt its coming. Let it encompass <u>every</u> situation and bring you peace. Not even faith is asked of you, for truth asks nothing. Let it [truth] enter, and <u>it</u> will call forth and <u>secure</u> for you the faith you need for peace. But rise you not <u>against</u> it, for against <u>your</u> opposition it <u>cannot</u> come.

As we've seen before, we're not required to give up our faithlessness; we must simply refuse to *use* it to our ego's advantage. Yes, we have the gun of faithlessness in our hands aimed at our brother's head, but if we just don't fire it no harm will be done. If we open our minds to truth, it will enter and take away the gun, giving us the faith we need to make every situation a means for truth and peace.

Application: Let's give the Holy Spirit the "simple courtesy" He asks of us. Think of a situation you're facing in which you are tempted to use your faithlessness, and say these words to the Holy Spirit:

> *Holy Spirit, I will not rise against truth.*
> *I will let truth be what it is.*
> *I will not intrude upon it, attack it, or interrupt its coming.*
> *Truth asks nothing of me, not even faith.*
> *When I let truth enter, it will give me the faith I need.*
> *I will let truth encompass this situation and bring me peace.*

> 3. Would you not <u>want</u> to make a holy instant of <u>every</u> situation? For such is the gift of faith, freely given wherever faithlessness is laid aside, <u>unused</u>. And <u>then</u> the power of the Holy Spirit's purpose is free to use instead. This power <u>instantly</u> transforms <u>all</u> situations into one sure and continuous means for <u>establishing</u> His purpose, and <u>demonstrating</u> its reality. What has been <u>demonstrated</u> [through the holy instant] has called for faith, and has been <u>given</u> it. Now it becomes a fact, from

which faith can no longer <u>be</u> withheld. The strain of <u>refusing</u> faith to truth is enormous, and far greater than you realize. But to <u>answer</u> truth with faith entails no strain at all.

Every situation becomes a holy instant when we refuse to use our faithlessness. By refusing to fire that gun, we allow the power of the Holy Spirit's goal of truth into our minds, which transforms every situation into a means to accomplish that goal. And as each situation actually does accomplish that goal, faith becomes easy. How hard is it to believe in something that has been *demonstrated* to be a fact? Believing in the Holy Spirit's truth will be as easy as believing in the law of gravity.

> 4. To you who have <u>acknowledged</u> the call of your Redeemer, the strain of <u>not</u> responding to His call <u>seems</u> to be <u>greater</u> than before. This is not so. Before, the strain was there, but you attributed it <u>to something else,</u> believing that the "something else" <u>produced</u> it. This was <u>never</u> true. For what the "something else" produced was sorrow and depression, sickness and pain, darkness and dim imaginings of terror, cold fantasies of fear and fiery dreams of hell. And it was nothing but the intolerable strain of refusing [Ur: your refusal] to give faith to truth, and see its evident reality.

The last paragraph referred to "the strain of refusing faith to truth." Before joining with another person in the Holy Spirit's goal, the idea that refusing His call to truth is a strain probably never occurred to us. It seems that there is a new tension in our lives between our ego's goals and the lofty new goal of our holy relationship. Yet the strain was always there; we just attributed it to different sources. We thought it was caused simply by living in this dog-eat-dog world full of pain and suffering. Yet the real problem the whole time—what really caused all our suffering— *was* our faithlessness to truth. Our newfound commitment to the goal of truth makes us realize what has really been going on all along.

> 5. Such was the crucifixion of the Son of God. His faithlessness did this to him. Think carefully before you let yourself use faithlessness against him. For he <u>is</u> risen, and <u>you</u> have accepted the Cause of his awakening <u>as yours</u>. You have assumed your part in his redemption, and you are now fully responsible to him. Fail him not now, for it has been given you to realize what your lack of faith in him <u>must</u> mean to <u>you</u>. His

salvation is your <u>only</u> purpose. See only this in <u>every</u> situation, and it <u>will</u> be a means for bringing <u>only</u> this.

Our faithlessness against our true Identity as God's Son started this whole sick dream. It crucified him. And we nail him to the cross again every time we use our faithlessness against our holy relationship partner or anyone else in our lives. But he is *risen*, and when we joined in our holy relationship we accepted the goal of extending resurrection to the entire Sonship. That is now our only purpose. We need to keep this in mind any time we are tempted to use faithlessness against anyone. Do we give our partner that tongue-lashing or do we heal our faithless thoughts with a "response to temptation" practice from the Course? We've progressed far enough to realize that the tongue-lashing will crucify *us*. Instead, we must learn to use the situation as a means for the Son of God's salvation.

Application: Bring to mind a situation in which you are tempted to use your faithlessness against someone. Now, repeat the following:

> *Let me think carefully before using my faithlessness against [name].*
> *To do so is to crucify him, and therefore to crucify myself.*
> *Let me see the Son of God's salvation as my only purpose in this situation.*
> *Thus will I recognize [name's] resurrection and my own.*

6. When you accepted truth as the goal for your relationship, you became a giver of peace as surely as your Father gave peace to <u>you</u>. For the goal of peace cannot <u>be</u> accepted <u>apart</u> from its conditions [that you become a giver of peace], and you had faith in it for no one accepts what he does <u>not</u> believe is <u>real</u>. <u>Your purpose has not changed</u>, and <u>will</u> not change, for you <u>accepted</u> what can <u>never</u> change. And nothing that it needs to <u>be</u> forever changeless can you now <u>withhold</u> from it. Your release is certain. Give as you have received. And demonstrate that you have risen <u>far</u> beyond <u>any</u> situation that could hold you back, and keep you <u>separate</u> from Him Whose call you answered.

Once we accepted the goal of our holy relationship, there was no turning back. We received our Father's gift of peace and therefore became givers of peace, for giving is the means to achieve the goal of peace, and no goal can be truly accepted without its means. Faithlessness just delays our inevitable release. So, Jesus says, don't delay. Let your life become a living demonstration of the goal you accepted. Use every situation as a means for the Son of God's salvation. Give as you received. Become a giver of peace, and you will recognize your own peace, your own resurrection.

About the Circle's
TEXT READING PROGRAM

An Unforgettable Journey through the Text in One Year

The Text is the foundation of *A Course in Miracles*, yet many students find it hard going. This program is designed to guide you through the Text, paragraph by paragraph, in one year.

Each weekday, you will receive an e-mail containing that day's Text section, along with commentary on each paragraph, written by Robert Perry or Greg Mackie. The readings contain material edited out of the published Course as well as exercises for practical application. This is the material that has been presented now in book format in our series *The Illuminated Text*.

By signing up for our online program, you will also receive:

- Weekly one-hour class recordings led by Robert Perry and Greg Mackie that summarize that week's sections and answer students' questions
- An online forum for sharing with others in the program
- Related articles on key Text sections e-mailed directly to you
- Your personal web archive, with access to all your commentaries and class recordings
- An unlimited "pause feature" for pausing your program while you're away

Want to learn more? Call us today on 1-888-357-7520, or go to www.circleofa.org, the largest online resource for *A Course in Miracles*!

We hope that you will join us for this truly enlightening program!